365 MEDITATIONS
FOR MOTHERS OF TEENS

365 MEDITATIONS FOR MOTHERS OF TEENS

M. Garlinda Burton, Pamela Crosby,
Lisa Flinn, Kay C. Gray,
Margaret Anne Huffman, Pam Kidd,
Anne Killinger, Marjorie L. Kimbrough,
LaDonna Meinders, Mary Catharine Neal,
Anne L. Wilcox & Mary Zimmer

DIMENSIONS
FOR LIVING
NASHVILLE

365 Meditations for Mothers of Teens

This book is printed on acid-free recycled paper.

Library of Congress Cataloging-in-Publication Data

365 meditations for mothers of teens / M. Garlinda Burton ... [et al.].
   p. cm.
   ISBN 0-687-10921-3 (paper : alk. paper)
   1. Mothers—Prayer-books and devotions—English. 2. Parent and teen-ager—Religious aspects—Christianity—Meditations. 3. Parenting—Religious aspects—Christianity—Meditations. 4. Devotional calendars. I. Burton, M. Garlinda.
   BV4529.A19   1996
   242'.6431—dc20   96-19805
                                                        CIP

96 97 98 99 00 01 02 03 04—10 9 8 7 6 5 4 3 2 1

MANUFACTURED IN THE UNITED STATES OF AMERICA

CONTENTS

$\mathscr{F}$OREWORD

No one understands a mother's joys and trials better than another mother. In this unique collection of daily meditations, twelve Christian mothers come together to offer reassurance, comfort, inspiration, and hope for mothers of teens. As you make your way through the year with these women of faith, you will be enriched by a variety of experiences and perspectives that provide practical and spiritual encouragement for the sometimes challenging, sometimes exhilarating experience of being a mother of teens.

Each month as you meet a new writer and her family, you will encounter new insights on some common themes of mothering during the teen years: the responsibilities and challenges of parenting teens in today's world; the assurances of faith for a mother's concerns; the emotional and physical demands of mothering; the necessity of spending time alone with God; the evidences of a deepened spiritual journey; connections with God as creator and parent and with the lives of other biblical women of faith; the joys, blessings, and insights that teens provide; and more.

The contributors represent a variety of lifestyles and family situations. Among them are biological mothers, adoptive mothers, stepmothers, and one foster mother; mothers who are "living" the teen years now and mothers who have been through that parenting phase and are able to share the wisdom that comes with experience and time; mothers who work outside the home and mothers who work primarily inside the home; mothers who are married and mothers who are or have been single parents.

It is our hope that the discipline of daily meditation and the thoughts that will be triggered by these pages will make every day more meaningful for you.

About the Writers

M. Garlinda Burton is the author of a book on overcoming racism and the editor of *Interpreter* magazine. She has two stepdaughters, Heather and Yukelia, and a three-year-old stepgranddaughter, Shermana. Garlinda and her husband, Larry, live in Nashville.

Pamela Crosby and her son, Adriel Watkins, live in Nashville. Pamela is an account executive at a denominational organization where she produces promotional and interpretive resources for various bodies of the church. She also is a freelance writer, whose work has appeared in *Alive Now, Interpreter, New World Outlook,* and *Orientation* magazines. Adriel is attending college where he is studying music and mass communications.

Lisa Flinn is a freelance writer and the author or coauthor of several books, including *Creative Ways to Offer Praise, Hooray for Children's Church,* and *Making Scripture Stick.* She also has taught at the elementary, high school, and university levels. In addition to writing, Lisa enjoys gardening, art projects, and collecting commemorative church plates and pottery. Lisa's oldest child, Emily, has recently left home to attend college. Lisa and her husband, Bill, live in Hillsborough, North Carolina, with their two younger children, Louise and Harrison.

Kay C. Gray is a pastor serving a church in Mt. Juliet, Tennessee. She is the single mother of two sons, Aaron, a senior in high school, and Hunter, a senior in college.

Margaret Anne Huffman is a community speaker and workshop leader and the author of *Second Wind: Meditations and Prayers for Women, Everyday Prayers for Women in the Workplace, Everyday Prayers for Grandmothers,* and a contributor to *365 Meditations for Mothers of Young Children* and *Flights of Angels.* She also is a former newspaper lifestyle editor and an award-winning journalist. Margaret Anne is a pastor's wife, a mother of three, and a grandmother. She lives in Shelbyville, Indiana.

Pam Kidd is a writer whose work regularly appears in *Daily Guideposts, Guideposts,* and various magazines and journals. Previously she has been a script writer and a magazine editor. Pam and her husband, David, have a son, Brock, and a daughter, Keri. In addition to being a pastor's wife and a mom, she enjoys cooking, writing fiction, and spending time at the family cabin. She lives in Brentwood, Tennessee.

Anne Killinger, who was trained as a concert pianist and once taught piano at Georgetown College in Kentucky, is a homemaker and writer who lives in Birmingham. She is the author of *An Inner Journey to Easter* and a contributor to *365 More Meditations for Women.* Anne and her husband, John, have two grown sons.

Marjorie L. Kimbrough is an instructor in religion and philosophy at Clark Atlanta University and the author of several books. She recounted her twenty-eight-year career in corporate America in her first book, *Accept No Limitations*, for which she was named Georgia Author of the Year in the area of nonfiction. She also is the author of *Beyond Limitations: Encouragement and Inspiration for the Start of Your Career, She Is Worthy: Encounters with Biblical Women,* and a contributor to *365 More Meditations for Women.* Marjorie and her husband, Walter, have two grown sons and make their home in Atlanta.

LaDonna Meinders is a homemaker, writer, and accomplished pianist and organist who lives in Oklahoma City. She is the author of *Leaves in the Wind.* LaDonna and her husband, Herman, have four grown children and three grandchildren.

Mary Catharine Neal is an associate pastor and program director for an organization that provides support to victims of abuse. Previously she has worked as a high-school counselor. Mary Catharine is blessed to be the mother of a biological son, Neal; two stepsons, Alex and John; an adopted son, Shane; and a foster daughter, Mary. She lives in Nashville.

Anne L. Wilcox is former Bible study columnist for *Today's Christian Woman*; the author of two books, including *A Woman's Workshop on Ruth*; and a contributor to *365 More Meditations for Women* and *365 Meditations for Mothers of Young Children*. She and her husband, Brian, have a thirteen-year-old daughter, Jaime. Anne also assists in teaching literature, math, and language arts courses at an elementary school in their hometown of Seattle.

Mary Zimmer is a writer and retreat leader on biblical women and spirituality and a former professor of Christian education. Mary and her husband, Steve, have two sons, Jacob, age twenty-one, and Michael, age sixteen. They live in Louisville, Kentucky.

$\mathcal{J}$ANUARY

LIVING A LIFE OF THANKSGIVING AND PRAISE

Marjorie L. Kimbrough

JANUARY 1   **Read Proverbs 3:6.**

I WONDER HOW MANY OF US actually keep the resolutions we make for the new year. I know that more of us make them than keep them, but I want you to try with me this year to make and keep the one that I offer: *This year I will live a life of thanksgiving and praise to God. I will acknowledge God every day. I will thank God for my life and for my children, and I will witness to his goodness in their presence.*

It is not enough for us to be silent Christians. We must live a life that actively witnesses to our love of and devotion to God. We must daily (and sometimes even hourly) offer prayers of praise and thanksgiving. We must be consistent in our attendance and support of our church, and we must be faithful in our study of the Scriptures. In this way our resolution will become a habit, and we will never have to make this resolution again.

"How will this help me in my efforts to be a better mother to my children, particularly my teens?" you ask. It will make you more appreciative of life and God's goodness, and therefore more patient with your family.

Once you have learned to give praise and thanksgiving to God, you will find it easier to give praise and thanksgiving to your family; and that will make a difference in all of your lives.

Lord, give me the courage to acknowledge you in all my ways.

JANUARY 2   Read 1 John 4:11.

THIS IS OUR SECOND DAY of actively offering praise and thanksgiving to God, but our praise and thanksgiving must not stop with God. We must also extend our praise to our children, especially our teens. They are struggling to be accepted in their social circles and in their family. They must know that they are loved and valued.

Today offer praise. Think of something for which you can compliment your teens. Be generous and sincere in your praise. Let them know how much you love them and appreciate them. Tell them how proud you are of them. Encourage them in their endeavors to be accepted at school, and be grateful that they are in school. Let them know how much you thank God for them, tell them that you have loved them all of their lives and always will.

Today is the day we will thank God for our teenagers. Today is the day we will praise them. Today is the day we will continue in our resolution of living a life of thanksgiving and praise.

Lord, thank you for my teenagers. Keep them aware of my love for you and for them.

JANUARY 3   Read Psalm 119:12.

I REMEMBER WHEN MY SON Walter reached the age of 15. All he really wanted was his learner's permit so that he could learn to drive. The "statutes" he was interested in being taught related to the rules of the road.

My husband was committed to teaching his sons to drive, so that task did not fall to me. For that I am grateful. Walter learned to drive, and by the age of 16 he had his license.

Seeing him drive away in a car alone—without an adult licensed driver—was one of the most difficult phases of letting him grow. He could come and go without either of his parents; he was independent; he was growing. I knew that he had passed that first step toward responsible adulthood. By learning to let him go alone, I was also learning to let him grow.

I worried those first few times he drove out alone, but then I spoke to my friend Sylvia, who has seven sons. She said, "Worry does no good. Tell them to be careful, send them on their way, and then 'let go.'" I took her advice, and as my second son reached that critical age, I learned to let him go and grow.

Lord, thank you for your constant guidance and protection. Every day I offer you praise.

JANUARY 4   Read Psalm 119:108.

AS MIGHT HAVE BEEN EXPECTED, one day my new driver had an accident. Thank God that it was minor; there were no injuries except to the car. But Walter was devastated. He felt that he had failed as a driver and vowed never to drive again.

You see, Walter is a perfectionist, and he finds few excuses for not doing everything perfectly. To have had an accident was for him a sign of failure. I assured him that accidents happen, that we needed to thank God that it was not more serious, and that we had insurance to get the car repaired.

I decided that it was a good time to teach him the "ordinances" of responsible driving. I insisted that he accompany me to the insurance claims office; I supervised his filling out the accident report; and I told him where to take the car for repairs. He was reluctant to drive again, but I explained that he could not let the car defeat him. He accepted the challenge. I praise God that since then he has been careful to follow the "ordinances" of responsible driving.

Lord, I have so much to be thankful for. Keep your arm of protection around my children, both on and off the road.

JANUARY 5   Read Isaiah 38:19.

OUR SECOND SON, WAYNE, found it more difficult to master the rules of the road. My husband often commented that he was afraid when he was teaching Wayne to drive. Wayne knew that driving had to be a piece of cake; after all, everyone else in the house was doing it. He drove fast and furiously, and he was plagued with accidents. I thank God that he is alive and has not injured anyone.

After his third accident and a significant increase in auto insurance, which was already exorbitant for a single male under twenty-five years of age, I began to pray that the insurance claims adjuster would declare the car totalled! That not only would give me an opportunity to reinforce the responsibilities of driving, but it also would give Wayne an opportunity to think about the inconveniences of not having a car. My prayers were answered, and Wayne found himself without transportation.

Wayne and I had long talks about driving safely, the cost of insurance, and the responsibilities of obeying the rules of the road. His father also had the opportunity to discuss how God is faithful to us and how being careful and responsible while driving is one way to demonstrate love of our neighbor and respect for God's creation.

After a few years, Wayne had saved enough money to help with the purchase of another car. He is still somewhat accident prone, but he is improving. Praise God!

Lord, thank you for children who are willing to listen to their mothers and fathers and who grow in an understanding of your faithfulness.

JANUARY 6   Read Exodus 15:2.

SOME DAYS WHEN MY SONS COME IN just having avoided some accident or danger, I remember the source of my strength. I feel compelled to praise God for sparing my sons and any others who might have been involved. I also feel that I must offer praise in front of my sons so that they may witness my expression of faith.

I often wonder if I am doing enough to show them their father and mother's God. Do they see me read my Bible? Do they hear or see me pray? Do they notice my singing the hymns of the church and the spirituals of our heritage? Or is it romance novels, telephone gossip, and rap or pop music that seem to provide the guiding light for my life?

I want my teens to know that I praise God. I want them to see me read my Bible. I want them to know that I offer prayers not only throughout the day but also every morning and night, and I want them to know that I can sing at least some of the verses of the hymns of the church without a hymnal. It is only then that I communicate the faith of our fathers and mothers. Without that background, how will I lead them to Christ?

Lord, help me to impart the source of my strength.

JANUARY 7   Read Psalm 139:14.

TODAY MY SON WAYNE NEEDS TO REMEMBER that he is wonderfully made. Sometimes he needs self-esteem building, and I consider that to be something I can help with.

I start by reminding him that he is wonderful; made by God; a person of great worth; a person that I love and for whom I thank God every day. I ask him how he intends to use all the gifts that God has given him. He looks at me somewhat awkwardly and asks, "What gifts?" Then I remind him of his beautiful smile, his pleasing personality, his physical strength, his charm and wit, and his keen sense of justice and fair play. I am honest in this assessment, for he knows his strengths and would not appreciate lies.

He asks me how he can use these gifts, and I tell him how much kind and sensitive people are needed in the world. I tell him about the groups in the church that could use a person like him, and then I tell him about the groups in his school that need a person like him. He begins to tell me about what he would really like to do, not only immediately but also in the future. I assure him that it is possible. All things are possible to those who believe. He smiles, and I believe that he can face another day. Life is tough when you're a teen.

Lord, thank you for making us so wonderfully. Teach us to recognize our gifts and to use them to your glory.

January 8   Read Psalm 144:1.

TEENAGERS FACE MANY WARS and battles each day. One of the most difficult is the battle with disappointment. I remember my son Walter coming in with less than a perfect report card or less than first place in the Science Fair and feeling that he had lost all of life's wars and battles. He was only learning to live with disappointment.

I had to help him remember to praise God. "God has not promised us that we will win all of the time," I said, "but he has promised to equip us for the battle." I often said, as have many other mothers, "It is not whether you win or lose, but how you play the game." Somehow that saying is just not meaningful to teenagers. They want to win, to come in first, to make all A's, to make the team, to be elected student body president or head cheerleader.

Learning to live with disappointment trains their hands for "war" and equips their fingers for "battle." We must help them to realize that God is their rock, their stronghold, their source of strength, and he will always be with them. They may not always win, but God is always to be praised.

Lord, help me to comfort my children in times of disappointment and direct them to you, Holy Comforter.

January 9   Read 2 Chronicles 5:13-14.

SOMETIMES WE PARENTS of teenagers find it difficult to live with all the musical noise that fills our homes, but this passage of scripture demonstrates the great number of instruments (over 100 trumpets alone) that were used to proclaim the glory of God. There was so much musical praise that the priests could not minister, but God did not need them to minister when his glory filled his house. God had the trumpeters and singers making themselves heard in unison in praise and thanksgiving, proving that there was more than one form of ministry.

Perhaps we as parents should encourage the lifting up of musical praise to God. Worship does not have to be silent or of a more traditional form. There are many ways to worship, and music seems to be one way that appeals to youth. We must stress unison, lifting up one voice, being of one accord, so that the glory of the Lord fills the house of God.

In every way and with every instrument, let us encourage our youth to praise the Lord.

Lord, help us to be open to the many and varied ways we have of praising you.

JANUARY 10   Read Joshua 7:19.

TEENAGERS ARE EXPOSED to many opportunities to participate in activities that are not pleasing to their parents or to their God. We as parents often need to remind them to give God praise by confession, for confession acknowledges that God is worthy and that we have sinned against him. We may be the intermediaries. If our children can confess to us, be open and honest with us, then perhaps they will find it easier to be open and honest with God.

Some teens were involved in harassing a fellow student who rode the school bus. The student was overweight and unpopular, and other students were cruel. One teen felt compelled to report the cruel treatment to her parents. She seemed to hear Joshua's words; and in order to give God glory and praise, she had to make a confession. She told what she had done.

Her mother was both ashamed and proud. She was ashamed that her daughter had participated in the cruel treatment, and she was proud that she had confessed. That mother asked to meet with all of the bus riders. She tried to make the cruelty real to all and asked them to put themselves in the place of the student who was being harassed. She took the opportunity to lift up the name of Jesus and to let the students know that it was their responsibility to praise God and not to harass others. Although the harassment did not stop, it lessened. I wonder whether I would have been able to live the life of praise that that mother did. Would I have used the opportunity to witness and to encourage others to praise God? I hope so.

Lord, help me to be open to the confessions of my teenagers, and give me the courage to turn their confessions into praise.

JANUARY 11   Read 1 John 4:7.

WHEN WALTER WAS IN HIGH SCHOOL, he liked to take my home-made chocolate chip cookies to his friends. They loved the cookies and looked forward to the days that Walter would bring them. Once when I had been working long hours and had not had an opportunity to make any cookies for some time, the teens began to ask for them.

All of Walter's friends were in the Science and Mathematics Academy at the local high school, and they participated in several city- and state-wide science fairs. They were very bright, industrious students who were serious about their studies; and I always looked forward to listening to their science project presentations when I attended the fairs.

It was time for the leading students to present their projects in the state-wide competition at the University of Georgia. All of the finalists had put in many hours of preparation. The bus was scheduled to leave the next day. Walter came home with an urgent message from one of his friends. She told him to tell me that she *needed* a chocolate chip cookie!

I laughed when I got the message, but I knew that the cookies represented the love and faith that I had in all of the finalists. They sincerely needed to feel and experience that love before participating in the final competition.

I stayed up late that night baking cookies and sent them with Walter to the state science fair. As it turned out, their school won the most medals. Though my cookies were not responsible for the number of medals, they did help the students to remember they were not alone. The cookies were my way of showing love, which comes from God.

Lord, teach us to show love daily to our teens and to their friends.

JANUARY 12

Read Psalm 139:7.

TODAY I MET A FIVE-YEAR-OLD GIRL in the county hospital where I volunteer. She became quite attached to me and wanted me to promise to stay with her until her mother came to visit. Her mother was a teenager who was known not to be very responsible, so I was afraid to commit to staying until she came. There was the possibility that she might not come.

The child needed a steady presence in her life. She had discovered that parents are not always physically with us, but she had not yet learned that the Spirit of God is.

When I explained that I could not promise to stay until her mother returned, I offered her an alternative plan. I would stay until she fell asleep. It was my hope that her mother would return by the time she awakened. Reluctantly, she agreed to my plan. I sat by her bed waiting for her to go to sleep. Each time she almost dozed off, she would awaken to see if I was still there.

Then she had a bright idea. She said, "Leave your purse." She had learned that women do not go anywhere without their purses. She felt confident that if she had my purse, I would not leave her. What she didn't know was that volunteers do not bring their purses into the patient area. When she found out that I did not have a purse, she gave in to sleep.

As I watched her sleep, I was reminded that it is our responsibility as parents to demonstrate for our teens what it means to be consistent in the care and support we give them, our children, in sickness and in health. We must teach them how to be good parents. It's never too early or too late to start.

Lord, help us become a source of confidence and support for our children and grandchildren as we lead them to you, from whose presence they can never flee.

JANUARY 13   Read Psalm 63:4.

SHARON'S TEENAGE SON did not get an opportunity to praise God for very long. His young life was tragically ended. After attending a basketball game with friends at a local high school, some sort of altercation broke out. There was gunfire, and two teenage boys were wounded. Sharon's son's wounds were fatal.

How would you respond if your phone rang and you were told that your child had been shot? What would be your first thoughts? Would you pray? Would you call on God's name? I am sure that Sharon prayed and asked for strength to endure the days and nights ahead. I am also sure that she asked why it had been *her* son. He was very bright and had such wonderful plans for the future. I am sure that she thought, "If I had not let him go to that game, he would still be alive." She might have even thought, "If I had praised God more often and given thanks more regularly, maybe my son would have been spared."

We are called for as long as we live and as often as we have opportunity to praise God's holy name. It is not ours to understand God's inscrutable ways, but it is a gift of our faith to know that God is with us always, including the times when we are asked to bear the most difficult burdens imaginable.

Lord, no matter how long or short our lives are, and no matter what our lives may bring, let us be constant in praise. You are worthy!

JANUARY 14   Read Psalm 68:19.

A FRIEND OF MINE has a teenage son who is troubled. Each time I see her, she has experienced another crisis with him. I remind her of this verse from Psalm 68 and let her know that God bears her up daily and is her salvation.

It is hard to be comforted by Scripture when the world around us is collapsing. Sometimes the Lord uses us to fulfill the Scripture. In other words, we must do the daily bearing up.

I begin by asking my friend to tell me what has happened. She tells me of something such as driving the car without permission or a license, violating curfew, being expelled from school, failing a course and jeopardizing high school graduation, or getting into a fight with a parent or sibling. This child is in trouble and needs prayer, attention, love, and counsel. This mother needs the support of friends and family. When we offer such support, we fulfill the Scripture.

Perhaps you are not the mother of a troubled teen. If not, stop now to praise and thank God. While you are praising, ask God to be a fence around those mothers who do have such children, and ask God to touch those troubled teens and help them find wholeness in the love of Jesus the Christ. He is their salvation.

Lord, strengthen me to be one who helps fulfill the Scriptures. All of those with whom I come in contact will know that I have found salvation in you. They can have salvation too. It is theirs for the asking.

JANUARY 15   Read Psalm 54:7.

TODAY WE CELEBRATE the birth of Dr. Martin Luther King, Jr. He was delivered from trouble, and in his last speech he knew that he would look in triumph on his enemies. Our teens were not even born when Dr. King lived his life of praise and thanksgiving, but he had a dream that we would all be delivered from every trouble, every prejudice, every hatred, every injustice, every war, every act of violence, everything that did not lift up the life and witness of Jesus the Christ.

As we look at our children, I wonder whether we are living that dream. There is only one way we can. We must make it *our* dream. Every day in every way we must seek to eliminate all that does not lift up Jesus. Jesus told us that if we lift him up, he will draw all men and women to him. That seems simple enough. All we have to do is lift up Jesus, and if we do, we are living the dream.

But do we want to? Are we willing to witness and teach our teenagers to witness? Are we willing to speak out against violence, oppression, and injustice? Or do we simply turn our heads and look the other way?

We will never live the dream until we decide to live lives that speak to the confidence we have in being delivered from every trouble and in praising the God who delivers us. Live the dream, for he is worthy to be praised!

Lord, help me to make the dreams of people such as Martin Luther King, Jr., become realities by adopting them as my own.

JANUARY 16   READ ISAIAH 11:6*b*.

IT WAS THE WEEKEND, and I was busy cooking food for the next week. I always cooked meals in advance when I had to be out of town on business. Wayne and Walter wanted to attend the Dog Show downtown; but with my schedule already full, I could not take them. Neither was old enough to drive, so I decided to drop them off at the Dog Show, giving them strict orders to be at the appointed pickup place on time.

When I returned, the boys were waiting. Excitedly they told me all about the show. My mind was not on the show but on a client I had to meet on Monday. I only half listened as they told me how the dogs were evaluated. They explained the point system, but I was not concentrating.

On Monday I met my client. I had been told that no one in our office had been able to relate to her, and we would probably lose the sale if I failed. Trying to make conversation, I mentioned the fact that my sons had attended a dog show over the weekend. Her eyes lit up, and she began to tell me about her show dogs. I quickly tried to recall all that my sons had told me about the show. I started asking questions about how the points were evaluated. The client thought I was terrific. We closed the deal.

I remember that experience and wonder how many times I failed to listen to my boys. How often did they speak words of wisdom that I missed? Sometimes a little child does lead us.

Lord, make me more attentive in listening to my children. I don't want to miss their cares, concerns, and words of wisdom.

JANUARY 17   Read Matthew 23:11.

MY SONS WERE 14 AND 16 years of age when I had a hysterectomy. They were accustomed to my being away on business trips; so when I told them that I would be away in the hospital for a few days, they were not overly concerned. My younger son, who likes to eat, asked if I could prepare enough food to last until I came home. I told him that I could and I would. The problem was that when I came home, I was still not able to cook. So, the boys and my husband had to fend for themselves.

To my amazement, they really did quite well. They found out that they can cook, set the table, do the dishes, and clean the bathrooms. It was a learning experience. They even found that they could serve their mother. They began to take pride in bringing me glasses of water and fixing my plate. They also began to realize just how much I had been doing for them.

Jesus was very clear when he told his disciples and the crowds that the greatest would be the servant. Sometimes mothers need to provide the opportunity for their teenagers to serve. I don't recommend major surgery, but taking advantage of a period of rest and confinement will give your family a chance to thank God for you and to extend some well-deserved praise. You all will be enriched by the experience.

Lord, help me to teach my children the art of serving.

JANUARY 18   Read Psalm 56:4.

TODAY THE STUDENTS at one of the local high schools had to pass through metal detectors as they entered the building. It is hard for me to imagine having to pass through a metal detector at school. But many of today's teenagers carry guns. They carry guns because they are afraid. Unlike the Psalmist, they are very much aware of what flesh can do to them. They can be maimed for life; they can lose their lives; or they can cause others to lose their lives. They are afraid.

There are many teenagers who praise and trust God. We do not need a metal detector for them. But there are so many more teenagers who do not praise and trust God, many of whom would, without the detectors, carry their guns into school and use them to harm others.

What can we as responsible, God-praising, and God-trusting adults do to help turn this situation around? We must thank, praise, and trust God openly. We must let our teenagers hear us sing the song of the freedom movement, "We are not afraid . . . God is on our side . . . We are not afraid today." When the freedom singers and the civil rights leaders sang that song, they *were* afraid, but the singing of the song gave them courage. By singing "We are not afraid," the words became reality.

It is my wish that one day we can do away with metal detectors in school. And so I pray that we will do away with the hatred, greed, envy, jealousy, and prejudice that have led many teens to believe that guns are the way to settle disputes. We will learn to live without fear only when we collectively learn to live a life of love, praise, trust, and thanksgiving.

Lord, make me and my children instruments of your peace. As we live lives of praise and trust, we will learn to live in peace—without fear.

JANUARY 19   Read Exodus 20:12.

As I READ THE COMMANDMENT found in Exodus 20:12, I think of Marcus who beat his mother up last week. She was so ashamed of her son's having hit her that she told everyone at work that she had run into a door. She refused medical treatment because she was afraid the doctors would be able to tell the difference between a left hook to the face and an accident.

What happens when teenagers fail to honor their parents? How does a parent respond? I have heard some say, "If you ever raise your hand to me, I'll kill you." I wonder whether some parents really mean that. Do they really feel that they brought their children into the world and they will take them out? What has gone wrong? How could a teen raise a hand against his or her mother? How could a parent raise a hand to kill her or his child?

Both parent and child need to experience the presence of God. A life of thanksgiving and praise would not allow time for violence. If every morning both parent and child would thank God for his goodness, praising him for his acts of mercy and asking him for the strength to be the best persons they could be that day, there would be no acts of violence. They would just keep so busy praising his name, there would not be time for anything else.

Lord, touch the hearts and minds of parents and teens who contemplate acts of violence.

JANUARY 20   Read Proverbs 10:1.

APRIL'S FATHER WAS NOT GLAD, and her mother was filled with grief. As far as they were concerned, April had acted very foolishly. She had participated in unprotected, pre-marital sex, and she was pregnant. Her parents thought their world was crumbling to pieces. They had no anchor.

Whenever they looked at April, they shook their heads or cried. What would become of all the plans they had for her? How would she finish high school and go to college? Should she marry the baby's father? What would happen to his future plans? What did his parents think about the situation?

April's grandmother was heard to say, "How can you say God is the anchor of your life if you can't make it through the storm?" What challenging words. If God is our anchor, our support, our sustenance, then we can and will make it through the storms. We learn to put our faith and trust in him; we praise and thank him every day; and we ask for guidance and direction through the storm.

I never faced the storm that April's parents did. But if I had, I hope that I would have been able to look at my son— or my daughter, if I had one—with love, realizing that my child had not acted wisely and praying that we would accept the situation and act responsibly in the best interests of all involved. We parents were once, and sometimes still are, foolish too. But God still loves us and forgives us and guides us through the storm.

Lord, help us to remember that you are our anchor when we are trying to make it through the storm.

JANUARY 21   Read Hebrews 12:6.

I HAVE NOTICED THAT SOME PARENTS of teenagers are afraid to discipline their children. They might be afraid of alienating their children. They might even fear physical retaliation on the part of a child who is bigger and stronger than they are.

This may be a sign of the times in which we live. All teenagers need discipline. It is a part of showing our love. We must have rules and regulations, and our children must learn to obey. They will never be law-abiding citizens if they have not learned to abide by the rules of the home.

The Scripture says, "Endure trials for the sake of discipline. God is treating you as children; for what child is there whom a parent does not discipline? If you do not have that discipline in which all children share, then you are illegitimate and not his children" (Heb. 12:7-8). We discipline because we love and because these are our children. They do not belong to anyone else, and they will not learn to live within the will of God if we do not share that will with them. We restrain and direct their activities so that they will be safe and successful in their lifelong journey.

Pray for your teens. Love them, but chastise them in love. If they are out of control, rein them in. They need your loving restraint. Do not be afraid. These are your children.

Lord, let us so love our children that they will know that they will be chastised when they are disobedient.

JANUARY 22   Read Matthew 5:9.

THERE ARE GANGS AT THE local high school. Some parents worry every day that their children will be attacked by the members of the gang. Other parents worry that their children are members of the gang. None of these gangs are known for being peacemakers. Wherever they go there is trouble, confusion, and conflict. No one would ever accuse them of being representative of the children of God.

Teens join gangs because they need and want to belong to a group, to feel accepted and loved. If they resist, they may be attacked, shot, even killed. I remember living in Chicago in a neighborhood that had been taken over by a gang. If any teenage male refused to joint the gang, he would be shot. Some were even castrated. One mother of a teenage male defied the gang by telling them that they would have to come through her to get her son. Her defiance and the appearance of the police turned the gang away.

I hope other mothers will not all have to resort to such drastic measures. Why can't we become peacemakers, mothers actively working for peace in our communities, peace without gangs?

Or better yet, our families could become the gangs that offer the acceptance, love, and group identity that our teenagers crave. How about a gang called the "Peacemakers, Children of God"?

Lord, help our children to resist the gangs of violence and join the gangs of peace.

JANUARY 23   Read James 1:2-4.

MARTHA'S SEVENTEEN-YEAR-OLD son got into an argument with his father about wearing a beeper. His father insisted that the only people who wear beepers are involved in drugs or some other illegal activity. The son insisted that his father did not understand modern youth who need to keep in constant communication with each other. The discussion became more heated, and blows were exchanged. Then the father ordered his son out of the house.

Martha did not know how she could count this as joy. She knew that it was a trial. She understood her husband's position, but she could not bear to see her son homeless. Social Services interacted and told Martha that her husband could be arrested for child abuse for locking his underaged son out of the house. Could all this be joy? Martha thought not.

Martha became a peacemaker between her husband and her son. She convinced her son to turn the beeper off in the house since his father objected. She convinced her husband to allow the son to return to the house on the condition that he would abide by the rules of the house. Those rules included no beepers.

There is now an uneasy peace. As soon as their son reaches the age of eighteen, his father could legally put him out in the street. Martha fears that will happen if either his behavior or her husband's outlook does not change. Martha is going through trials; but as she continues to play the role of peacemaker, she is growing in Christian maturity and in endurance, which enhances her faith so that she lacks nothing. Count it all joy. Praise God in spite of. Hallelujah, anyhow!

Lord, sometimes it's difficult to give thanks and praise when our world seems to be falling apart. Give us strength to endure the trials and remind us to "count it all joy."

JANUARY 24   Read Psalm 34:1.

WHEN MY SONS WERE TEENAGERS, they participated in a church basketball league. I would often leave work early to be in the stands when their team played, and I was always disappointed in the number of parents who actually came out to support our team.

It had been so different when they were in Little League. Then I was just one of many parents who supported those games. It seemed that the pattern of failing to support teenage efforts existed in many areas. While there had been many parents attending PTA meetings at the elementary school, there were very few at the high school meetings. Often parental support and praise of our children taper off when they reach the teen years.

Just as the Psalmist pledged to bless the Lord at all times and to continually praise him, I believe that parents ought always to bless and praise their children in their wholesome efforts and activities. One day I sat in those stands as our church basketball team walked onto the court. I noticed that our coach had not arrived with the other players. However, my sons had brought a carload with them, so there were five players to begin the game.

The referees called our team to the sidelines. I continued to watch. Then my son motioned for me to come onto the court. I knew that something was wrong, and I hurriedly walked onto the court. My son explained that they would have to forfeit the game if there was not an adult with them serving as coach. He said, "Mom, you can do it!" I took off my jacket and gathered the boys around me. Some looked disgusted, thinking that there was no way they could win with a mother as a coach. But their eyes brightened when I asked, "Are we going to play zone or man-to-man?" My question gave them confidence that I at least knew something about the game.

I wish I could say that we won, but we lost by one point. That did not matter to either me or my boys. We had worked together, and when they needed an adult, I was there—praising them and encouraging them to give it their best!

Lord, help us always to be supportive of our children. They need us for all of their lives. Even as we always need you, they always need us. Praise and blessings should continuously come from our mouths.

JANUARY 25   Read 1 Corinthians 10:13.

A MEMBER OF OUR CHURCH who played on the local high school basketball team asked my husband, his pastor, to attend some of his games. My husband agreed, and even sat near the bench with the players. He became another coach or perhaps, more accurately, an honorary chaplain. He tried to instill in the players the desire to win, but he always reminded them that winning was not everything.

At times there were many obstacles to winning. Star players were injured, referees made bad calls, team members failed to play like a team, and games were lost. The coach and my husband talked with the players about their being tested. Sometimes obstacles became stepping stones. The team had to be reminded that others had faced and overcome similar tests; but, the God they served would not allow them to be tested beyond their ability to endure.

The presence of a pastor who prayed for them and encouraged them made the team members aware of their need for God to be active in their lives. They found joy in praising God, and several players as well as a coach who were not already members joined our church.

Teenagers are hungry for adults who are not afraid or ashamed to witness to their faith. If we become a people of praise and thanksgiving, even when we are tested, I believe our youth will be saved.

Lord, help us to witness wherever we are so that our youth will know you as the center of our lives.

JANUARY 26   Read Psalm 48:12-14.

As I AM WRITING THIS, it is my aunt's ninety-sixth birthday. God has blessed her with a long life, but I wonder whether she has lived a life of praise and thanksgiving. Has she told the next generation about our God who is ours forever? I don't remember her ever talking to me about her faith. I don't remember her teaching me the words of the Scriptures or testifying about what God has done in her life. I don't even remember ever seeing her read the Bible. All I know is that she has lived a long time, and I respect her advanced age.

I want the teenagers who look at me to be able to do more than respect my age. I want them to be able to tell the next generation the stories of Jesus that I have told them. I want them to be able to say that I testified about the goodness of the God who is my God forever. I want them to recall having seen and heard me pray and study the Scriptures and provide words of encouragement to those who were struggling to reach maturity in life and in the faith. I want them to be able to call the names of those I led to Christ. I want them to respect my age, but I want them to respect more than that. If I live to reach my ninety-sixth birthday, I hope I will be living a life of praise and thanksgiving. What about you?

Lord, bless us with long years, and let them be years of witnessing to the next generation about your goodness.

JANUARY 27   Read Matthew 6:19, 21.

WHEN MY SON WALTER was in graduate school in Raleigh, North Carolina, he worked as a counselor in the Regional

Detention Center. One of the youth incarcerated at that time was a fifteen-year-old drug dealer. He was reputed to be the biggest drug dealer in the city with a weekly payroll to his pushers of more than $1,000,000. When he was apprehended, more than a quarter of a million dollars in cash was found under the floor boards in his house.

My son had several conversations with the youth. Walter tried to tell him that while he was consumed with material things, there were values that were more important. The fifteen-year-old had a baby daughter, and my son tried to let him know how his drug dealings would affect his daughter. But the youth wanted money, lots of money. The fastest and easiest way he knew to make money was to deal drugs.

Walter spoke to him of graduate school and the long-term contributions that education meant to his future. He told that young man how proud I was of him even though he had little money and often needed my financial assistance. The teenager replied, "You have to wait for your mother to send you money to help you pay your rent. Well, I can buy my mother any house she wants." He was consumed with material things. He did not even hear what my son was saying.

Too many of our teens are similarly consumed. They want everything they see, and they even feel that they need everything they can think of possessing. Perhaps if we spent more time in thanksgiving and praise and less time in buying and selling, our children would be less consumed with the treasures of this earth. Let us try harder to help our teens lay up treasures in heaven.

Lord, help us to set the example of storing up heavenly treasures.

JANUARY 28   Read Matthew 6:25.

RECENTLY I READ A NEWSPAPER article that featured teenage models dressed for proms and other important dates. The teens were dressed in the latest fashions and were in poses that suggested the most elite training. The fashions were all available at local department stores and boutiques, and they were designed by the hottest designers.

At first glance I noticed how attractive the youngsters were. Then I thought how mature they looked. Then I looked at the prices of the clothes they were modeling. I was in deep shock! Who in their right mind would spend that kind of money on clothes for teens? So I started to read the article. Words about how your child would be the envy of all the others and how your child deserved the latest in fashion filled the page.

I began to think about the values we instill in our children. Isn't life more than clothes? Why do we worry and teach them to worry about what they will wear? I wish the article had been about teaching our children the proper manners to use as they attend proms and go out on dates. I wish the article had talked about non-abusive behavior so that we would not have to worry about drunk drivers and date rape. I wish the article had talked about wrapping our children in the love of God and in thanksgiving and praise for their many blessings.

One mother wrote a letter to the editor stating feelings very much like mine. She said that if we clothed our children in love, we would never have to worry about the sizes in which those clothes were available. One size fits all!

Lord, help us to teach our children that life is more than food and the body is more than clothes.

JANUARY 29   Read James 5:16.

OUR CHURCH HAS EXPERIENCED a spiritual renewal since it has become a praying church. The first Sunday morning worship service begins at 8:00 A.M., but at 7:00 A.M. members of the church meet for prayer. They pray at each pew for all who will sit there during the various worship services; they pray at each instrument and at each pulpit chair; they pray at each choir stand pew and for each choir member.

Out of this praying atmosphere there emerged a group called the Prayer Warrior Moms. It is a prayer ministry composed of women who pray every day for their children. They are willing to fight for their children. They are warriors, and they know that by heartfelt prayer they can fight against the forces of evil that surround their children.

The moms are divided into groups of seven, and they pray on their specified day in the privacy of their homes. On their day they pray for their own children and for all the other children on their list. In this way each child is prayed for daily, seven days a week, 365 days a year.

Just think. What if in every church we would organize Prayer Warrior Moms? What if every day someone was praying for our teenagers? What if all mothers were fighting for their teens through prayer and praises? Why don't we all commit today to become Prayer Warrior Moms?

Lord, make us every mindful of the power of prayer.

JANUARY 30   Read Luke 18:1.

DO YOU EVER FIND YOURSELF praying the same prayers for your children again and again, yet the concerns of your prayers still persist? Consider the story of the persistent widow found in Luke 18:1-8. She was wronged by her adversary, and she went to the judge for justice. She had nothing to bargain with but her persistence; she had no bribe to offer; and she had no man to protect or accompany her. It was well known that the judge was unjust, but she hoped to wear him down with her persistence. She eventually did just that. She wore him down to the point that he finally granted her justice just to get rid of her.

Jesus told this story to illustrate the virtue of persistence and to make clear that even an unjust judge would grant a petition if one just kept asking. If an unjust judge would grant a persistent request, surely a righteous God would and will.

We, as parents, must never stop praying. After all, this year we are living a life of praise and thanksgiving. Prayer is composed of these elements. Our righteous God will grant our petition. And, as the parable suggests, when Jesus comes back, he wants to find us still praying. Pray on!

Lord, we praise you for your righteousness, and we ask for the faith to be persistent in prayer.

JANUARY 31   Read Psalm 146:2.

AS WE HAVE REACHED THE END of this first month of the new year, I hope we are all firmly committed to living a life of thanksgiving and praise. Suffering, disappointment, and death are a part of life. We never know when any of these will find us or our teenagers, but we can be assured that our hope is to be prepared to meet them by living a life of thanksgiving and praise.

Thanksgiving and praise strengthen us and equip us by helping us to draw closer to God, and God holds our future. For some of us, this will be a banner year. For others of us, it will be a difficult year.

I pray each day for strength to meet the challenges that lie before me. I know that I cannot fight the battle alone. I need God, the source of my strength. As I rely on my faith to sustain me, I want the way I live my faith to be a witness to all teens. I want them to see me and realize that if they follow me, I will not lead them astray. How many of us would be willing to let a teenager follow us for a week, a day, even an hour and be assured that we would not lead them in the wrong direction?

We do not know what lies ahead, but God knows. He holds the future. All we have to do is praise him!

Lord, I will praise you my whole life long!

FEBRUARY

ALWAYS GROWING

Anne Killinger

FEBRUARY 1   **Read Ecclesiastes 3:4a, 7b.**

MY MOTHER GAVE ME some remarkably sound advice when our first son, Eric, was born. It didn't come from Dr. Spock or any psychology book. She learned it from raising six children. "Laugh at half of what he does," she said, "and ignore the other half."

When Eric and his brother, Krister, reached their teens, I understood her meaning, for like all families with teenagers, we had a few trying times. Sometimes our boys let their grades fall. I didn't scold very much. I chuckled because I remembered my own difficulties with geometry. The high school principal lived up the street from my family and volunteered to tutor me; but even he finally gave me up as "hopeless." Good marks are wonderful, but sometimes they are impossible to obtain.

Once, Krister dropped a decorative vase that broke into a thousand fragments. I regretted the accident because I had purchased the vase with a Christmas check from my father. But seeing the stricken look on his face swiftly diverted my attention from the vase. My truly precious treasure was standing there before me!

Laughing and ignoring can't win out all the time. Some situations are obviously far too important to let them go unheeded. But most offenses can be handled lightly, for they won't really matter a few years from now.

Lord, I hope you can laugh at half of what I do and ignore the other half. I promise to try to do the same for the children you have lovingly entrusted to my care.

FEBRUARY 2   Read 1 Samuel 17:39*b*.

I REMEMBER MY FIRST PAIR of high-heeled shoes. Wearing them, I wobbled down the church aisle like a newborn colt. Smiles followed me, as older women remembered their first experience with heels. I was only fourteen, but I felt absolutely grown up!

I didn't acquire those shoes without a struggle, though. My father wanted me to dress *sensibly*. He had been a farm boy, and his idea of a pair of shoes was laced-up brogans that could withstand the rigors of ploughing and hoeing. He never understood why my mother didn't force me to wear the pair of lace-ups he purchased for me. They lay untouched on the closet shelf until I left home. I never even dusted them. It was a simple matter of the older generation's not understanding the younger generation's need for personal identity.

Unnecessary conflicts result when parents try to outfit their children in what they wore when they were young. Teens are individuals like the rest of us, and need to express themselves by what they wear. Oh, we adults may have to step in and explain why certain clothes may be inappropriate, but by and large, young people have to wear their own styles even when we think they look ridiculous. They have their own journeys to make and need to get accustomed to them in their own ways.

Help me to remember, God, what it was like to be young and to want to dress like my friends, and then to realize how natural it is for my child to want the same thing.

WHEN HE WAS VERY SMALL, Krister would always measure his dinner fork against Eric's to be sure his brother's fork was not longer than his. Later, when he was a teenager, he sometimes did the same thing as a joke. Then, as an extension of the fun, I would tell him I always gave a larger one to Eric because I loved him more. Then we would both convulse with laughter.

I thought about this ritual recently when I was administering an exam to a class of college students. I looked at the students' faces and wondered if any of their parents had shown more love to their siblings. What about the girl with an earring in the side of her nose and the fellow with his cap on backwards, who sat facing the other students instead of arranging his chair beside theirs? Were they trying to make statements about themselves because they had been told they weren't as important or clever as a brother or sister?

As a mother, I sometimes pity poor Esau in the biblical story because his mother, Rebekah, favored her son Jacob. Children are such sensitive creatures, and feeling that they aren't loved as much as other children can mark them for life. It is so important for our children to know how much we care about them—just as it's important for us to know that God cares about us.

I know you love me, dear God, but sometimes I forget how much. Help me to live with a daily awareness of that love, so that I may live in the overflow of joy and excitement.

MY MOTHER ONCE TOLD ME, when our boys were teenagers, that I loved them too much. I thought that was a ridiculous thing to say. How could a mother love her children too much? The only thing that was wrong with the world, I believed, was a *lack* of love.

Then I began to notice what happens to parents who love their children "too much."

I had a friend whose fourteen-year-old son would not respond to her when she questioned him. He merely grunted or shrugged his shoulders. One day she became so upset with this that she yelled, "If I didn't love you so much, I wouldn't care whether you talked to me or not!"

Hmmm, I thought. Her love for the child was giving her pain.

Another friend had a fifteen-year-old daughter who had a personality disorder. She rarely told the truth, and sometimes she became unreasonably violent. The mother gave the child extra doses of love, but was chagrined to learn that love didn't cure the problem.

Hmmm, I thought, there it is again. Love often leads to pain.

Maybe my mother was right. Should we try to love less so that the pain won't be so great? I reflected on God's sending his only Son into the world for our redemption, and how he was rejected and brutally killed. That surely caused God more pain than we can ever imagine. But God didn't withdraw from loving because of that. If anything, he seemed to love us even more. So we too cannot withdraw. We have to keep on loving despite the pain it may bring us, because loving is the best thing we can ever know to do.

Your pain must have been enormous, dear God, yet you didn't hesitate to let your Son die on the cross for our sin. Help me to understand what that means about your great love for us and to be willing to endure the pain of my own love.

FEBRUARY 5   Read Luke 10:19*b*.

NOTHING WILL HURT YOU. I wish I could hold that saying over my children like an umbrella of protection all their lives. There are so many things in the world to hurt them.

One day Eric came home from school with his shoulders sagging. "What happened?" I asked.

"Nothing," he replied.

"Come on, you can tell me."

His math teacher, who had a reputation for belittling students, had really chewed out the class that day. The students had been having trouble grasping a concept he was trying to teach, and he told them they were ignorant. Why, he said, his dog was more intelligent than they were!

Surely the teacher had no idea of the dismay he was injecting into his young students' hearts by such an outburst. But I realized there was little I could do to protect my child from such abuse. The world is full of it. The best thing I could do was explain to Eric that people often say things like that when their own lives are filled with rejection or disappointment, and then surround him with the affection and acceptance that would fortify him for dealing with disappointments in the outside world.

It must have been like that when Jesus told his disciples that nothing would hurt them. Surely he knew that a lot of things would hurt them. But he also realized that down inside, where the world didn't see, they would be shielded by his love and the things he had taught them.

I pray for my children, Lord, that they will always be shielded by the love you and I have given them, so that whatever befalls them they will survive with joyous and positive spirits.

FEBRUARY 6   Read 1 Samuel 17:29a.

OUR TWO BOYS BOTH HAVE two-syllable names: Eric and Krister. I have always suspected that one-syllable names lie flat on the tongue and don't command as much attention as two-syllable names. I could be wrong about that. My mother could say "A-unne!" in a way that made even my toes perspire! Whenever I heard my name pronounced that way I always wondered, "Oh no, what have I done now?"

Teens do a lot of provoking things, some on purpose and others because they're neither fish nor fowl, and often tempt their parents to call their names in that way that only parents can. I tried to realize, when Eric and Krister were teens, how I felt when I was their age. I didn't want to embarrass them with questions and accusations just because they were at a different place than I was on the journey of life.

It is sometimes difficult to confront teenage children when we think they are in the wrong. We know how likely they are to respond, "What have I done now?" which is really a way of saying, "What are you accusing me of this time?" or "What right do you have to blame me for my actions?" This always has the effect of turning the reprimand back on us, which makes us angry.

There isn't any more important time in our relationships to remember to trust in God with all our hearts and not rely solely on our own insights. God will hear us when we ask "What do I do now?" and open a path for us.

Give me patience, O God, to treat my children with the kind of civility and consideration I would expect for myself, and help me not to react to their irritation or unhappiness with rudeness and unkindness; for you are never rude or unkind to me.

FEBRUARY 7   Read 1 Samuel 14:1.

HOW MANY TIMES, when our children have come home late and we have asked "Where were you?" have they answered "Out with friends"? No details. No explanation. No real account of their whereabouts or their doings.

This happened to Mary, the mother of Jesus, too. They had been to Jerusalem and were on their way home a whole day's journey when Mary realized her son was not with their caravan. It was a first-century *Home Alone!* Mary and Joseph began a frantic search and found their son in the temple. Mary must have been livid! "Son," she asked, "why have you treated us this way? We have nearly died of anxiety!" Jesus answered, "Why were you searching for me?"

Sometimes I imagine I hear God asking me, "Where have you been, child?" And my answer usually sounds like some teenager's excuse: "I've been busy."

"But I've missed you."

"I've had a lot on my mind."

42

"Can I help?"

"Well, you see, it's a problem."

"I'm listening."

"God, I don't understand my son. He has this way of going off and not telling me where he's been or what he's been doing."

"Same as with you and me?"

Give me the strength, O God, to raise my children well and to commit them to you. In the process, maybe I will learn to commit myself to you as well.

FEBRUARY 8   Read 1 Sam. 1:27*a.*

IT HAS BEEN DIFFICULT FOR ME to give my children totally to God. God allowed me to become a parent, and I have always tried to honor my role by protecting and guiding them. But even though I have always prayed for my children, sometimes when they were growing up, I didn't allow the heavenly Expert to influence their lives as much as he might have. I asked God to watch over them; but I still felt that my watchful presence was necessary wherever they were and whatever they were doing.

I did say "God, he is yours" when Eric took his first communion. And when both Eric and Krister were baptized, I felt my heart swell as I mentally gave them to their heavenly Father. Yet I really had trouble letting go. I wanted to remain necessary as their caretaker, as the person who would make everything all right in their lives.

Then one night Krister was in an accident. The VW he was driving dropped a wheel over the edge of the pavement and flipped over five times. His head went through the windshield. But miraculously he walked away from the car with a few minor scratches and his curly hair full of bits of shattered glass.

Krister was taken to the hospital for a checkup. When I walked up to his bed and our eyes met, we both began to cry. What a close call it had been! I held him tightly and felt totally helpless. I knew I could not protect him from the cru-

elties of life, some of which might even prove fatal. I relent-
ed. God had to be the master Parent.

That doesn't mean that God always makes the road
smooth and easy for his children. The hurts and tragedies
we parents sometimes endure can be faith-shaking. God
never promised us that there would be simple solutions to
some of the heartbreaks we experience. But whatever happens, I must try to remember that God is a far better caretaker than I. God understands the whole picture; I am trying
to cope with only one little part of it.

*I have tried to be a faithful parent, O God, but now I realize that a large
part of being faithful is turning my child over to you for your love and
blessing. Help me to do that and then to share your joy.*

FEBRUARY 9   Read Lamentations 3:25-28a.

I WAS HOME ALONE one hot summer afternoon. My husband,
John, and the boys had decided to get out of the house, but I
opted to curl up in my favorite chair with a book. I had been
feeling excessively tense and haggard and needed some solitude.

After I had read a few pages, I noticed that the house was
deathly still. The dryer wasn't running. The refrigerator was-
n't humming. There was no music. No dogs were barking.
There wasn't even a fly buzzing in the room. The stillness
became palpable, as if it had a life of its own.

I listened to it. I thought I could hear the distress signals
in my body—the fatigue in my weakened limbs, the deep
sigh of a troubled heart, the paralyzing neurosis of my spirit.

Then I thought about God and listened again.

This time I heard something else. I heard my soul turning
toward heaven. I heard the sound of soft weeping, as if my heart
were shedding tears of joy. I heard a fresh breeze that carried
new promises. Finally, I heard a quiet voice saying, "My child!"

I felt whole and rested again. The process had taken only
a few minutes. Yet something had renewed me. The stillness
had borne me back to God.

Sometimes we mothers are so busy attending to the needs of our families that we forget our own needs. Take time to wait and listen for God today.

There is nothing more refreshing to my spirit, O God, than being alone with you. Teach me to be still more often.

FEBRUARY 10   Read 1 Corinthians 13:13.

ROBERT COLES, THE PROMINENT child psychologist, did an extensive study of the children of the wealthy and the children of the poor in America. He discovered that the children of the poor are generally happier than the children of the rich because their parents spend more time with them and give them more love. The wealthier the parents, the more likely they are to lead extremely busy lives and to give their children *things* instead of love.

I got a glimpse of this when our sons were growing up. They went to a private school attended by many children of affluence. Some of these children, we learned, had never eaten a meal with their parents. They were usually fed by maids in the kitchen so their parents could dine alone at a later hour or go out socially with friends.

These children considered it a treat to be able to come home after school with our boys. Invariably, they wanted to hang around the kitchen and help me bake chocolate chip cookies. They laughed and talked and popped chocolate chips in their mouths. I rarely got more than one pan of cookies from a batch because they had eaten so much of the raw cookie dough.

I have often thought about those children and how important that small domestic gesture was to them. In the overall spectrum of their existence, it was only a tiny thing. But to them, starved for love and attention, it was probably more important than anything else.

There are so many love-starved children in the world today, Lord. Maybe it's part of what's wrong with the world. Help me to love the children in my life and give them the little joys that translate into happy adulthood.

FEBRUARY 11   Read James 1:5.

I DON'T LIKE TO BE TOLD what to do. I never have. My mother used to say, "Ask Anne to do something and she will do it gladly, but don't ever *tell* her to do anything." One time she and I went shopping together. I tried on a number of dresses. Mother told me not to get the purple one, it didn't look good on me. I bought the purple one, even though I didn't really like it. If mother told me my hair needed cutting, I wore it even longer. If she said I should wear pale lipstick, I wore bright red.

Why should it surprise me to learn that teenagers rebel against their parents?

I hate to admit it, but I have even felt rebellious when my heavenly Parent wanted me to do something. I would make excuses, or even go so far as to tell God it was my life and I should be able to do with it as I wished.

Now that I'm older, I realize that my mother really wanted the best for me, and I probably hurt myself by not listening to her and trying to please her. It is the same with God. I know my life would have been richer and better if I had always listened to him and tried to do what he wanted me to do.

James 1:5 promises that if we lack wisdom, we only have to ask of God and he will give it to us. Maybe it is in the willingness to ask that we really gain wisdom—the willingness to admit we don't know everything and God does. I hope I can remember that and practice it. I'm only hurting myself when I don't.

I am truly sorry for my rebellion, O God. I pray that you will take it away and give me a radiant, compliant heart. And I ask the same for my children.

FEBRUARY 12   Read 1 Corinthians 13:4-8a.

I ONCE HEARD A MINISTER make the statement that mothers never get away from being mothers. I wasn't terribly excited at that news. Eric and Krister were teenagers at the time, and I didn't relish living as the mother of teenagers for the rest of my life.

It wasn't that they were difficult or unmanageable. Far from it. They were practically model children. But they were so active, so inquisitive, so *active*—there, I said it again!—that it was a fulltime job just keeping up with them. I was tired. I sometimes wanted to resign from motherhood. When the boys would call "Mother" I would answer, "Your mother doesn't live here anymore. Why don't you go look for her?"

The next Sunday, the same minister spoke about how impossible it is for parents to impart to children everything they know. Then I realized why I was so tired. I *wanted* to teach my children everything I knew. I wanted to give them the secrets of the universe. I wanted them to possess all the wisdom I had gained through making mistakes without their having to repeat those mistakes. And it was impossible!

What a freeing revelation that was. I didn't have to fill my children's cups to overflowing. I could concentrate on loving them and let them learn about life on their own. I could hug them and send them out to gain their own wisdom. Suddenly I could relax. The future of the world didn't depend on me. I could be human again. I could thank God for the chance to share my children's lives and then turn them over to him for the future. These were some of the best words I ever heard!

God, you have taught me a lot in life, but you have also given me room to learn on my own. Help me to do that with my children. They have a right to their own discoveries, and even their own mistakes

FEBRUARY 13   Read 1 Timothy 4:11-12.

I RECENTLY ATTENDED MY FATHER'S one hundredth birthday party. It was a sweet-sad occasion, seeing all the relatives, young and old, gathering to celebrate the life of one man who was responsible for the existence of us all. I especially enjoyed watching the teenagers. There was an outspokenness about them, a sort of devil-may-care attitude about what they said, that could easily have been misunderstood as rudeness. I wondered what my father might have said to them, had he possessed the mind to do so. Would he have echoed the biblical injunction, "Let no one despise your youth" (v. 12)? Would he also have added, "And don't ever despise your elders"?

It is sometimes difficult not to dislike what we don't understand. I'm sure my father was not especially comfortable with some of the children and the way they were dressed. Girls didn't wear such short dresses when he was young, and boys didn't wear their hair in ponytails. By the same token, I expect some of the children were not comfortable with my father, who grew up in an authoritarian age and still expects young people to be submissive in the presence of their seniors.

But we all got along beautifully. It was as if we felt something very special in the presence of one who had lived an entire century. And I couldn't help thinking about God, who has been here forever, and how special we should feel in his presence. We really should, shouldn't we?

Before the mountains were created or the seas sprang up between the lands, O God, you were there. Teach me reverence, that I may number my days and be glad, and help me to teach reverence to my children.

FEBRUARY 14   Read Amos 9:11.

A FRIEND'S NEPHEW WAS IN THE process of obtaining a divorce. But because he wanted the marriage to work, he kept delaying signing the papers. He frequently telephoned his wife and asked if they couldn't try again. He accepted all the blame for the problems they had had and told her how much he missed her and the children. But she was adamant. "You want a Beaver Cleaver family," she said, "but Beaver Cleaver families simply don't exist anymore."

The world has greatly changed for families. Now both parents usually work. Children come home to find the house empty. There are few of the old-fashioned dinners where the whole family gathers around the table and prays or reads the Bible together. Life has become very chaotic, and we all suffer from it.

What's a mother to do in such a situation? Maybe the answer is in the ancient book of Amos, where God promised to rebuild the fallen city of Jerusalem. The former inhabitants of the city couldn't do it. They didn't have the resources or the ability. But God could do it. It may be that the most we can do in a fragmented world like ours is to spend more time in the presence of God, asking God to rebuild our homes and our culture. And then maybe God will lead us to do our small part in that rebuilding, showing us what we can do through loving and caring and serving others to lead our families into times of blessing again.

I feel helpless to make things right for my family, O God. But in your strength I am able to face the demands of every day. Give me courage and wisdom and love, for everyone's sake.

FEBRUARY 15   Read Joshua 24:15.

A *NINETY-FIVE-YEAR-OLD WOMAN* once told me that a teenager is "a person in the process of maturing." I thought at the time that the remark was rather obvious, that what she was saying was that teenagers are experiencing a lot of volatility in their growing up and it sometimes makes their behavior appear immature. But the more I have pondered her remark, the deeper its truth has appeared. I realize that she was actually talking about the life process itself, and how we are always in process, regardless of how old we are. Maybe the teen years are more difficult because one's hormones are changing and the way one feels and views the world is undergoing rapid alteration. But every period of life is part of the process.

It is one of the ironies of life that most parents are going through midlife, which psychologists say is a kind of second adolescence, at the same time that their children are going through adolescence. This makes things doubly hard for both the children and their parents, for the hormonal imbalances in their bodies and shifting perspectives of their psyches tend to make them edgy and uncomfortable. Both are facing constant decisions that will affect the remainder of their lives.

Joshua was an old man when he confronted the Israelites with the choice of whom they would serve, and he understood the importance of their choosing properly. He knew that whatever their age, young or old, they would not go wrong if they consciously decided to follow God. Maybe that is the most important thing to know about the process of maturing: We are never too young or too old to seek the guidance of our heavenly Parent.

The children aren't the only ones who still have maturing to do, O God; so do I. Please give me the serenity and determination to continue growing, that I may be wiser tomorrow than I am today.

FEBRUARY 16   Read Leviticus 19:3*a*.

MY HUSBAND, JOHN, AND I were walking through our neighborhood recently and heard a teenager shouting at his mother. "Don't tell me what to do," he said. "What I do is my own business, so just shut up! I hate you!"

"Whoa!" I said to John. "If that had been one of our sons, I think I might just have broken my vow of nonviolence."

I wondered how the mother must have felt after such an outburst. I would have been devastated. Had she just arrived home from work? Had she had a hectic day? Was her patience thin? Was she a single parent doing a double shift? What had her son been up to that led to a confrontation? Had he failed an exam? Had his favorite girl snubbed him in front of friends? Was he lonely and scared?

I wanted to put my arms around both of them, because I knew they were both hurting.

We walked on and thought about our own sons. They had never yelled at us that we could remember. I know they were sometimes angry with us and thought we were old fogeys, but they never lashed out like that young man. Why? We decided it was because they had respect.

Respect for us.

Respect for God.

Respect for the created order of things.

Respect for themselves.

When people have respect for God and themselves, they revere everything else in the world. I prayed for that mother and child to recover their respect. It would put everything in order again and restore their joy in living.

I respect you, God; help me to respect you more. Let the fact that you are always beside me enable me to walk with serenity and love in your world.

FEBRUARY 17   Read Ephesians 4:32a.

MY FATHER, AS I HAVE MENTIONED, is more than 100 years old. He is confined to a bed or wheelchair, and his mind doesn't always function at full efficiency. While he usually doesn't recognize family members at first, a few minutes of conversation about the past will soon engross him and put him back on track for a while. On my last visit to see him, he was very lucid, and we had a very special time together.

I asked him if he remembered playing the fiddle. His eyes lit up, and he told me he taught himself to play when he was a small boy. Music has meant a lot to him through the years. He still whistles old hymns and favorite songs.

I asked if he remembered his farm, and that opened up another world he loved. He talked about it for an hour, recalling the plowing and planting; the good, cold spring where his mother had stored her milk and butter; the winter snows; the tall hickory trees with squirrels in them; and dozens of other cherished memories.

Then a shadow seemed to pass across his consciousness, and he began speaking of some of the hard times and difficult passages of his life. He took my hand and stared at me. He told me he had always tried to do his best but might not have succeeded.

When I was young, my father had been an extraordinarily

strict parent. There were years when I wasn't sure I liked him at all. A few times I even thought I hated him. But there by his side, with those dark, brown eyes pleading for affirmation, I quickly forgot all that and remembered instead the things my father had given me. There had always been a roof over my head and plenty of food on the table. There were times of merriment and love when I was a small girl. There were the indomitable virtues of honesty, hard work, dependability, and fortitude. There were the music lessons that had meant so much to my life. My heart melted and I assured him that I loved him and was proud that he was my father. Whatever unpleasantness there might have been was forgotten; all that mattered was a father and daughter and a sense of forgiveness.

Dear God, I pray that my own children will be able to forgive me for any mistakes I have made in raising them, and that I will grow old with their love and devotion.

FEBRUARY 18   Read Isaiah 12:2.

THERE ARE FEW THINGS IN LIFE more important than trust. The human heart requires a sense of trust before we can relate well to others, sleep at night, do our work, and fulfill our individual natures. Yet the history of humanity is a history of broken trust and disappointment. Even the Bible is filled with stories of infidelity and disillusionment. Cain rose up against his brother Abel and killed him. Jacob outwitted his brother Esau and deceived their father Isaac. David sacrificed his soldier Uriah in order to have Uriah's wife. Peter denied knowing Jesus, and Judas betrayed Jesus for money.

It is sad that children, who are born completely trusting and dependent, must be disillusioned and must learn to live in a world of hypocrisy and disloyalty. I was dismayed recently to hear a thirteen-year-old girl say that she didn't want her divorced parents to get back together because she and her mother could not trust her father. How will her experiences and lack of trust affect her for the remainder of her life? Will she ever be able to trust people with the kind of confidence she might have had if her father had proven trustworthy?

I have always wanted our children to understand that their trust can be betrayed—that friends will desert them, people will misrepresent the truth, and even those closest to them may sometimes try to manipulate them for selfish reasons. Learning this important lesson is part of their education for living safely and self-protectively in the world. But at the same time I have always wanted them to know that it is vitally important to create their own little centers of trust and fidelity in the midst of the world's falsehood and deception, for this is the only way to live happily and positively and not slip into cynicism and despair. I hope I have taught them to imitate Jesus, who was faithful to the end despite what anyone did to him, and to value friends ad loved ones whose trust is a match for theirs. If they have learned this, they will be both vulnerable and secure in the world, and will help others to see the worth of truth and devotion at a time when such qualities have been devalued by society.

Please help the children of the world to grow up with a sense of trust, O God, so that their lives on earth may begin to experience something of the joy you have prepared for them in heaven.

FEBRUARY 19   Read Luke 15:11-13.

WHEN WE DROVE OUR YOUNGER son, Krister, to college for the first time, he sat in the back seat sullen, withdrawn, and grumpy. We could hardly get him to say a word. I thought he was mad at us for insisting that he go on to college when he had wanted to say home and work for a year.

But his mood was totally different when he came home for a visit a few weeks later. He hugged me so tightly I thought he would break me in two. He ran excitedly from room to room, investigating the house to make sure it was the way it had been when he left. He devoured his favorite meals and desserts. He laughed a lot, played the piano, and swam happily in the swimming pool with his father and brother.

I had misinterpreted the signs. I thought he was angry with us on the way to college, when he was actually fearful and anxious about what his new life would be. He was shy about plunging into a world of new experiences, wondering whether he would be able to survive away from his parents.

I wonder about the prodigal son in Jesus' story: Was he really as rebellious and resentful when he went away as we have often thought? Or was he merely trying to psych himself up for the dreadful business of learning to get along in the world by himself?

I am sometimes quiet and withdrawn when I meet new people or enter new situations. It is because I am guarded and afraid and don't know if I can respond or interact the way people expect me to. I hope I can remember this and always try to be sensitive to the moods of those around me, especially teens for whom the world can be a very frightening place.

Forgive me, Lord, if I sometimes seem quiet and moody even with you. It is because life can become heavy and I am preoccupied or afraid. Teach me to trust you so thoroughly that I have fewer and fewer of these times and can live with radiant presence among my friends and family.

FEBRUARY 20   Read 2 Samuel 18:33.

IT MUST BE TERRIBLE when a parent loses a child, as David did. My heart breaks whenever I heard of such a tragedy. My parents lost a baby daughter, and my mother talked about her until the day of her own death. A family in a church my husband pastored lost a teenage son who fell from the twenty-first floor of a hotel building. I couldn't understand how they survived the loss. Another friend lost her only son when he was in his forties. "No parent," she said, "should ever survive a child; it isn't natural."

But accidents and tragic illnesses can happen, leaving us suddenly devastated. None of us is immune to the possibility. It is best then to be prepared, to know it could happen and to think about how to cope with it.

The brevity of life should make us grateful for each day we have. It should remind us of the fragility of human existence and help us to get our hearts on eternity. And it should help us to take the long look about the small things our children do that don't matter all that much. We should often ask of the mistakes they make or the little episodes of bad behavior, "What difference will this make a hundred years from now?" Then we can love them for who they are, as if we might not have them forever, and give thanks to God for the joy of having shared their lives for the time we've had them.

Thank you, God, for our children's lives that have given us happiness and fulfillment. Help us to entrust them to you, so that whatever happens we will know they are always in good hands.

FEBRUARY 21   Read Psalm 28:4*b*.

AFTER ERIC AND KRISTER reached the age of sixteen, we required them to work at summer jobs. We believed it would be important to the formation of their character. Eric always sought indoor jobs; Krister preferred outdoor jobs. Eric never complained about working; Krister complained incessantly.

Sometimes I felt guilty about making them work. I knew they wanted to sleep till noon, swim till dinner, and party with their nonworking friends. And in some ways they were still children, even though they were driving the car and thought they were fully grown.

But whenever I felt too bad about it, I remembered a wealthy friend's son whose life was one big party. Everything he could ever want was handed to him on the proverbial silver platter. By the time he was in his late teens, he had become bored with life; and this had made him cynical and obnoxious. One day he overdosed on drugs and called his mother at her club to say good-bye.

I didn't want Eric and Krister to ever feel that way about life. I wanted them to enjoy their work as much as they had enjoyed play, and to feel a sense of pride and accomplishment because they were earning their own money. The Bible, after all, endorses work. It says that God told Adam and Eve that they must earn their living by the sweat of their brows. Jesus worked as a carpenter, and Paul paid his way as a missionary by making tents. We owe it to our children to give them the gift of work. It may in fact be one of the finest gifts we ever give them.

Thank you, dear God, for the joy of working with our hands and our brains. It enables us to feel as if we are involved in creating our world. Help us to impart to our children a sense of the sacredness of labor, which will add to their satisfaction all their lives.

FEBRUARY 22   Read 2 Samuel 11:1-4a.

SOMETIMES WE THINK we live in the most immoral age that ever was, but there is nothing new under the sun. These words come from one of the most lurid stories of sin and betrayal in the Old Testament. They are about King David, who saw a beautiful woman, desired her, had her brought to his palace, and arranged the death of her husband.

I'm probably an old-fashioned mom, but I'm really concerned about the pall of immorality that hangs over our young people today. What terrible pressures they experience to smoke, drink, take drugs, and have sex before marriage. Sometimes it seems that everywhere they look, the message is that they ought to gratify their desires, feel good, and not worry about the consequences.

What can a mere mother do to stem the tide of such immorality? Plenty, if she really wants to. She can make sure her children learn the values of her faith, and understand the difference between right and wrong. She can help them to see the importance of valuing themselves and their bodies in the light of God's caring for them, and not merely in the view of Hollywood and Madison Avenue.

Oh, there will be times when her children will probably stray from the path and get into trouble. That is to be expected in a culture that is so thoroughly secular and hedonistic as ours. But I've always liked something the mother of Phillips Brooks, the great New England preacher, once said about raising children. She said: "You have to give a child some rope; but if you hold on to your end of it, the child will always come back."

Dear God, please save our children from making irreparable mistakes in their lives. And even when they make mistakes, help us mothers to be there to take them back and help them overcome the consequences.

FEBRUARY 23   Read Matthew 6:12.

HOW MANY TIMES have you heard someone say, "I'm never going to forgive that person"? How many times have you said it yourself? Sometimes we become so angry over something someone does—even a spouse or a child—that we think we will never be able to put it behind us. This is very unfortunate, for it means that the anger always lies there as a barrier between us, inhibiting the natural flow of love and fellowship.

A friend of mine told about the time when he was an awkward teenager and spilled a can of acrylic paint on his mother's antique Oriental carpet. He was horrified! But she was at work, and he thought he might be able to correct the problem before she returned. First he tried to soak up paint in paper towels, but the gooey liquid simply wouldn't enter the towels. Then he tried to clean up the mess with water. But that only smeared the paint into a larger surrealistic mass. In desperation, he attempted one more thing. He took some darker paint and tried to repaint the design over the top of the discolored area. Perhaps his mother wouldn't be able to tell the difference.

My friend died of cancer last year, and even until the final weeks of his life he was chuckling about that incident. The beautiful thing was that his mother never mentioned the paint on her carpet. She saw it, of course. What woman wouldn't see such an obvious mess! But she had the grace to pretend that she didn't. My friend said it was one of the nicest things he could ever recall about his mother, and he loved her for it.

God reacts the same way to a lot of the messes we make. It isn't that God doesn't know about them. It's just that God loves us so much that he doesn't say anything. God is able to forgive anything we've ever done. In fact, God has already forgiven us. We can stop pretending God hasn't noticed and accept his forgiveness with grateful, penitent hearts. Then we can enjoy God's love even more.

I hope I'll always be forgiving to my children, dear God, the way you have been forgiving to me. Don't let me ever waste my time or energy being angry and fretful, when there is so much in the world to love and enjoy.

FEBRUARY 24   Read Ecclesiastes 3:1.

"QUALITY TIME IS MY FAVORITE time of the day," says Lili Tomlin in *Edith Ann: My Life So Far.* "But with my busy schedule, it's hard to find time for it."

Nearly everyone today can resonate with that statement—especially mothers. Everything in our schedules seems to conspire against our having time for the things that really matter. We cook, clean, wash clothes, iron, shop, sweep, run errands, oversee our children's schedules, carpool, and (often) work outside the home. By the end of the day we are drained of all energy, and most nights aren't long enough to restore it.

What happens to God in a typical day? God gets banished somewhere to an occasional prayer as we're stuffing the washer or making a bed or driving to work. And we feel even more harried because we don't have time for our deepest needs and aren't providing for the restoration of our souls.

The wise writer of Ecclesiastes knew that there is a time for everything—even the things we think we don't have time for. The important thing is to find the time for the most indispensable things in our lives—for gentle loving, for solitude, for meditation in the presence of God. When we do this—when we literally *make* time for the things that matter—all the other things take care of themselves, often more beautifully and gracefully than if we had not been centered.

My time is in your hands, O God. Fill me with your divine energy, and even in my busyness, never let me forget to bless you for it.

FEBRUARY 25   Read Job 35:9-10.

A *FRIEND OF OURS WAS PASTOR* of a church next to a large university. When his daughter went to the university, he gave her a key to his office so she could slip in and study there when the dorms got too noisy. Sometimes they exchanged notes left on his desk. One morning he found this note: "Daddy, how do you sing the sad songs of life?"

The father was deeply touched by the note. Obviously his daughter was running into some of the problems we all have to face and handle in life, and it was making her sad. "How do you answer a question like that when your child asks it?" he said. "I wasn't really sure what to say."

The problem of evil in the world is age-old. Job encountered it in his day, and didn't know the answer to it. There was no reason for the calamities he suffered, no rationale for the great pain in his body. Then he had an experience with God, perhaps in a dream or in a state of hallucination. God showed him all the great wonders of the world, including such mythical beasts as Behemoth and Leviathan. Finally, Job collapsed in awe and humility, and apologized for having even questioned the wisdom of the creation. "I despise myself," he said, "and repent in dust and ashes" (Job 42:6).

Our children too want to know how to sing life's sad songs. The only ultimate answer lies in the mystery and greatness of God, and in the love that has led God to prepare a future for us beyond the trials and inconsistencies of this existence. Job understood in the end that human beings weren't made to ferret out *all* the secrets of life; some remain to humble us before the majesty of God.

It is hard to explain suffering to my children, O God, when I don't understand it myself. Help me to live so constantly in your presence that explanations become paltry things beside the great love I experience.

FEBRUARY 26   Read Matthew 5:9.

MY MOTHER CONSIDERED HERSELF a peacemaker. Her idea of making peace was to get everybody to capitulate without escalating a quarrel into a larger conflict. "Peace at any price" was her motto. On a minor scale, her eagerness to settle disputes usually worked.

But I don't know what she would do in the complicated world we live in today. There are enormous tensions on the modern scene. People seem to be battling over almost everything—politics, education, the environment, homosexuality, contraception, abortion, the role of women, medical ethics, and dozens of other "hot" issues. Our futures are being forged in the crucible of public conflict. How does one live as a peacemaker in such a society? What does one teach one's children about right and wrong?

Sometimes children and parents end up on opposite sides of a disputed matter. Children echo their teachers, their peers, what someone said on television; and the parents contend for a viewpoint they always considered traditional and sacrosanct. How can there possibly be peace in such a convoluted world?

I don't have an easy answer to give. Occasionally, in the history of the world, there are times when everything seems to be up for grabs again and people have to live through years of contentiousness before the disputes are settled. Maybe we are in such a time now. The best I know to do is to turn to the Master Peacemaker, who sometimes stilled the storms for his disciples. That's why I keep this ancient Celtic benediction taped to my refrigerator door:

Deep peace of the Running Wave to you.

Deep peace of the Flowing Air to you.
Deep peace of the Quiet Earth to you.
Deep peace of the Shining Stars to you.
Deep peace of the Son of Peace to you.

And I pray . . . Give peace in our time, O Lord, as you did to those who were troubled long ago.

February 27   Read Matthew 6:8.

MY HUSBAND, JOHN, AND I once saw the great British actor Robert Hardy portray Winston Churchill in a play. The action took place during World War II. London was under heavy bombardment from the Nazis. Nothing seemed to be going right for the British. Churchill was in his underground war room studying all the bad reports. Suddenly he curled up like a small child and cried out, "I need my nanny!"

Mothers and nannies are indispensable in the lives of their children—even their independent teens. They provide comfort and solace in a world where things go wrong. They make hurts feel better and encourage broken spirits.

I remember not so long ago when I was going through a bad time in my life. Everything seemed to have gotten too heavy to bear, and I wasn't sure I could go on carrying the load. I stood in the kitchen one morning and said, "I want my mommy!" What I wanted was someone to rock and care for me, someone to cradle me and let me be a little girl again.

Then the strangest thing happened. I felt the presence of God come over me and wrap around me like my mother's arms. I even thought I heard God say, "Hush, little baby, don't you cry. Let me carry your load for you."

Isn't it wonderful to know that in the midst of mother-hood, when others are depending on us for their strength and comfort, we can depend on God the same way? All we have to do is turn to God for help. God has promised that he will always be there to give us the love and support we need. And he even knows what we need before we ask!

Dear God, teach me not to try to endure everything alone but always to turn to you for peace and encouragement, for you never fail to give it.

FEBRUARY 28   Read Revelation 11:15.

WHEN ERIC AND KRISTER WERE living with us, we used to celebrate everything. We didn't need much of an excuse to have a party. We even went through the calendar and created special holidays in the months when there weren't any holidays or family birthdays, so we'd all have something to look forward to with eagerness.

Sometimes the parties were spontaneous. There was the time, for instance, when they went off to field day at school. Both were determined to win a lot of ribbons in the races, broad jumps, and field events. But one was athletic and the other wasn't, and the one who wasn't came home at noon tired and discouraged. He hadn't won a single ribbon. We injected a little hope and sent him back to try again that afternoon. But it was the same story late in the afternoon, only this time he was more weary and disappointed than ever.

"You'd better get something cool to drink out of the refrigerator," I said.

He opened the refrigerator door and his eyes lit up. Knowing how much he liked root beer, I had gone to the store and gotten a huge bottle. Then I had made a big blue ribbon to put on it, with the golden words "Root Beer Champ" stitched on it. His entire mood changed, and we all began to sing and dance and have a good time.

Life can be awfully discouraging, both for children and for parents. But when we know what the writer of Revelation knew, that "the kingdom of the world" will eventually become "the kingdom of our Lord and of his Messiah," we can laugh and celebrate even in the depths of our disappointments.

Thank you, O God, for the hope buried as a seed in all our despair, for the promises that will be fulfilled when life has run its course and we are gathered up into an eternal celebration.

$\mathscr{M}$ ARCH

LEARNING TO SOAR

Anne L. Wilcox

MARCH 1   **Read Psalm 91.**

WHAT IS THIS FRANTIC FLAPPING against my hands? Once down-covered and unpretentious, you cried for fundamental things—food, warmth, and love. How did I miss the down evolving into stiff wings? In fact, every part of you embodies stiffness and resistance these days!

You're constantly pecking at my hands to give you more room. You perceive these palms, which simply want to protect you, as locked cages of restriction. So I've started opening these hands—or have you pried off each finger determinedly? However it has happened, you soar regularly now.

I hold my breath . . . the air contains more pollutants than when I was a child. The predators have multiplied in number and in ability to deceive these days. As you expand flight patterns, my worry expands exponentially!

And of all things, sometimes I think you're flying completely in the wrong direction at a time when you rarely circle back to the nest. I'm convinced that adolescent hormones erase all homing instincts. However—and fortunately —you still get hungry.

How can I let you fly this high with such little experience? And yet . . .

How will you ever be ready for life if I keep you tethered to my arm?

Lord, guard my high-flying teen—only you can reach that far. May both of us find your faithfulness a powerful refuge during these years.

MARCH 2   Read Psalm 145.

DAILY LIFE HAS SUCCESSFULLY dismantled my passion. Laundry, errands, car-pooling, bills, job, grocery shopping—all of it has simply disabled my ability to experience wonder. The closest thing to wonder I achieve is to *wonder* what I'm going to fix for dinner! Sometimes I think I'm so busy being responsible and conscientious that I'm missing every chance to "celebrate . . . God's abundant goodness" (Ps. 145:7).

Then you show up. I rant and rave that you need to take more responsibility and do your chores without being reminded. But there you go—escaping my lectures to go roller blading. Somehow my words seem hollow as you take a few moments to simply enjoy being alive, reveling in the wonder of motion.

Maybe I need to stop harping about the chores. Maybe the younger generation has much to teach the older generation. My push to get you to adulthood is simply killing wonder. After all, the one screeching about responsibility hasn't pulled out the roller blades you got her for Christmas and joined you for a long time.

In all this faithful training about duty, I must remember to allow you time to spin and soar—unencumbered for just a few moments by the cares and worries of life.

Even adults, especially adults, need to take time for such moments. Maybe my passion for life would recover if the teacher became the learner today.

Lord, grant me enough wisdom to learn from this spontaneous teen. May wonder and responsibility find a skillful balance in both our lives.

MARCH 3   Read Job 11:7-9.

I DON'T THINK I'VE PREPARED you for mystery. When you were younger, I bought Scripture memory packets—perfect for the sequential child. Then we discovered you are random in your learning style. I also tried devotional books assuming you'd get into a daily routine. Sporadic, however, is your operational style. So I bought the latest apologetic helps. Finally, we are armed with well-documented answers for questions you're not asking yet.

In all this frantic effort to give you the information you need to walk a life of faith, I think I've forgotten to leave a place for mystery. Some days I feel like I'm force-feeding your mind. I have been wanting you to formulate your beliefs for a lifetime—sort of like preparing a house for the certain hurricane. But mysteries cannot be documented; they must be felt.

All my training plans, all my discipling tools, all my desires for apologetic prowess have their place. But a sacred place for mystery may be the most important of all.

When the dust of child rearing clears, I hope you're left unafraid of the messiness of faith. Whether you scale mountains of apologetics to see what you truly believe or whether you endure seasons of doubt, I hope you're ready for mystery.

Lord, grant this teen a mother who is not constantly overthinking the mysteries in this information age, but who models a wrestling with and an enjoyment of your mysteries.

MARCH 4   Read Psalm 139.

THE CHILD PSYCHOLOGISTS SAY your age is a time of formulating opinions about who you are . . .

Well, what do you think? Besides all the questions other teens ask during this time, you get to add one more about your adoptive heritage. We've talked a lot about your birth and adoption stories. But who are you first—even before bloodlines and legal standings?

Before any of these things transpired, the days of your life were written by unseen hands (Psalm 139:16). Therefore, in one sense, your true mother tongue is communion with your Maker.

I'm afraid your parents only speak English—so you didn't have the wonderful chance of becoming multilingual early, which seems crucial in your international generation. However, discerning this mother tongue may be your most significant linguist feat.

With other languages, the sounds seem strange at first. With this one, you'll have instant recognition. Words of faith will draw your attention. Interventions of God, even when experienced by others, will seem familiar. You'll experience a quiet, certain guidance or a joyous burst of touching God's sovereignty.

Through these things you will hear your native tongue—a language deeper than English, clearer than the Spanish you're studying in middle school, and even more certain than the genetic codes that determine so much of who you are.

The sound of it will create a yearning—a desire to one day hear it face to face.

Lord, our first language is communion with you. Give my child fluency in the mother tongue of faith.

MARCH 5   Read Hebrews 12:11.

WHAT A WEEK! Report cards were due and parents were eager to have conferences—but that was only at school, my workplace. At home a family get-together was approaching, and I was to be the hostess. Did I have it all or was I losing it all? That was the question in my weary eyes when you approached with middle-school needs.

A major homework assignment was due the next day. All of a sudden you needed help this very minute. Starting early had not occurred to your spontaneous teenage heart. However, this time 911 was overloaded.

I offered some suggestions and pointed to some possible resources. When, at this last date, that wasn't enough, I realized it was time to let you feel the heat of poor planning.

Grades were at stake. What would parental love have me do?

I stepped aside and let the ball drop. I was not abandoning you—although the angry cries from you made it seem so. My goals for you are greater than one major homework assignment. The A+ I want you to get is in life. In this case, the real lesson is how to plan ahead to achieve an important goal.

So I closed my eyes and let you fall. One eye kept popping open, however, wondering if I had done the right thing. I could have prevented the bruising, but if I keep breaking your falls now, the stakes will only get higher. I must allow you to feel these bruises now to prevent major fractures later.

Lord, give me the courage, in our fast-pain-relief culture, to let this teen experience the pain that brings us all to maturity.

MARCH 6   Read Matthew 10:16.

SO MUCH OF WHAT YOUR YOUNG eyes see, I never knew existed in my adolescent years. Through the visual input all around you, you have access to everything from shots of other galaxies to microscopic particles unheard of when I was a teen.

So much of it is thrilling. Your eyes are privileged. And yet, you also have access to other things I never knew about when I was young—things not so innocent. What do I attempt to keep from your reflecting eyes? What do I let you see? When are you ready to move from innocence to knowledge? In our fallen world, wisdom can be found only in grappling with the tension between Eden and hell.

What of Eden do you dream about? What dreams can I encourage? What of hell—a fallen world—will you be asked to face? How can I get you ready for these two competing facts of life?

You must be aware of evil—no one lives well or fights

skillfully without keen understanding of the enemy. You must also have moments of playful innocence, or bright eyes can turn dull and hopeless. How do we ride the wave of your generation? How do I stay alongside you and throw you appropriate guidance that will keep you buoyant in this culture and this time?

Lord, how can that playful sparkle in my teen's eyes continue—and still be variegated with keen awareness and wisdom? Help me to find the right balance.

MARCH 7   Read Micah 6:8.

WE USED TO MAKE IT THROUGH college, and a career was waiting on the other side. No longer. You live in a world where jobs are tenuous and economic factors are fickle—so what should I hope for you? Do I push for top grades so college choices are wider, so jobs are better, so you'll have a fulfilling career? As life becomes more and more uncertain, what do I *really* wish for you? What would be a worthy goal through this period of your life?

Maybe our most important career is to act justly, love mercy, and walk humbly with our God. I doubt there will be a college class on that one. Don't misunderstand me—I do wish for you a fulfilling career—work that uses your gifts and abilities. But in all this college/career preparation, how do we also concentrate on your true career?

Excellence in justice means developing discernment that unclouds the complexities of right and wrong. Succeeding at mercy is remembering that justice has limitations overridden only by forgiveness. Graduating with honors in a humble walk with God is an impossibility. That piece of it can only be walked by awareness of our continual need for new training—and our constant need to be carried.

Lord, grant me wisdom to move us both closer to our "real" career—the true one that doesn't have to stop when the market crashes or that isn't spoiled by prosperity.

MARCH 8   Read Romans 8:12-17.

GERARD MANLEY HOPKINS, a nineteenth century Anglican priest, created in his poetry an image of the Holy Spirit that seems crucial to our parenting of teens. In his poem "God's Grandeur," Hopkins contrasts the thoughtless spoiling of the natural world with the sustaining grace of the Holy Ghost.

His "bent world" is described as "seared with trade" and wearing "man's smudge." Although the poet's main concern is with nature being disrupted, I see that "smudging" occurring philosophically in the days my teen is apathetic about spiritual things. In her world, the obsessive attempt to separate sacred and secular has a "searing" effect on the potential delight and wisdom about life. Her generation often assumes a strange blend of immortality and temporal pleasure.

But Hopkins wrote of something more—an insight creating great hope in his day as well as ours. He spoke of the Holy Spirit brooding over the bent world "with warm breast and with ah! bright wings."

It is easy to see the need for brooding—and forget the brightness. Protecting is crucial, and we parents of teens are constantly petitioning to that end. But celebration must also enter our prayer vocabulary. Someone with bright wings cares warmly for these emerging young adults in a very bent world.

Brood closely to our children, Holy Spirit. They are running so fast, thinking at Pentium speed. May they discern your brightness and be drawn by the profound relevancy of your life protecting theirs.

MARCH 9   Read Proverbs 31:31.

ROADBLOCKS ARE A GIVEN. Diversions clutter the road at every point in our journey. It seems that life is more about navigating around obstacles than deciding on a course and making a run for it.

You encountered a huge barrier the summer you really wanted to go to camp but finances were tight. You could go only if you could earn half the tuition. At first it seemed impossible to drum up that much money. But you refused to see "impossible."

All of a sudden the desire to reach the goal awakened a new energy and resourcefulness. Babysitting opportunities were never turned down. Shared responsibility on a paper route was taken on. Extra chores at home were initiated. Working and saving and working some more all earned not only half the camp tuition, but a bit of spending money as well.

You blazed through with flying colors—and replaced the discouragement that could have come from roadblocks with a new sense of accomplishment. You experienced the creative power of determination. You rallied the wit and strength needed to conquer the goal. No amount of my talking or modeling could have accomplished what you taught yourself that one summer.

Lord, desired goals are not always attainable. Sometimes the determination learned from the attempt must be enough reward. But thank you for the success of determined ingenuity to remember when the next set of obstacles present themselves.

MARCH 10   Read Hebrews 12:1-3.

HALF-FINISHED EVERYTHING! The homework paper was half-completed. The new, exciting cross-stitch project started with such enthusiasm lies half-started in a dresser drawer. The music lessons are now abandoned. The craft project for Christmas didn't quite get done in time.

How do I teach you the importance of finishing—and of counting the cost before choosing to start?

Hebrews coaches us to stay focused if we want to finish this race. Running has never been your favorite sport, and this passage is filled with images of the marathon athlete. It's about keeping your head down, staying focused, and refusing to be distracted.

When your preference is to do your homework with CD

blasting, television on, and telephone graphed to one ear—how can "focus" even have a definition in your mind? How can this generation who feast on the jumping, chirping, blinking, and clicking of Nintendo screens formulate a definition of singleness of anything—much less the heart?

How can running the race before you with eyes only on Christ be something you can even begin to understand in a world containing a million windows, all of which can be clicked on and pulled down in multi-layered fashion?

You say you'll finish when it is really important—and I want to believe you. But finishing small is how you learn to finish big. Completing piece after piece when things are insignificant is what gives the grit to complete the significant.

Guide us, Lord, one focus, one Face, and the ability to finish—intent on one purpose—to love and obey you.

MARCH 11   Read Proverbs 19:11.

WELL, THERE YOU ARE slumped angrily in an overstuffed chair—overstuffed with self. The grouchy aura has spread from the bedroom through the kitchen and now is fogging up the living room. Everyone else is happily occupied today. But not you; you are determined to make your misery felt.

How could we possibly ask you to set aside the telephone one moment to disconnect from peers and reconnect with family? You've had several gracious invitations to join the game in this corner, the puzzle in that corner, the walk at the beach about to begin—but no one your age is around, so you grump and stare angrily at the ceiling—hoping it will fall on everyone over fourteen.

There are so many who want to love you today—to enter your world—to have some part in your life. Holding off all that love is making you miserable. How strange to see the sources of affection as the antidotes to your happiness.

Every patient attempt to penetrate your icy shell of resistance merely signals the "grump" troops to gather reinforcements. How do I back off—without giving up?

Detachment is a strange dance. I need to retreat without any thought of giving up on the war. I must recircle with hopes of getting a few darts of love to penetrate that adolescent armor.

Lord, when the difficult days come, grant me enough patience to get through the day and enough impatience to guide a very precious teen through a very obnoxious attitude.

MARCH 12   Read Lamentations 3:22-23.

THIS SLUMPING IN THE CHAIR just didn't reflect your usual sunny self. Your answer to "What's up?" was a report of the BORING Spanish teacher. As the year progressed, your grades reflected your continued frustration in that class. It made me wonder how to talk with you about your duty to study hard even when an instructor is far less than exhilarating.

Faithfulness ultimately involves both duty and passion. To remain dutiful through difficult circumstances is the greatest test of faithfulness and maturity. Especially during these teen years, it seems as if only the fun, exuberant teachers are worth your attention and energy. But passion is the volatile element of faithfulness. In a perfect situation, duty and passion would be intertwined, with duty guarding passion and passion energizing duty.

However, duty must sometimes act as a cast when passion is absent. Casts seem, for a time, so restrictive, so stifling, so itchy! But premature removal results in further injury. Bursting out of duty before it accomplishes its work can result in more shattering and more brokenness.

If you let a boring Spanish teacher kill your love of language (and ruin your grade point average), you will be the loser. You cannot control her effectiveness; you control only your choice to remain faithful.

You must learn that it is appropriate to live weeks, months, even years in duty-mode. Doing the right thing day after day will eventually provide a place where passion can again return.

Lord, this mix of passion and duty is so delicate. Help our teens to see the wisdom of employing duty when passion has evaporated for a time.

MARCH 13   Read Genesis 1:1-2.

To MAKE ORDER OUT OF CHAOS is to mimic God—somehow bedrooms of teenagers are more challenging than the cosmos.

The laws of gravity have pulled everything out of drawers and off hangers to create formless heaps on every square inch of floor. The delicate spin of a planet on its axis and its precise rotation around the sun is another galaxy away from this room.

What will make you want to speak order into this microcosm? Each suggestion of tidiness from me is greeted with an equal and opposite reaction. I have confiscated the nicer clothes; they can be purchased back when you want to wear them—twenty-five cents an item is a great reminder to pick up. Yet even that desperate intervention has not changed the laws of your universe.

We clash over this because we live in the same quadrant of space—under the same roof. We could draw lines and grant laissez-faire policies, but we are not equal nations. You are in training. How do I balance training with freedom—and instruction with privacy?

Somehow our peace negotiations need to include changes from both sides of the bargaining table. What I would like to see is a new stewardship of your space prompted not because of my threats, but because your world is important and meaningful to you.

Somehow the music of the spheres needs to continue in harmony between these two generations.

Lord, how on earth (or even in heaven) do you create a desire in someone for orderliness? May your answer come quickly—before this universe explodes.

MARCH 14 Read Deuteronomy 31:6.

"*THE GUY I REALLY LIKE IN* that video game is Rahul. All you have to do is push A, B, A, B, seventeen times real fast, and he electrocutes everybody around him. It's really cool."

I looked at my young teen and wondered if anyone has thought of creating game heroes that appeal to something besides annihilation? What is the agent that will ennoble the next generation? Right now the closest thing to courage seems to come from a blinking monitor where buttons are pushed. Where are the heroes who steady others through the shattered dreams that are inevitable in every life? Where are those who refuse to be rebuffed by rejection, but patiently wait for a chance to express kindness?

I guess they wouldn't fit into a game very well. It's not very action-packed to portray someone whose gaze is constant regardless of what another's eyes may hold. Unswerving loyalty is a bit difficult to capture for joysticks. Someone strong in character but humble in expectations or a person of strong principle who also has enough gentleness to heal others' wounds—how could that be played out on the screen?

How will all this be transferred to the next generation when the "cool" stuff of life comes after seventeen AB's and an electrocution explosion?

Lord, simulated courage is not going to be enough, especially when the most severe battles occur in the heart and character of our children. Give them ways to see and emulate real courage.

MARCH 15 Read Colossians 3:13.

THE CAR WAS FILLED WITH thirteen-year-olds all competing for the air waves. As I attempted to sort through the barrage of words, I realized that the best story or the latest info on peers achieved the gold medal. I kept the traffic and my daughter's face in the rearview mirror. I wanted to see how she would handle the fray.

In the first round, she received two verbal blows—one about her lack of gossip info and one about her physical appearance that day. Neither were up to snuff according to the others in the competition. I knew she was wounded, but I stayed silent to see how she would respond. She grew quiet and decided to withdraw from the arena until the others secured their pecking order. Then she reentered with topics that didn't create competition.

I was surprised to see her so undaunted. She seemed to understand the battle. She chose to withdraw from a ridiculous competition, forgive her offenders, and go on. But had she truly forgiven others—or was she denying the wounds?

To truly forgive, the full impact of an emotional injury needs to be recognized. When we reached home, I asked her about her hurt.

"No big deal," she said casually as she headed to her room.

Lord, give our teens the courage to feel the hurt as deeply as is needed for true forgiveness. Let them diagnose their hearts fully.

MARCH 16   Read Proverbs 27:9.

THE NOTE WAS STUFFED IN a jeans pocket. I was merely checking to see if I should save the scrap or toss it out before the pants were laundered.

My quick glance revealed words I had no idea were in your vocabulary. A friend had written it—one of my favorites in your circle of friends. The author was obviously experimenting with new language; life is more earthy in your middle school than your naive mother had anticipated.

After the first few words, I realized I had read enough to know that you probably didn't want me reading it. Experimenting with coarse words is one thing—putting them into lengthy notes is quite another. It was time to talk.

I thought you would at least faint when you discovered that I had the note. Jeans pockets are no longer safe—you were thinking. I was thinking your whole life was unsafe. If friendship is to be as refreshing as perfume, where did this fit? If the pleasantness of a friend springs from her counsel, how do you treat counsel filled with dirty words?

We talked long and hard through it. This was not quite the perfume of a healthy friendship.

Lord, mature our teens when they feel the need to try out new, inappropriate language. Give them a graciousness that will pull them beyond their experimentation. Help them provide one another with friendship as refreshing as perfume.

MARCH 17   Read 1 Samuel 1:1-2:12.

THERE YOU ARE SLUMPED in front of the T.V. again, devouring ice cream with eyes glazed by the consumption of images. Sometimes I want to pack us all up and head to the country. I'd find a farm somewhere where there's no time to sit and watch T.V. and where you have so many chores to do that you fall exhausted into bed each night. There would be no need for the anesthetizing effect of television waves.

What would enliven you—in this setting? The needy are certainly all around us. In fact, we just fed the homeless teens in downtown Seattle. You remarked that they have the brand-name jacket and shoes I refuse to buy for you because of the high prices. Hmm—somehow that backfired.

How will I ignite you for true service, for living life as Christ would want us to live? Do I know how to model such things? I keep wondering what will deepen you—what will you want to give your life to? What captured me at your age was people— people who loved Christ in a genuine, sacrificial way. Watching and waiting isn't easy; but, like Hannah, I will hold on to faith.

Lord, sometimes this place seems to be "the wrong place at the wrong time" for the maturity of my teen. It must have felt that way for Hannah as she sent Samuel to live with Eli—a man whose sons rejected the faith. May your purposes for my child not be thwarted despite this less than ideal environment for spiritual growth.

JUSTICE HAS ACHIEVED more popularity these days than mercy. After all, justice assures my personal rights, comforts, and safety. Mercy is less showy and less able to attract the marketing experts. In fact, we live in a world afraid of mercy—as shy as this virtue is.

Those who express tender kindness are often exploited. People with merciful hearts endure much scarring. Drawing assertive, justice-filled boundaries is much more useful in today's culture of preoccupation with individual rights.

True justice, of course, is always appropriate to express, but how do I help you wrap it in mercy? Mercy, though more elusive and retiring than justice, has achieved incredible things. It is mercy that has achieved for us new hope at the resurrection of Christ. It is mercy that secures an inheritance that can never perish, spoil, or fade (1 Peter 1:3, 4).

Often we withhold mercy because we're afraid of losing something. But how interesting that the greatest things—the imperishable things—are given wrapped in mercy. Indeed, the only way they can be conveyed to us is through the vehicle of mercy. Justice cannot carry the things most important to us.

Lord, in this parental battle to train and equip my teen, the balance is quite heavy on the side of justice—consequences for rules violated and rigid expectations of responsibility. Help me to see appropriate times to express mercy—not a permissive counterfeit, but authentic expressions of mercy that will help my teen see that true justice is often clothed in mercy.

MARCH 19   Read 2 Corinthians 5:17-21.

THE GIRL ACCUSED YOU of flirting with her boyfriend—a serious accusation in an inner-city middle school. Owning one another is an important issue for those who own very little else. Anyway, your friends rallied around the false accusation and traveled en masse during the lunch hour to your accuser's table. Threats and majority backing silenced the girl's taunts towards you. But I wonder, does muscle flexing ever really solve misunderstandings?

What would true reconciliation have looked like? Talking through the behavior that had left her feeling threatened might have helped—if she had been willing to talk. A desire on both sides to sort through the issues is crucial—but at this age she simply felt threatened and you simply felt bewildered. Desiring to possess can create many skewed images of jealousy.

You will continue to meet those who are unreasonable. And you must check your own rationality first, then deal carefully, cautiously, and wisely with others—always trying reason first. Then, I'm afraid there will be times to marshall a few protective resources. But making a reasonable attempt at reconciliation in an unreasonable world is one of the greatest Gospel tracts ever to be handed to anyone.

Lord, you have given us the ministry of reconciliation because we are yours. Grant our teens wisdom to initiate healthy compromises in a way that reflects your character.

MARCH 20   Read Ephesians 4:25-27.

ANGER IS INEVITABLE—it comes with being alive. Although I want you to be more comfortable with gracious, conciliatory attitudes, I also want you to be befriend anger.

Anger is often an invaluable signal. You became angry yesterday when your friends didn't follow through with a promise. Violation of trust is an appropriate reason to feel angry. You also became angry when I didn't listen to you and insisted on certain chores that shouldn't have been done if I had taken the time to comprehend your report of a fever. Anger was the only fitting response in both cases.

You will also feel anger when it isn't appropriate, but the point is that anger will be there, just like breathing—because we are alive. But we are more than alive; we are creatures capable of choice.

Therefore the art of anger involves taming the inevitable

and making choices about its expression. Anger signals that something isn't right. However, anger must be bridled before its energy can be unleashed for good. Learn to ride it well—you will often find yourself in its saddle. And when you fall off, which happens to all of us, time and forgiveness mend many things. There is always time to remount and learn "be angry but do not sin." Learn to see it as an alarm needing attention before the sun goes down—not as something to overcome.

Lord, your anger works righteousness; ours often does not. Give our emerging adults wisdom in handling anger.

MARCH 21   Read 1 Corinthians 13:4-7.

ONE MINUTE YOU WANT CLOSENESS; the next minute you want distance. The only thing predictable is your unpredictability. How can love be patient, kind, and persevering when the object of love is strangling you with needs one minute and telling you to take a hike the next? This yo-yoing between your competing needs is creating a crucible for the authenticity of 1 Corinthians 13.

You need me to keep connecting with you, but my attempts to touch must never be attempts to grasp tightly. You are changing so rapidly that the minute I figure out how to effectively get in touch with you—you've grown out of that method of joining.

So here I sit wishing time would stop just long enough to let me communicate with you before you move on again. I also feel in competition with your peers. The pull of their lives on yours is frighteningly strong. I must not try to seize something that by its very nature cannot and should not be possessed. No relationship survives grasping.

My touch must have as its impulse the desire to love, serve, and disciple—never to own.

Lord, keep me from using strangle holds on my teen, but also keep me patiently loving when no matter how I try to touch, it just isn't the right way.

HOW DO I TEACH YOU TO PRAY? At first I thought my consistent "quiet time list" meant prayer. Then I discovered that prayer more closely resembles bleeding when this fallen world explodes my manicured list. Then there were years where I wondered if a planned prayer time was even appropriate because prayer seemed more like breathing—both in frequency and sustenance. Since then, I've decided that prayer defies a restrictive definition.

Abraham Heschel, a wise Jewish rabbi, says that "prayer is our humble answer to the inconceivable surprise of living . . . it is like a beam thrown from a flashlight before us into the darkness."

There is much darkness in your generation, but there is also much light. You live in an era where microscopically and telescopically more things are being unveiled than ever before. But as more is known, so are more mysteries being exposed. Our five amazing senses are limited. We need the light of prayer. 1 Corinthians 13:12 says we see through a glass darkly—but it is that dim perception that gives the brightest light to the other five senses.

So, what definition can I give you for this crucial communion with God? Its essence falls somewhere between our intense helplessness and our bold yearning.

Lord, prayer cannot be pinned down anymore than you can. Give our teens a vibrant prayer life before you.

THE EXPERIMENTING HAS BEGUN! And although the eyeshadow was a bit heavy this evening, I would say it was a very successful first try at reasonable make-up usage!

We are all drawn to beauty. We desire to create it, enhance it, and keep it at all costs, especially in our faces. You are blossoming right now, which requires a look at this whole notion of beauty.

Beauty will simply come and go. At best it is a fluctuating attribute. It varies daily, mostly because of the beholder. Something or someone of great attraction to one person holds no interest to another. (For instance, how about your perception of beautiful music and mine!) Even with objective beauty, the flowering is often brief.

Time, that element which can cut through mountains and rust through steel, also works on our faces and against our make-up strategies. We cannot hope to stop its certain erosion. It must be supported by something unalterable.

Kindness and purity resist time's relentless erosion. Those can grow stronger while everything else recedes and wrinkles. If we cling to fluctuating beauty, it will escape us. It escapes everyone.

Right now, though, enjoy the freshness of youth. There is much beauty there. At the same time, use beauty wisely—not to define yourself, but as an outward exuberance of inward virtue.

Lord, all of life is fleeting, especially beauty. Give our teens, who are certain of living forever, a reverence and a desire for the beauty that can never fade.

MARCH 24   Read John 17:13.

MARK TWAIN SAID THERE WERE only two disappointments in life—not getting everything you want and getting everything you want. Maybe looking at disappointment is even the wrong side of the issue. I don't see you avoiding disappointment as much as I see you pursuing happiness and pleasure. You want a continuous flow of both. However, I must inform you that those two evaporate quickly, leaving a more persistent thirst.

You need an underground reservoir of something reliable—something impervious to fluctuating watertables and harmful pollutants. In John 17, Christ defined this resource as joy. The words of this chapter are his prayer for his disciples and for "those who will believe in [him] through their word" (v. 20). Therefore it is his prayer for us.

This joy is very different from happiness or pleasure. It refuses overprotection (v. 15) and refuses to be governed by the acceptance or rejection of others (v. 14). Just imagine being sustained by this reservoir even through the peer ups and downs.

Christ went away to achieve this resource for us (v. 13), and he desires a full measure to be ours. In all the fluctuation of emotions during these years, may you begin to rely on a reservoir designed by One who knew, first hand, what you would need to assuage your thirst in an often capricious fallen world.

Lord, may we drink deeply of your joy and see its sustaining superiority over happiness and pleasure.

MARCH 25   Read Psalm 19:8.

YOU ACT AS IF SNAKES WERE HISSING in your face. What is this protected stance when others are introduced to you for the first time?

The woman you were meeting was about my age. She even had a son your age and knew the smoke screen young teens throw up in the face of unsuspecting adults. She greeted you warmly and wouldn't let your lack of eye contact derail her graciousness.

Slowly she coaxed you out of hiding. Up came your head; your eyes met hers more consistently. When she said goodbye and gently touched your shoulder, you didn't shrink. What is this teen-taming all about?

Could it be a discomfort with yourself? Are you asking if you truly have something to offer? Are you wondering if your eyes are worth pouring kindness into another's eyes while in conversation? Are you debating whether or not you have enough to invest energy and eye contact into another?

This investment is different than all others. The less you hoard, the more you have. Courtesy requires you to step out of the protective coverings and risk a bit of kindness—learn to think about the other person. She coaxed and tamed you—now it's time for you to acknowledge and appreciate her.

Lord, help our teens move out of themselves and learn to highly esteem others. May eye contact begin to be something they can give and receive graciously.

MARCH 26   Read 1 Corinthians 13:12.

YOU'RE SPENDING A LOT MORE time in front of mirrors these days. I couldn't help watching you fix your hair for a party last night. I wonder what you perceive as being reflected there. No matter what generation or what culture we are in, we are curious about our own image. We face the reflection and evaluate.

Right now I'm noticing the area around my eyes that is signaling some significant aging. Time does refuse to pause. For you it's the adolescent war with acne. Whatever age we are, there will always be something not quite perfect reflected there. Some spend hours trying to change this or that. Some spend hours painting over this or that.

What will you do with the imperfections? How will you look past the reflection to the image? How will you learn to value your uniqueness, rather than wish for something someone else has? More significantly, how will you learn to look past reflections to deeper realities?

First Corinthians 13 also uses the image of a mirror and our imperfect or clouded perceptions of spiritual realities. We do only know "in part," but the exciting insight of this passage is a hope for someday knowing fully as we are fully known.

I'm not sure which is more exciting—the prospect of future complete knowledge or the present reassurance that we are fully known by our Lord.

Lord, mirrors at best reflect a secondhand image. How comforting to be known by you deeper and more significantly than those reflected images.

MARCH 27   Read Ephesians 3:14-21.

YOU WERE PUNCHING VIDEO game buttons so fast I couldn't even begin to follow. The bounding, twirling, gyrating figures on the screen, which enthrall you for hours, simply give me a headache. Such a different world you live in. So many screens, such massive amounts of information—and all at the touch of a button.

With all that you have—will it enhance or restrict imagination? The tenacity to try to get past certain levels in the video games *may* be helpful in developing persistence. But what will train the imagination? What will happen when the push of a button doesn't materialize your dreams?

Will you have the determination and the self-discipline to keep working toward the desired end? Will your dreams be towards eternal things and worth pursuing with a lifetime of creativity? Will your imagination be drawn towards the wonders Paul spoke of in Ephesians?

There he speaks of power—not through the clicking of buttons, but power in the inner person. This power does access information—but this knowledge is unique. Grasping how wide and long and high and deep is the love of Christ goes beyond any CD-ROM program. In fact, it goes beyond knowledge and beyond imagination.

Lord, spark our imaginations with this power that works within us. Give us dreams that further your glory "in the church and in Christ Jesus to all generations, forever and ever. Amen" (Ephesians 3:21).

MARCH 28   Read Psalm 1.

YOU ARE A PEACEMAKER—an includer—the one who makes sure everyone is comfortable.

Therefore, how can you grow to have noble convictions? Convictions are dividers, rather than uniters. However, unity at all costs is no unity at all. Some things cannot be negotiated; some things have no compromise.

In your generation, what criteria can be used for sifting through it all? You live in a world where tolerance is often more god than God. How strange it is, however, that people really do desire someone with unwavering (please note I do not mean obnoxious or rigid) loyalties.

If there are no firmly planted trees, if there is nothing taking root, and if reality is only what you think at the moment, then there will be miles of wasteland. This acreage may be able to sustain some hollow life forms, but the soul and spirit will shrivel.

You must remember that tolerance is not always appropriate; unconditional love always is. Tolerance often grows disinterest and distance. It can actually be the opposite of love, because neglect and apathy often create a deeper hell than hate.

Lord, give our young peacemakers wisdom not to deify tolerance. At the same time, give them the skill to plant themselves firmly and winsomely in your truth, which is always filled with the fruit of reconciliation.

MARCH 29   Read Jeremiah 30:23-24.

SOME DAYS I WILL NOT be reasonable. I love you too much. Some days we will not sit down and discuss quietly the distance between us. Some days you will not see me gently, peacefully bringing your name before our Lord.

Indeed, some days my voice will raise passionately! I just might lose all poise. Love is like that. It storms and rants and raves. It explodes out of reasonability and will not be contained. Believe me, teens are not the only ones with emotions that overflow the boundaries.

The prophets, those reflectors of God's heart, reveal many emotional explosions on God's part. Don's misunderstand me—God never loses control, but he is passionate. Jeremiah describes the "storm of the Lord" bursting and swirling "until he fully accomplishes the purposes of his heart" (Jer. 30:24 NIV). In the next chapter of his prophecy, God speaks of Ephraim as "my dear son, the child in whom I delight"

(Jer. 31:20 NIV). It was no accident that God revealed himself in the metaphor of parenthood.

There will be times I need to explode—from frustration, or anguish, or love—and you will need to see it. For regardless of how far we stand back to let you fly, our love never goes away. And believe me, it is a passionate, less reasonable love as we begin to watch you make life-impacting decisions.

Lord, your fervency as a parent comfort and encourage me to feel fully the passions of parenthood.

MARCH 30   Read Luke 18:17.

ONCE AGAIN YOU FORGOT—several things: your lunch, your textbook, your chores, your coat, your paper that was due! When will you grow up—and only forget one or two things like I do?

Everything I tell you to do—every correction I make—says grow up. How do I say please grow out of *childish* but never out of *childlike*.

Childishness is selfish and unthinking. Just like the little girl we saw screaming in the store today. She wanted what would have harmed her; and because those who love her said no, she blamed them for her unhappiness. Childishness is also not learning from mistakes but repeating them over and over to the harm of yourself and those caught in the wake of your mistake.

Childlike is trusting—add adulthood to it and you get a discerning trust. I hope you never lose the eagerness to trust. Childlike also means that faith comes easily. It's an assumption that you are loved and will be taken care of.

There are many children whose circumstances never allow them a point of reference for childlikeness. I hope you'll always be able to retain a childlike approach—not naive and unwise—to the years ahead.

Lord, make my teen discerning and childlike—while I diligently train out the childishness.

YOU AND I BOTH LOVE to analyze things. I read literary criticism—for fun, of all things. You take a homework outlining task and master it in minutes. The main idea is always obvious to you, and the supporting details are sequenced adroitly. It's a good thing we are the way we are in this communication age which is piggy-backing on the information age, which stands atop the age of Reason.

But how are we at worship? Through reason and analysis one can *see* the good, but only through worship can we *want* the good.

David seemed to understand this in Psalm 40. Trust and wonder characterize this Hebrew song. There are many references to rescue and desire, rather than to reason and analysis. If reason were governing this psalm, verse 6 would be changed. After all the instructions about Old Testament law, it only seems *reasonable* that God would desire the elements required in the law. But David realizes that a deeper desire than sacrifices and offerings lies in the heart of God—and in his law. Verse 8 reveals the superiority of worship over reason. David, in worshipful response to his Savior, *desires* to do the will of God.

Don't misunderstand me and throw reason to the wind. We have been given invaluable gifts of reason and analysis to steward our world. (And I sense you will have many more outlining projects in your academic career.) But reason must be governed by worship because desiring the good is far superior to merely seeing it.

Lord, in a world that values reason and analysis, may my teen value it, too—but only as it is informed and ruled by worship.

APRIL

OUR OLD GREEN DOORS

Pam Kidd

APRIL 1   **Read 2 Corinthians 2:12.**

IT WASN'T EXACTLY MY DREAM house. But as my husband, David, and I walked through the empty rooms, we realized that the house did, indeed, meet our most immediate needs. At the time, Brock, our budding teenager, needed "space." David needed a private study, and Keri, our daughter, was looking only for enough room to spread out her Barbie dolls.

"Oh, David," I remember saying as we stepped out onto the front porch, "look at these horrible green doors. They have to go!"

In the years since, those doors (still green, of course) have witnessed the comings and goings of one, then two teenagers, eager to step out into the big world—and two parents just as eager to hold them safe.

Angry words, loud accusations, and fearful pleadings have passed the entrance to our home. The doors have seen tears and heard countless prayers prayed with a desperate hope as taillights have melted into the bend of the road beyond.

The doors have known great victories, too, as well as joyous greetings and silly surprises. Countless tape marks and thumbtack holes remember congratulation posters and happy birthday banners.

On this first day of April, I'm tacking a welcome sign

across our old green doors. Step into our lives and you'll find a family struggling to find their place in God's good plan. It's still a far cry from a dreamhouse, but come on in! As mothers of teens, let's learn from our wins and our losses as we grope for balance in this greatest adventure of parenthood.

God, mark our door post with your grace. Come into our homes, and bless our mothering in the month ahead.

APRIL 2   Read Luke 2:49.

I WAS RUNNING AS FAST as I could. Passersby would have guessed that I was into a pretty serious fitness routine. Actually, I was distancing myself from a surly twelve-year-old. "I should never have been a mother," I was saying to God as I pushed along.

Motherhood had been pretty simple until now. My job, I thought, was to create a safe place, a home where our children would flourish. But at twelve, Brock no longer wanted what we had. He didn't seem to like me anymore; he had become a belligerent stranger.

If I didn't have eight-year-old Keri, all sweetness and sunshine, to reaffirm my faith in parenthood, I think I would have just kept running.

"What have I done wrong, God? Where did I lose my way?" I prayed. God's answer came like a small miracle: *"Jesus was twelve."* Three words. They came to me straight from the morning sky. I stopped dead still.

"What?" I said out loud. But already I was realizing that I had been handed a gift.

Walking home, I recalled Luke's story. Jesus, twelve years old, had been missing for three days. His mother was frantic.

"Don't you see I have to be about my father's business?" he said when his mother found him in the temple. Putting myself in his mother's place, his words sounded . . . well, let's be honest, belligerent! And yet, I knew Jesus' actions were not an affront on Mary's motherhood. He was simply seeking his purpose.

God seemed to be offering a clear message as I teetered on the brink of teen-mothering—an insight that's certainly made my mothering easier.

Loving God, help us see our children's move into the future, not as a threat to our mothering, but as the healthy unfolding of your great plan.

APRIL 3　　　　　　　　　　　　Read Luke 2:51.

AFTER THAT FRANTIC EARLY MORNING run, my thoughts often drifted to Jesus and his mother. The similarities were certainly there. Brock, my twelve-year-old, was pushing out, eager to find his place in the teen-aged tribe. I was holding back, wanting everything to stay the same.

David and I had been careful parents. Years before, we had vowed to make "home" our first priority. Now, any place but home was where Brock wanted to be. If we went to the mall or the movie, Brock made an effort to walk a few steps ahead. He didn't even want to be seen with us!

It sure hurt my feelings then. But, looking back, I laugh at my silliness. Brock was about his Father's business. He was struggling to become the individual God had created him to be.

I wish I had been wise enough in the beginning to see his efforts to separate as a healthy sign rather than as an insult to my mothering. It took me a long time to figure it all out, to understand that a willingness to let our children *become* is the best gift mothers have to offer their teens.

I wonder how long Jesus' mother pondered her son's move toward independence before she understood. I wonder how many times she questioned her ability to mother and how many nights she lay awake fearing what might happen to her child before she accepted him as the gift he was and then simply did her best and gave him back to his Father.

Comfort comes in my wondering and slowly gives way to a new understanding. Isn't this what mothering a teen is all about: to simply do our best and then trust God to do the rest?

Heavenly Father, we want to be good mothers. It's difficult to know when to let go. Be gentle with us as we learn.

IT'S INTERESTING HOW THE STORY goes. Jesus, at twelve, wanders off from his parents, worries them to death, and makes no apologies when they finally locate him in the temple. Then Luke brags that this same twelve-year-old "increased . . . in favor with God" (2:52 RSV).

There seems to be yet another "mom message" here. Before we leave Luke's account of the boy Jesus, let's take his words "increased . . . in favor with God" as a clue, a measure of our response to our own fledgling adult behavior.

In hindsight, I realize that my reactions to Brock's and later Keri's teen behavior would have been well served by centering on the behavior that gains our teenagers "favor" with God. Yet, for years, I had this extraordinary talent for overreacting to the things that didn't really matter. Keri was well into her teens before I began to distinguish between behavior that really mattered and behavior that simply favored my own ego. In all honesty, how important are made-up beds and unstained carpet—even perfect grades and team trophies?

On the other hand, teaching our children to value honesty, to act kindly, to seek justice, and to treat the world and the people in it with love, as Jesus asked, is probably a pretty safe heading for the "gaining favor with God" category.

Today is a good day to re-evaluate our responses to our children's behavior. Two lists emerge: What doesn't really matter, and what does. For me, that means bragging less about Brock's and Keri's so-called "worldly" accomplishments: Brock's investing success and Keri's invitation to a prestigious honor society. Instead I'm going to put that same ego-energy into nurturing Brock's genuine concern for the customers in the investment department at the bank where he works and affirming Keri's focus on a local justice issue.

We are offered a clear choice. Wouldn't it be a shame to give a "C" in math more attention, and thus more importance, than that flash of Christ-like behavior we see in our teens—when we really look?

O God, how we long for our children to find favor with you. We long for your guidance. Show us your way.

APRIL 5   Read John 19:26.

AS I PREPARE FOR EASTER, I often think of Jesus' mother, Mary. I wonder if, on that awful day when Jesus was crucified, Mary was thinking of the fresh-faced youth who ran off to the Temple years before. She must have wondered how her boy's life could have come to this, the darkest of all nightmares: Death.

Cold chills come as I imagine Mary standing beneath the cross. I am afraid. I know the darkness can come to my children. I think of my friend Elaine. Her daughter, Melissa, was Keri's age. In one crazy, mixed-up, unexplainable moment, Melissa, in her beautiful fifteen-year-old innocence, died of an overdose of a prescription medication. My friend Elaine has stood at the foot of the cross with Mary.

In that moment of pain, I think all mothers ask themselves: "Is loving worth the risk? If my worst nightmare comes to pass, could I bear the cross?"

The fear of what might happen rolls over us, swallows us up. On the hill near Jerusalem, called Golgotha, Mary's boy was nailed to a cross. As he was dying, he looked down and saw his mother. Some of his last words relayed his love for her.

Close your eyes and see Mary there. Standing strong for motherhood, she shows us how to hold on to our faith through the dark nights that come to us all.

Father, how we love our children. And loving them so, we are afraid of the dark. We thank you for offering us an example of faith through Mary's pain.

APRIL 6   Read Mark 15:40-41.

THIS IS THE SEASON of expectation, a time of waiting. There is the promise of spring and the promise of the Resurrection. Yet we must wait. It is a time of not knowing: Just hoping.

When Keri was fifteen, she became terribly depressed over the unjust death of a cousin she loved very much. She rebelled against God and everyone who had taught her that the world was good. She turned from me with a vengeance.

I was distraught. I had no answers to her angry questions. I thought I had failed my daughter, and I didn't have a clue as to what I should do.

I prayed furiously—meaning I begged, demanded, pleaded. And one early morning as I was cajoling, "Please, God, please help me," God answered.

"Trust her," God said to me as clear as day.

I was too surprised to argue.

So I sat Keri down and said, "God told me to trust you, and now that I think about it, he's right. I know the wonderful person you can be. I not only trust you, I believe in you."

It was the best I could do, so I let go and hoped that my best was good enough. And naturally, she tested me. Wanting to know if I really believed in her, she pushed me to the limit. She dared me to stop trusting her, because she needed to know for sure that I did.

For all mothers, the day of waiting comes. Like Jesus' mother and the other women who looked on after the crucifixion, we hope against hope and hold on for dear life to whatever grain of faith we can muster.

Help us, God, to hold on in unsure times. Our children need to know that someone believes in them. Let us never stop trusting.

APRIL 7   Read Mark 16:1-6.

THE DAY IS BREAKING, and the women step slowly toward Jesus' grave. As I imagine the scene, Jesus' mother is with them. Her heart is too heavy to notice the loveliness of the dew-drenched grass, the smell of the jasmine, the bird's song. She rounds a bend and the tomb is in sight. Up ahead she sees the stone rolled away—in her mother's heart, I imagine she already knows. The angel's words simply confirm the good news. He is risen!

In all of history this one juncture takes our task of teen-mothering from bearable to triumphant. We can do our best, then rest in faith. In the end, nothing can separate our children from God. No matter how deep the hole they fall into, God is there. The Easter story says: On the other side of the dark door, there is endless light. For mothers, that means loving—even with the chance of losing—is worth the risk.

My own Easter story ends—or rather begins—with a note Keri left on my pillow last week as she returned to college: "Mom," it says, "Your thoughts and encouragement make all the difference. Thanks for believing in me."

My friend, Elaine? "Since Melissa's death," she writes, "I have felt her with me. I truly believe she has appointed herself to be my guardian angel."

How can we understand God's goodness? We can't, of course. But we can trust God's Easter promise. And trusting, we can cut ourselves free to jump headlong into the day, with a song of hope in our hearts.

O God, in this day of new beginnings, roll away my fears. Fill my heart with hope. Give me courage that I might be a beautiful mother.

APRIL 8   Read Ecclesiastes 3:1, 4.

IN MY FAVORITE CHILDHOOD poetry book there is a poem by Bertha Adams Backus that suggests building a box; putting all your troubles, fears, and broken dreams inside; and then: "Fasten the strong box securely. Then sit on the lid and laugh."

Not bad advice, especially for mothers of teens. The truth is, we have a lot to laugh about.

Already I have seen Brock reach the ripe age of 20. This is proof that I am, indeed, capable of surviving a teenager. And Easter's message makes me brave. So when I discover Keri and her friend Kristen sitting out front, puffing on very large cigars, I laugh. Much to their disgust—and later their delight when they retell the story to their friends—I'm still laughing as they dash through the kitchen with a green pallor on their faces.

Of course, we choose our reactions, and laughter is not appropriate for dangerous, destructive, or rude teen behavior. But on the other hand, there are lots of things we fret over that could just as easily be laughed about. Even a river of milk spreading across the kitchen floor can be pretty funny—and we already know we're not supposed to cry over spilled milk. Why *not* laugh?

So build yourself a box and label it "Easter." Toss all your fears, frustrations, and worries inside and fasten the lid. Sit on top and tell God you're going to trust him.

From this unique vantage point, make a real effort to enjoy your teenager. Then laugh, and laugh, and laugh!

Mothers need to laugh more, God. Help us to remember!

APRIL 9   Read Joshua 24:15.

IN THIS COMPLICATED WORLD, it's more important than ever to produce young people who are capable of making their own choices. Most teenagers choose their friends, their after-school activities, what they wear, their hair-styles, and their hobbies. Yet there's one area where my children have never had "a choice." In the Kidd house, church has never been a choice.

Throughout Brock's and then Keri's high school years, Sunday meant three sure things: Sunday school, church, and evening youth group.

Please understand: There was nothing easy about David's and my stand that going to church is as important as going to school. Believe me, those green doors of ours have witnessed a lot of foot-dragging and have heard plenty of "no fairs" and "Joe's parents say you should never force religion on anyone."

The doors have also heard: "We're not forcing our religion on you. We're simply following a rule we made when you were born. If you live in the Kidd house, you have to go to church. Period."

Brock is 23 now. He has graduated from college and has just begun his career as an investment counselor at a bank. He's living at home, saving to buy a little house of his own. We no longer enforce the Kidd church rule. Brock comes on his own, explaining, "It's my choice now."

And Keri, a freshman in college, has passed her earlier "I'm the only teenager in the world who has to go to church" stage. I'll bet you can guess what tops her must-do list when she comes home for the weekend. You got it: church!

Help us, Lord, to teach our teens to love your church.

APRIL 10   Read Ephesians 2:19-20.

SHARING OUR CHURCH-is-not-a-choice rule with you yesterday set me thinking. I hope I didn't come out sounding like super-mom, because I have to credit my survival as the mother of teens to that very rule.

You see, being part of a church is a lot like membership in one of those big extended families of bygone years. You've heard the saying, "It takes an entire village to raise one child." To David and me, church is that village.

If you get involved in a church—contribute your time, talents, and money; volunteer to change things that need changing; reach out and help those who need help; take your children along on special projects such as delivering meals to those who are sick or need a lift—this incredible thing happens: You find yourself surrounded by a church-family that turns out to be a lot like a huge gathering of grandparents, aunts, uncles, and cousins.

When that proper lady who sits two rows behind you reprimands your son for passing notes in church, or the chemistry professor who sings in the choir helps your daughter with a math problem, you find yourself sighing in relief. By the time your kids are teenagers, you are no longer proud. By now, we moms know we need all the help we can get.

Father, in you we are all one big family. Show us how to help one another.

APRIL 11   Read Matthew 6:8.

CHURCH, IT TURNS OUT, is a very wise investment. You put a certain amount of your time, resources, and energy in and require the same from your teens. The return comes just when you need it most.

For years a remarkable couple served as leaders of our church youth group. Early on, the kids dubbed them Mama and Papa. And for good reason: they were always there for the kids. They listened. They cared. Every teenager in the church knew they could trust them.

In the years when Brock considered his parents "dorks" and later when Keri saw us as incapable of understanding how she felt about anything, this couple was there. Helping our kids through the rough times, even putting in a good word for a tired dad or a frustrated mom from time to time, they were instrumental in nurturing our children through many rough seasons of growth. I know that Brock and Keri are better people because of these friends and others who were there for them when David and I simply didn't fit the bill.

Let's face it. Teenagers invariably turn from their parents toward some other person or persons during their growing-up years. Chances are good that if you "make" them go to church, they will find that "other person" to confide in there. That's when the interest on your church-investment begins to yield a high-quality kid!

God, your return on our investment is exactly what we need. Thank you!

APRIL 12   Read Ephesians 6:10.

A GROUP OF MOTHERS from our church have been asked to participate in a panel on mothering. Mothers of all ages gather in a circle. The conversation flows freely from toilet training to adult children and divorce. It makes me feel good to hear the mothers return again and again to the importance our church plays in bringing up their children.

"Emily is a teenager now, and I don't worry as much as I might, knowing that she finds her center here," one mom says.

"There's no doubt that the teen years are the most difficult," another mother says. "As parents, we seem to lose our influence, but it's funny how much my teenager still cares about what some of the older folks here at church think about the youth."

Their words take me back to a time when Brock, as a junior in high school, found himself in a bit of trouble. He had attended a party where under-aged kids were drinking. The police were called, and when they arrived, they issued citations to everyone in attendance.

A few days later, David, Keri, and I went downtown with Brock, where he had an appointment to "clear his name" with juvenile authorities who deal with such matters. I'll never forget Brock's voice of concern as we approached the police station. "I sure hope Mr. Allen, from church, doesn't drive by and see me going in here," he said.

Remembering Brock's words, I smile to myself. The moms on the panel are right on track. I'll never know how many times a momentary "What would Mr. Allen think?" turned Brock or Keri away from trouble. I do know that without the influences of our church family, my mother role would be infinitely more difficult.

God, we need the help of the family of faith as we raise our teens. "Let us work together for the good of all," especially for our teens.

APRIL 13   Read Matthew 5:16.

I HAVE A CLIPPING TAPED inside my kitchen cabinet. It reads: "Don't tell me how to be good. Show me."

As the mother of a teenager, you've probably already discovered that no matter how good you try to be, your teen has become a master at pointing out your flaws. Maybe this teen tendency is one of God's great gifts to us moms.

With teenagers near to keep me honest, I've found that admitting my own failures is a part of "being good" that my teens really need to see. One of the best pieces of advice I've ever been smart enough to heed—probably offered out of kindness, as I was overdoing one of my "when I was your age, I never would have done that" soliloquies—was "be vulnerable with your teens."

An important part of that "show me" is being honestly vulnerable. Instead of acting perfect (which we are not!), try telling your teen the truth about your own math grades, or the time you acted like a complete jerk to a friend, or your guilt over a bad decision you made when you were fifteen.

Holding back on my inclination to judge others is a constant struggle for me, one that requires a lot of honest confession and equally honest prayer. It's not easy to stop myself in mid-sentence and say, "I'm sorry I'm saying this; I don't really want to be critical of others." Even more difficult is saying "I'm sorry" to one of my victims! It's never much fun to confess your personal flaws—especially in front of the people who are most important to you: your family. But I've noticed that when I do, I'm showing rather than telling—and that's when my children listen and learn!

Gracious God, we want to show our children "good." Point the way!

APRIL 14   Read Ephesians 4:32.

THERE'S A LOVELY SONG WE SING in church from time to time: "They Will Know We Are Christians By Our Love." Isn't this our biggest challenge—not only as mothers of teens, but also as citizens of this run-away world?

"But as a Christian, how do you love people you don't like?" I ask an older friend who somehow seems to love everyone with whom she comes in contact.

At this particular time in my life I am struggling to act civil to a girl who often shows up at our house when Keri's friends gather. To be honest, the girl irritates me. She finds something negative to say on every subject and throws caustic comments, like tiny darts, toward the other girls. And when she's not insulting someone else, she's fishing for compliments. "I got my hair trimmed yesterday," she whines. "Didn't you notice?"

Let's face it, Moms, one of our great tests in these years of raising teens is our reaction to their peers. And I definitely need to change my feelings toward this girl.

My wise friend's response to my question surprises me. "Well, my dear," she says, "though I can't always manage to love or even like everyone, I can certainly call upon that Bible verse we all learned as children and be kind to them."

Such a simple and profound answer. Try it, and you'll be a believer!

Make up your mind to be kind to each and every teen who crosses your threshold. Offer a snack or some help with a school project. Inquire about their favorite activity. Be interested. Be kind.

And don't be terribly shocked when that very kid you couldn't stand runs up, throws her arms around you, and says, "You're the neatest mom I know!"

Forgiving God, let us be kind, tenderhearted, and ever forgiving.

APRIL 15   Read Luke 15:11-24.

"MY MOM GAVE ME THIS book when I graduated from college last year," our friend Elizabeth says, pointing to a copy of *The Runaway Bunny* in the bookstore where we are shopping.

I pick up the book, written for preschoolers, by Margaret Wise Brown. It tells of a mother rabbit's unconditional love for her bunny.

My thoughts go back to a time during Elizabeth's high school years when her mother, Mary, was to be honored at a prestigious event. Hearing that Elizabeth would be making a talk at her school on the same day, she turned down the invitation to the important gathering so that she could "be there" for Elizabeth. Later I expressed admiration for her decision, and she said simply, "A year from now, who will care whether or not I attended the meeting? Elizabeth will always remember that her mother was there to hear her first speech."

As moms of teens, maybe we should reread that classic tale of the little bunny who wants to run away from his mother: No matter where he runs, his mother lets him know that she will be there waiting. "If you become a bird and fly away from me," says the bunny mother, "I will be a tree that you come home to."

It reminds me of a story Jesus told about a father and a wayward son. Self-less unconditional love.

I smile. The book was a sweet graduation gesture. Yet the promise to "be there" was nothing new for Elizabeth. Her mother has been living the book's message since Elizabeth's birth twenty-three years before.

Lord, we see your love in the lives of good mothers who have raised fine children. Let us learn from their example.

The Runaway Bunny by Margaret Wise Brown (New York: Harper & Row, Publishers, 1942)

APRIL 16   Read Isaiah 40:31a.

WHEN WILL I EVER LEARN to keep my mouth shut? I ask myself as I stand in the kitchen, reeling from a nasty confrontation with Keri.

Moments before, she had stormed into the house, "I hate my French teacher," she had announced with a vengeance. "He's so unfair. He wants everyone in our class to fail. He gave me a 69 on my mid-term, and the highest grade he gave anybody was a 74. He's trying to punish us because he's a dork. He's jealous of the students because *we have a life.*"

"Keri," I answered sharply, "I can't believe you failed the test. You can blame your teacher all day, but you are the one who failed."

"Great, I should have known you'd take *his* side," she yelled as she made a hasty retreat and slammed the door behind her.

In the kitchen, I try to make sense of what's just happened. I am angry with Keri—because she failed the test and also because she shifted the blame to her teacher. But she's a senior in high school now, and if I'm ever going to learn to handle such situations in a way that doesn't simply fan the flames of her wrath I had better learn now.

As I scrub potatoes and peel carrots for supper, I pray, "God, show me a better way to respond to Keri's troubles. Right now I'm not a very good example. All I did was blame her the way she blamed her teacher."

And then I wait for an answer.

Help me, God, to be wise enough to wait on your wisdom. I want to be an example to my children, not a critic.

APRIL 17   Read James 1:19.

AFTER MY CONFRONTATION with Keri over her French grade, I am trying to keep myself open to God's presence as I prepare our evening meal. Later I turn the stove to low and go into the living room to sit quietly for a few minutes.

Once there, I decide to search our family Bible for a bit of guidance. In the concordance, the word *anger* catches my eye. There was plenty of anger in our exchange: in Keri's reaction to her teacher, in my response to Keri, and then in her reaction to my chastisement. So I read on.

"One who is quick-tempered," says Proverbs 14:17, "acts foolishly." *That's me; I get an A+ in foolishness*, I think to myself.

"One given to anger stirs up strife," Proverbs 29:22 reminds me. *I've stirred up my share of strife*, I admit again to myself.

"Do not let the sun go down on your anger," Ephesians 4:26 implores.

I glance out the window. The first shades of pink and orange tint the sky. I say a quick prayer and walk down the hall to Keri's room. I knock softly.

"Come in," Keri says. She's propped up on her bed amid pillows, stuffed animals, and books.

I sit down and begin: "Keri, my daddy used to warn me, 'Engage brain before putting mouth in gear,' and I'm afraid I forgot to do that a little earlier. Let's start over about this French grade. This time, I want to listen instead of talk."

God, I want to be a good listener in this time when teens so desperately want to be heard. Give me patience to listen. Help me respond with wisdom.

APRIL 18   Read Matthew 11:28.

AS MOTHERS OF TEENS, it seems we are always tired. The challenge to balance day-to-day maintenance of a household and other demanding responsibilities, the struggle to convince our teens to do their fair share of the housework, the long nights of waiting for that car to turn into the driveway—will it ever end? *Will I ever feel rested again?* I wonder.

For years I have spent my best energy creating a home for my children. That translates into a lot of meal preparation, dishwashing, kitchen mopping, bed changing, and so forth. You have a similar list, I'm sure.

There's a Spanish hymn that speaks of serving. "In my tiredness," it says, "let others find resting." Every time we sing that song in church, the words remind me that the opportunity to serve others is the very heart of our Christian faith. Aren't the most inspiring Christians the foot-washers, the hand-holders, the ones who spend their lives doing something beautiful for God?

As we mother our demanding teens, maybe we should call "time out" occasionally and evaluate the worth of these tiring years. Sure, we are weary, worn, and tuckered. But nobody ever said building tomorrow would be easy. In our tiredness, Moms, we need to remember this: Serving is our most important mother-work!

And so we chisel on. Within a rough world, we carve a safe resting place for our teens and their tribes of friends. The work is relentless; but God made us mothers, and we are equal to the task!

In our tiredness, Father, give us the rest of knowing that we serve our children in your love.

APRIL 19   Read Philippians 3:12-14.

WHAT DO YOUR CHILDREN call you? There are many words for Mother: Mommy, Mom, Momma, Ma, Mummy.

I call my own mother Bebe. It's a name my older brother gave her when he was very small—actually a derivative of Baby, which was our father's pet name for her.

Several years ago Keri grew fond of calling me Pam, but now she favors Momma. Brock simply calls me Mom.

There are many other names for Mother. Check a thesaurus and you'll find words such as procreator, protector, originator, producer, and author. My dictionary refers to Mother as source, and society calls us caregivers, nurses, and matriarchs.

But I believe God-inspired characteristics take the concept of mothering to its highest level. Take mercy, grace, forgiveness, and peace. Add sacrifice, self-giving, and unconditional love. Roll all of these into a tidy package and voila! A picture of Mother emerges.

We have chosen, you and I, to take on the name of mother. It is a challenge that begins anew each day. It's silly even to suggest that we might be perfect in the role. And yet, with God's help and the guidance God offers in Christ's teachings, we are pressing on, moving forward. Our goal is to become the best Mother, Momma, or Mom we could hope to be!

God, help us in our mothering always to "strain forward to what lies ahead," stretching to meet and expand the definitions of motherhood as they are acceptable and pleasing to you.

APRIL 20 Read Matthew 7:15-20.

AS A PART-TIME FREELANCE writer, I have learned that if you really want to cut to the chase in an interview, you ask this question: "How would you like to be remembered?"

The question shifts even the most self-important interviewee away from talk of prestigious honors, business acquisitions, and prominent zip codes. Answers tend to center on more fundamental values, such as "a good person," "an honest person," and "one who loves my family."

Asking myself this same question from time to time leads me back to some equally basic fundamentals of motherhood. *Is this the way you want Brock and Keri to remember you?* I ask myself in the midst of an infrequent but volatile housecleaning fit. The possibility of being remembered as a hateful mother with an extraordinarily clean house usually stops me in my tracks.

Imagine being remembered for
—driving a car too fancy to stuff with smelly kids.
—wearing expensive clothes that make you act restrained.
—never picking flowers, sharing your possessions, or using your good china.

On the other hand, with a little effort we *can* be remembered for:
—laughing a lot.
—always having room for one more at the table.
—having a home with an open door, a comfortable couch, and a well-worn dining room.
—"being there" as the heart of our home.

We are known and remembered by our fruits. May we bear good fruit!

Lord, I want to become a mother who will be remembered with a smile. Show me how.

APRIL 21 Read Psalm 95:3-5.

TOMORROW IS EARTH DAY, a day to both celebrate the beauty of our planet and to safeguard its future. To prepare ourselves for the celebration, let's consider some bad news and good news.

The bad news: Headlines warn of a depleting ozone layer, the rainforests disappear before our eyes on national television, and locally there are dangers of impending chemical spills, tainted water supplies, and hazardous waste disposal problems. We know that greed is a major player in most of our environmental problems: Land stripping for immediate rewards, irresponsibly disposing waste, and choosing convenience over responsible problem solving all take their toll on the earth's natural resources. No wonder our youth are less secure than the offspring of prior generations. What, after all, are we telling them has worth: profit or people?

The good news: As mothers, we can help safeguard the future of this planet. We can do this by recycling, composting, avoiding disposable products when possible, and adding our voice to local, state, national, and international environmental concerns. By doing this we become a living witness to our children. We reflect a message of faith: God's creation is sacred. We are its caretakers. Any effort we extend toward the betterment of this planet is worthwhile.

Our name for earth is "Mother." Let's vow to show our teens how a mother should be treated.

Father, we sing with the writer of Psalm 96, "Let the heavens be glad, and let the earth rejoice . . . let the field exalt, and everything in it." Give us the courage to make the song come true.

APRIL 22   Read Matthew 7:24.

ON THIS EARTH DAY, let's consider the long-range results that come when we, as mothers, make a point of honoring the sacredness of God's creation.

It's been said that we build a foundation of security for our children when we teach them a reverence for life. When you think about it, it must be pretty scary to grow up in this throw-away society.

As mothers, shouldn't we live an example of respect? I

well remember a day when I carelessly tossed a candy wrapper on the ground as David and I strolled through a lovely park. To my horror, a bent old man stooped over, picked it up, and put it in a nearby trash can. Needless to say, I never littered again. That embarrassing moment inspired me to walk through life with a greater awareness of my duty to take responsibility for whatever space I'm occupying at the moment.

Let's vow to commission our children, through our own example, to consider themselves accountable for the portion of the world they occupy at any given moment. Let our motto be to leave a room, a house, a street, a park, a world better than we found it. Such actions will enable our teens to build their life on a rock-hard foundation of honor, respect, and yes, with a sense of permanence.

God, we long to give our teenagers the proper building materials for a secure life. Give us the wisdom to build in your style.

APRIL 23   Read Ezekiel 18:31.

AS I'M WRITING THIS, today is the first day of the Days of Remembrance, a week set aside for us to remember some six million people of Jewish faith who were killed by the Nazis during the Second World War. During this week we recall stories of mothers who had their children torn from their arms, mothers who saw their babies tossed in furnaces, beheaded by bayonets, and herded into gas chambers. And yet these horrific Holocaust stories contain the hope of mother-love: Mothers starving so that their children might eat, mothers offering their own lives so that their children might live.

As you hold this book and read these words, consider what you might do to pay homage to the suffering of the mothers of the Holocaust.

Tonight when our family gathers, I will remind them of the Holocaust. I will talk of prejudice and its part in the darkest point in human history. I'll describe my personal struggle to live a color-blind, status-oblivious, religion-tolerant life. I'll share my goals of seeing the good in others—in people who are different from me—and learning to praise that good.

Today I'm going to ask my children and my husband to help me become a person of mercy and grace. Because, in truth, I know that a better, brighter world begins with me and with you and with every mother who bears influence on the hope of tomorrow's world.

O Lord, I remember the mothers of the Holocaust and my heart hurts. From this terrible mother-pain, sow your seeds of hope. Give me a new heart and a new spirit.

APRIL 24   Read 2 Corinthians 5:17.

As I CONTINUE TO THINK of the Holocaust, I am reminded of something I all too often forget: my freedom to *become.* We have the incredible blessing of living in a country that makes few restraints on our choices. We can choose our religion, our occupation, our life-style. We can travel without hindrance from place to place. We can support whom we choose for public office. We can influence our local education system, community government, and religious organizations simply by becoming involved. And even better than all of that: We can become who we want to be as mothers, wives, friends—as unique and beautiful individuals.

You can become who you want to be by visualizing that person, naming her traits, then spending a lot of time talking to God about exactly who you want to become and why. Today is "no excuses" day—a good day to free yourself from "if onlys," accept the freedom *to be,* and run with it.

We live in a world of excuses. But we don't have to be one more victim of the excuse-making epidemic. It's a terrible thing to have bitter memories of a difficult childhood or abuse or bad breaks, but isn't that all the more reason to stop the cycle and make your own child's growing up years different?

What a grand power we moms have. We are free to create

a better, happier, kinder world for our teens. And we can start today: Good smells from the kitchen, a board game laid out in the den, a sign on the front door saying "I'm glad you're you."

Keep trying, Mom! If today doesn't work—no excuses—do it again tomorrow, until you get it right!

God, make us "new" mothers and begin today.

APRIL 25   Read Psalm 91:11.

"*DO YOU BELIEVE IN ANGELS?*" I don't know how many times I asked that question as I prepared to write the script for a documentary on angels last year. Are you surprised to know that most people said yes?

A recent *Time* magazine poll tells us that 69 percent of Americans believe that angels exist. The Bible mentions angels approximately 300 times. Documented accounts of near-death experiences frequently include face-to-face encounters with angels.

The truth is, even without statistics and an unending supply of angel stories in every bookstore, I can't imagine raising teenagers without the hope of angels! Since Psalm 91 indicates that angels watch over us, I rarely hesitate to call on them on behalf of Brock and Keri. After all, there's just so much a mother can do without a little outside support!

Seeing Keri off at the airport, I ask God to put an angel on each wing of the plane. When Brock backs his old car out of the driveway, I visualize a couple of angels riding on the hood. I refer to Keri's angel as the swan angel, thinking of a lovely being whose big feathery wings shield Keri from harm. I see Brock's angels (I always think in pairs for Brock, who seems to need extra protection!) as the muscle angels: big, burly, and beautifully strong.

OK, call me crazy and I won't care. As I've said before, we mothers need all the help we can get. Since the Bible says angels are at hand, I'm going to keep calling on them and trusting that they can hear.

God, your word promises that angels are near. We claim their protection for our teens.

APRIL 26   Read Deuteronomy 5:16.

WE MOUTH THE WORDS "Honor your father and your mother" but we don't do what we say. Oh, we may honor our own parents, but do we honor older adults in general? How dare we ask our teens to respect us, to honor us, when they see the low premium we often place on older adults. One of the most distressing aspects of our throw-away society is our inclination to dispose of senior citizens. I have come to believe that such an example instills a reckless attitude and a deep disrespect in our young people. We can't change the whole of society, but, as mothers, I believe we *can* change attitudes within our own family.

Here's how the Kidd family approached this problem. If you follow our lead, I guarantee that your teens will hem and haw and drag their feet—at first. Later they will come to respect and even honor you, their mother!

The plan: Choose an older person from your church, neighborhood, or even a local retirement home. Pick someone who doesn't have a family nearby. Throw a birthday dinner for this person in your home. Make this an annual tradition. Invite your new family over for Christmas. Let your teen take responsibility for filling a Christmas stocking for him or her. Include your friend in a family cookout in the summer. If your teen drives, put him or her in charge of picking up your special guest.

I'm itching to tell you stories of the wealth of character and compassion Brock and Keri have gained as we've added elderly friends to our family circles—but I'm not going to. Instead I encourage you to try it yourself and watch your family flourish!

Lord, I know firsthand of the love, the respect, and the joy that comes when we include older people in our family circle. I pray that every mother who reads this book will discover this wonderful truth for herself.

YESTERDAY WE READ THIS same Scripture passage from Deuteronomy. But today we look at it from a different perspective. Today we focus on the one who made our motherhood possible—your child's father.

Some of us are married to our child's father; others of us are divorced, remarried, widowed, or single. None of us can escape this truth: When you honor your child's father, you empower your child.

My husband, David, and I are blessed with a good marriage. I've always considered myself lucky that David is who he is, and yet there are times when his behavior leaves me less than starry eyed—just as there are times when my behavior doesn't thrill him! Whenever David has done something to irritate me, I try to mentally shove whatever it is out of my thoughts and replace it with something wonderful about him. I take time to remember at least one reason I married him. Then I ask myself this burning question: "Pam, what have you done today to make yourself lovable?" Needless to say, the process leaves me humbled and ready to start again.

For those of us who are married to our child's father, working on our marriage is one of the nicest things we can do for our child. Even those of us who are married to someone other than our child's father give a precious gift when we model a healthy marriage relationship.

Regardless of our marital status, all of us can resolve to find the good in our teen's father—and then talk about that good. We can honor our teen's father by complimenting his positive traits. And those times when we're having trouble seeing any redeeming qualities, we can honor him by affirming that he, too, is a child of God, precious in God's sight.

Whether close up or from a distance, you will never regret the effort you make to honor your child's father.

Heavenly Father, give us mothers the grace to honor the men who fathered our children.

                              Read Job 9:25a.

IT'S A UNIVERSAL STATEMENT: "They grow up so quickly." Yet it's hard to believe when you're up five times a night with a crying baby or folding your seventh load of laundry for the day. Then suddenly you find yourself waving good-bye to your baby at the bus stop, then sitting white-knuckled in the passenger's seat while your teen drives around the block for the first time. College is difficult to imagine, but it too comes in time. They do grow up so quickly!

My "baby girl," Keri, is eighteen now, my "big boy" is twenty-three. I find myself at that strange stage when other parents look to me for advice. The advice comes quickly and from deep within my heart. "Enjoy them more," I say. "Laugh more."

I've never regretted time spent catching lightning bugs with my kids. I'm sure sorry for a lot of the time I wasted cleaning house. To tell the truth, I wish I had climbed more trees and taken more impromptu picnics. I'm sorry I didn't learn to roller blade. I'm really glad I helped Keri save all those tadpoles the summer our pond dried up. The punch bowl was never the same after that; actually, there's still something sort of lovely about serving teapunch to church friends and remembering the year the bowl was ringed with muddy pond water. It makes me smile a secret smile.

Go for the secret smiles, Moms, the belly laughs, the wild extravagances. Buy live lobsters, walk in the snow at midnight, wake the family up at 3:00 A.M. for the falling stars of August. Live, laugh, love—then laugh some more!

God, the days fly by. Wake me to their glory moments!

                           Read Psalm 100:4.

JUST YESTERDAY DAVID walked through the kitchen carrying a brand new bucket of soft white paint.

"Have I got a surprise for you," he said. "After all these

years, I'm going to paint the front doors—a bit of sanding, then I'll fill in all those tack holes . . . and before you know it . . . "

I stand and stir the soup that bubbles on the stove. I think back to the day that Keri won the seventh grade creative writing award. In a hurry, I hammered the congratulations poster to the door with a flat head nail—hole's still there. Later that year, I pulled away a sign that praised Brock's move to the starting line-up on his high school football team, and the tape pulled two strips of ugly green paint right off the door. Many triumphs scar those doors: Brock's first Christmas home from college, Keri's pre-med scholarship—so many memories.

"Wait, David, I'm not so sure. What I mean is . . . I've kind of grown fond of these old green doors. Why not use that paint to trim those windows around back?"

As mothers of teenagers, we're a bit worse for wear. We have our wounds: marks of disappointments, broken dreams. We are on a first name basis with failure. Yet, some say its our scars that make us beautiful.

Meanwhile, our teens never stop painting rainbows of hope across our hearts. So we continue to believe. We post our praise and pray our thanks. And we count ourselves blessed to be an active member of the best of all professions: the God-given privilege of being someone's mom!

Thank you, God, for letting me be a mother.

APRIL 30   Read Isaiah 49:16.

HERE'S THE BEST NEWS, saved 'til last. *You* have a friend, waiting to help you raise your teen. This friend is waiting out in front of your house every morning, hoping you'll make time for him. Set your clock thirty minutes early and go out into the first light of day to take a walk and have a talk . . . with God.

Tell God about your teen, about your hopes and your

fears for this child struggling toward adulthood. Describe your successes and your failures. Ask for help with the problems you'll be facing during the day. Thank God for the good things that have come your way.

This is, perhaps, the best gift you can ever give yourself—this time alone with God. It requires so little. A bit less sleep, a tiny effort to get dressed and close the door behind you.

God knows all that's inside you, yet he wants to hear the truth from you. So be honest with God, as you walk along. Honest about your own failings, your insecurities, your stumbling blocks. Lay out your mistakes and your regrets before him.

You are God's child. God loves you, as you love your own child. There's nothing you can do to make God love you more than he loves you now. There's nothing that will make God love you any less.

Take God's love. With it comes the courage, the strength, and the faith to be the best mother you can be. He's waiting for you. Why, he actually has *your* name written on his hand!

God, how good you are to wait for me. How patient is your hope that I will come. And I am coming . . . to talk with you.

$\mathcal{M}$AY

LIVING "AT THE READY"

Mary Zimmer

MAY 1   **Read Judges 4:4-5; Proverbs 2:1-6.**

IN MY PART OF THE COUNTRY, the weather during the month of May is a good image for the beginning of the teen years. It is mostly unpredictable with wide swings between gloriously beautiful days and thunderstorms that can bring a cold wind. After all, adolescence primarily is about change and growth.

When people comment on my sons' rapid physical growth, I often comment jokingly, "They don't ask your permission!" Those genes and hormones start pumping in the blood, and there simply is nothing anyone can do to stop it!

Because we can't control the process, we mothers of teens have to live "at the ready." We need a stockpile of skills we can call on to meet whatever day arises, whether sunny or stormy. These skills include an ability to let go and let natural consequences happen, a willingness to have the most important conversations when we are really sleepy, an ability to choose our battles carefully, and, most of all, a sense of humor.

When the storms of adolescence rage in our homes, a primary skill may be to know when to be like Deborah and go to whatever is the place of our own "palm tree" in order to seek the wisdom of God. As mothers of teens, our most common prayer may be, "O God, give me patience and give it to me now!" But growth for most teens is a matter of two steps forward and one back. So we must have patience with *their* process.

Spend a moment now in prayer. What follows is a prayer *suggestion* rather than a written prayer. My hope is that you will take this opportunity to personalize your prayer and talk intimately with God about the specific needs and concerns as well as the joys in your life *right now*. Pray in whatever way is most comfortable for you, and believe in the power of prayer!

Prayer suggestion: Today pray for any particular storm happening with your teen and for wisdom in responding.

MAY 2   Read Psalm 146:9.

THE CLEAREST EVIDENCE OF impending adolescence in our house was that all of a sudden my sons, Jacob, now twenty-one, and Michael, now sixteen, started using the floor of their rooms for an all-purpose closet, trash compactor, and junk collection site. The energy and time they saved from hanging up clothes and putting away "stuff" could then be utilized in hours spent in front of the bathroom mirror checking their looks and brushing their hair. This phenomenon happened with both boys shortly after their twelfth birthday.

I have learned that boys are just as concerned about physical appearance as I was as a teenager. And I have had to choose just how important the battle over a clean room is going to be. For the most part, I have concluded that my own time and energy are better invested in chauffeuring to activities, staying in touch emotionally, and doing clear supervision than in nagging about neatness. The door can just be closed.

As my sons approached the teen years, I knew there were battles they were going to have to fight, and they would need my steadfastness and encouragement. They would have to navigate the muddy, tumultuous waters of teen friendships, where the greatest pain is betrayal by a "best" friend. They would have to figure out how to resist the temptations of being "cool" or escaping pain through drugs or alcohol. They would have to learn how to relate to young women, who are so fascinating and mysterious. They would be called on to make big decisions about school and career long before they felt ready.

Psalm 146 assures us that God watches over "the strangers." At times our teens seem like strangers to us. For those times we are called to be "watchful," keeping an eye out for whatever the most significant threat may be and being available for consultation when asked.

Prayer suggestion: Contemplate the area of your teen's life that seems to need watchfulness. Pray for the wisdom to know when to step in with parental leadership.

MAY 3   Read Luke 2:41-51.

ONE OF THE MOST IMPORTANT things to remember about teens is that they are learning so many new things. Never before have they had so many new experiences and responsibilities, such as helping to select their classes—and perhaps even their school—and learning to drive. Dating is another new experience that brings much anticipation but also much anxiety; many teens simply do not know what to expect. Working and relating to a supervisor for the first time can also be challenging for teens, who do not yet know all of the things we learn from on-the-job experience.

They will learn, but often it is their own experience, not our wisdom, that teaches them. Some children are simply "born rebels," and they don't follow any predictable path. But they do learn. And often the rebels are the ones who are most creative.

To complicate matters, we parents of teens are still learning too! But we have to put up a good front and make them think we know what we're doing! One day a friend and I acknowledged that when we were young, we thought our parents were certain about their answers and rules. Only as uncertain mothers ourselves did it occur to us that our parents were making it up as they went along, just as we are. So we don't have to know all the answers on the morning of our first-born's thirteenth birthday.

In the second chapter of Luke, Mary and Joseph are frantic when they cannot find Jesus, who has stayed behind to talk with the rabbis. When they confront him, his response stretches them as parents. He is no longer a child; he has a purpose independent of them: to be about God's purpose for him.

May we stretch with our teens as they grow in independence and become the unique individuals God has created them to be.

Prayer suggestion: Pray that as your teen grows physically, mentally, and emotionally, he or she also will grow and mature spiritually.

MAY 4   Read Ecclesiastes 3:1-8.

WHEN JACOB WAS FIFTEEN, one day I had a revelation about what being fifteen really means developmentally: Fifteen is the "average" of twelve and eighteen. One day Jacob seemed to feel and act twelve years old, and the next day he seemed to feel and act eighteen years old. Fifteen, then, was in the exact middle.

Generally speaking, fifteen-year-olds bounce between these two poles, seeming to return to childhood and then trying on adulthood for several blessed days at a time! Just imagine what it would be like for us adults if every year we felt this pull between the stereotypical carefree life of a child and the purposeful responsibility of an adult. There are years for all of us when this is true.

When I am feeling optimistic, I think it is a good design that teens often have parents who, at some time during their children's teen years, go through a midlife crisis. At least we ought to have some understanding of one another when these developmental storms rage! This is especially true if one parent feels the call of an unfulfilled adolescence in the middle of the teen-parenting years.

Family developmental theorists tell us there are certain stages in family life when the stresses and strains are more aggravated than others. One is when the oldest child becomes a teenager. Another is when the oldest or youngest child leaves home. When we are living in the middle of one of these times, we need to remember the word of the preacher in the book of Ecclesiastes: "For everything there is a season, and a time for every matter under heaven" (3:1). This time will not last forever.

Prayer suggestion: Pray about what "time" it is in the life of your own family right now.

MAY 5   Read Proverbs 4:10-11a.

ONE OF THE PARADOXES of being a parent of teens is that the stronger your relationship, often the stronger the push and pull of their growing up. That is, teens often push hardest against the ones they need to be certain will hold firm.

Being a mother of teens means learning the fine art of negotiation so that you can navigate this passage to adult-hood together. Will you set a curfew? What will it be? How will it compare to the curfews of their peers? How will car privileges be determined? What will the consequences be for broken rules?

Jacob had a curfew when his best friend did not. In fact, his friend had his parents' blessing to go to all-night parties at age fifteen. My point of view was and is that there is little left to look forward to as an adult after that kind of adolescent freedom.

With Jacob we negotiated and renegotiated over the years, gradually adding both responsibility and freedom. Now we're doing the same with Michael. For the most part, it has worked. But there have still been nights when I have lain awake waiting for the front door to slam shut, announcing my son's return.

I have told Jacob and Michael that if I had to choose between their being safe or their being happy, I would choose their safety first. If they were safe, then they could be happy. But if they weren't safe, then happiness would be a real long shot.

A good deal of being a parent of teens is knowing or intuiting when to stand firm and when to let your teens take responsibility for their decisions and behavior. It is a balancing act. And most of us lose our balance a few times during each child's teen years. The good news is we don't have to balance the load alone. God is always there, ready to give us guidance and wisdom.

Prayer suggestion: What is the current issue of negotiation between you and your teen today? What kind of wisdom do you need from God?

MAY 6   Read Proverbs 23:15-16.

TEENS DON'T ALWAYS KNOW what they want from week to week or even day to day. If you have a good relationship with your teens and they trust your strength, sometimes they will use you as a bouncing board for their emotions. Some days we mothers feel like a basketball backboard with multiple dents!

I remember promising myself as a young teen that I would never use the phrase "because I'm your mother and I said so!" Jacob and Michael would have to testify whether or not I've broken the vow—they are certain to remember. But at one time or another, we all pull out the "because I'm the adult here" or "because I pay the bills around here" phrases that keep the roles clear.

Keeping the roles clear is important when "everyone else's mother lets them do it." After all, until our teens reach that magic age of eighteen, we are responsible for them and for any consequences of their less-than-prudent actions. But more important, we want what's best for our teens. We want them to be wise and to do what is right. And when they do, souls rejoice.

But we have to remember that good judgment takes a number of years to develop. It is not magically conferred when our teens grow taller than we are or when they get a driver's license. Our teens need opportunities to develop their judgment, to make decisions, and to learn from their experiences. So sometimes we have to take a back seat.

Still, they always need to know that we are in the wings, ready with the car insurance forms or clear advice or reminders about the house rules. Most teens really don't want to leave the nest just yet, but they have to make some practice flights.

Prayer suggestion: What is the particular push-pull issue today for your life with your teen? What do you need from God as encouragement? What has your teen done to make your soul rejoice? Remember to give thanks to God.

MAY 7   Read 1 Corinthians 13:11.

THE PRIMARY RITE OF PASSAGE in American culture is that wonderful day when your teen passes the driving test and is loosed on an unsuspecting public as a new driver in *your* car. For Jacob and Michael, this step really did function as a mythic rite of passage. I saw them become significantly more mature in various ways once the larger society recognized them as qualified to drive.

Rites of passage are important parts of growing up. Because there are not enough of them in our culture, it is very difficult for young people to know exactly when they are truly considered adult by their "tribe."

Both extended family and church family can help carry out this responsibility by looking for those particular events and passages that move teens from childhood to adulthood. The development of rituals that recognize and bless these transitions can provide both symbolic meaning and a message to teens that they are "putting away childish things."

Think for a moment about those defining times in your own teen years, times that conveyed to you that you were truly becoming an adult. It might have been a first date, a first "real" job, a trip without your parents, or, of course, high school graduation. These may be vague memories for us now, but for our teens these times are crucial and significant events deserving dramatic emphasis. Though letting go is never easy, it's important that we celebrate joyfully with our teens as they "put away childish things."

Prayer suggestion: What "rite of passage" does your teen need to experience? What form of "tribe" (family, friends, neighbors, classmates, church family, youth group) could help you create that for your teen?

MAY 8   Read Isaiah 66:13-14.

THE MEMORY WILL ALWAYS haunt me. One day when I was in seminary, I was headed to school for a test when the phone rang. A friend from church called to tell me that one of the most vibrant, energetic young women in our church youth group had been killed in a car wreck on the way to school.

I stopped to pray, and then I went on to school to take the test. I planned to be home to tell my older son, Jacob, myself. I had not counted on the teen network among the high schools. He beat me home, having already heard the news. His grief was inconsolable. As I hugged him, rubbed his back, and listened, I realized that he was far too young to have to be faced with the questions that came to him.

I followed the time-honored custom and took soup to the family's home, stilled and bereft of a teen's noise. I made Jacob his favorite cake, explaining that grief somehow compelled me to cook.

Somehow we lived through those first days, made it through the funeral—the sanctuary was filled with weeping teenagers—and tried to learn what lessons there were for our lives. Jacob wanted to focus on making memories for himself and for others.

There is no good answer to the question *Why?* about such

tragedies. But our Christian faith gives us reassurance and comfort. Isaiah 66:13-14 tells us that God does seek to comfort us in times of grief and bewilderment. Perhaps this is the best "answer" we can give our teens at such difficult times.

Prayer suggestion: Consider what recent griefs both you and your teen have had and seek God's ever-present comfort for them through prayer.

MAY 9   Read Proverbs 1:8.

BEFORE BECOMING A MOTHER of two boys, I never knew there would always be a round ball in my living room. I didn't know that the very last thing I would pick up for the umpteenth time before company walked in the door would be a basketball, or a baseball and bat, or a soccer ball, or now a set of golf clubs with little hard white balls bouncing everywhere on hardwood floors. I didn't know that one of the primary litanies for me as a mother would be "Stop bouncing that basketball/soccerball/superball against the wall! Stop!"

For me, one of the revelations of parenthood has been how many times I've had to repeat the instructions and lessons. Part of the dynamic, I think, is that children and teens have their own agendas for each day. Even if it is only a bowl of cereal and cartoons, they know what they want.

The daily grind of homework, chores, and personal hygiene are not often on the top of the list. So sometimes I push and sometimes I pull and sometimes I offer rewards just to get the basics accomplished. The reward for me is knowing that someday my sons will have to be just as dedicated to the details for my grandchildren!

This is where the lesson of consistency and modeling comes in. Teens are even more astute than children at noticing whether we are consistent about the rules, and much more important, whether we follow our own rules. This is how we truly teach morality.

Prayer suggestion: What are the most important teachings that you hope your teen will not forsake?

MAY 10 Read Matthew 6:5-6.

THE OLDER I GET, THE MORE I believe that people really are, by nature, introverts or extroverts. Maintaining a balance when there is a mix in your family can be a delicate matter. Introverts need a good deal of privacy, and they usually know it. Extroverts also need privacy, whether they know it or not.

Teens will start establishing privacy when they need it, whether by the closed bedroom door or the ubiquitous cassette player earphones. They need time and space to think about what's happening in their lives, to work through problems, and to daydream about what their futures may be like. Someone has said that what we cannot imagine, we cannot accomplish.

I made a personal rule as my sons entered adolescence: If the door to their bedroom was closed, I would be certain to knock and then wait for an answer before entering. I wanted to convey respect for their privacy and personal space.

Parker Palmer says that in education, hospitality is creating a space where obedience to truth is practiced. We do a lot of educating at home, whether we realize it or not. And our teens need space to practice obedience to the truth of who they are becoming. They need this in order to become integrated, consistent human beings rather than artificial people who wear a series of masks for each social role.

Our teens also need space to practice obedience to the Truth, to practice obedience to God. If our teens are to become all that God intends them to be, they must spend time alone with God. As they grow in so many other ways, they also must grow spiritually.

What are you doing to model the importance of spending time alone with God?

Prayer suggestion: Where do you find and establish privacy for your own spiritual reading, prayer, and nourishment?

MAY 11 Read Proverbs 22:6.

NO MATTER HOW POSITIVE our relationships with our children may have been prior to the teen years, generally those relationships undergo some changes in adolescence. For teens to become adults, they must break the bonds of childhood. Some go slowly and easily. Others make a few, often dramatic breaks to distinguish themselves from their families. Sometimes the child you have felt is most similar to you in personality traits and approaches to life is the one who breaks out in ways that hurt the most.

Our children know things about us that we have never explicitly told them. They watch and listen, and they know what hurts us. If our teens' urge to feel separate is overwhelming and we give them little or no permission to break away, often they will use anger and hurt to make the break.

These attempts to break away can challenge our identity as mothers. If our experiences with our children have, for the most part, been positive, we may find these moves for separation very painful. But just as our teens are letting go, we have to let go too. Sometimes letting go simply means giving ourselves permission to recognize and feel powerful negative emotions.

There will be days when we just don't recognize these persons we have mothered, cared for, and tenderly watched. There will be days when nothing we do pleases or gets a positive response. On those days we need to remember that our children are not abandoning us or the things we have taught them—at least not permanently; they are merely stretching and testing their wings. On those days we need the comfort of Scripture and prayer.

Prayer suggestion: What specific kinds of comfort do you need from God as a mother of teens today?

MAY 12   Read Romans 13:1-7.

ONE EVENING JACOB CAME HOME with a very sheepish look on his face. As it turned out, he had gotten a speeding ticket on the way to school one morning and had tried to handle it himself by going to court. His plan had been to pay the fine;

but he found himself assigned to traffic school, which would necessitate his using the car on several evenings. So he had to tell us the whole story.

Some might think my husband, Steve, and I reacted strangely. What did we do? We had a good laugh and reassured Jacob that there would be no additional punishment. You see, we believed that the experience itself was both punishment and education. Experiencing the justice system firsthand and having to go to traffic school would teach him the lessons he needed to learn.

As many of us discover, our lectures and warnings about the responsibilities of driving a car are not nearly as effective as the experiences of the first speeding ticket and the first fender bender. Sometimes experience teaches our children more than we ever could.

There comes a time when we have to let the "larger systems" of our society—such as school regulations, work policies, and civil laws—function as they are supposed to and provide consequences for our teens. This does not mean that we abdicate our responsibilities as parents; rather, we allow these systems to reinforce our parenting and help us teach our teens how to live in a world that is much bigger than the immediate family. For some of us this is difficult, because we believe our teens are too vulnerable. But we must remember that our teens actually need these "practice runs" of adolescence if they are to make their way in the world.

Prayer suggestion: What arena of protection or "education" do you need to relinquish to the larger world? What assurance do you need from God in order to relinquish it?

MAY 13   Read Ephesians 2:19-22.

"IT TAKES A WHOLE VILLAGE to raise a child." This African saying is gaining acceptance in our highly mobile and often alienated society.

When I thanked a departing youth minister for helping to raise Jacob and Michael, he looked a little puzzled. So I explained that one of the best things I had done as a parent was to provide roots for my sons in a vibrant church that became the "village" for them.

By participating in youth choir, youth group, and church mission trips, both Jacob and Michael have had the opportunity to build camaraderie with peers as well as to work side by side in home repair with adults in the church. Through these experiences they have become friends with adults who have cheered them on during musical productions and sent them off and welcomed them home from mission trips to Scotland and Zimbabwe.

Our family is fortunate to belong to a church with a commitment to the future shown by its commitment to children and teens. In addition to being a place of worship, learning, and fun, our church has become the "village" that has nurtured my sons—watched over and watched out for them through their growing-up years. For Jacob and Michael, our church defines what "community" feels like.

Teens need this sense of belonging to a village, even when they seem to prefer only their peers. Nothing can compare to the feeling they get when an *adult* friend affirms something they've done or welcomes them home.

Prayer suggestion: Where is the "village" for your teen? What strength do you need from God in order to support and enhance this community?

MAY 14   Read Matthew 23:37*b*.

THERE COMES A TIME when our children are not as receptive to our hugs, kisses, and other demonstrations of affection. As Jacob and Michael moved out of childhood into adolescence, the evening ritual of reading a book and being "tucked in" had to change. They opted for backrubs and head scratches. For a while, our evening bedtime ritual looked a lot like the grooming rituals of larger primates!

But there was deeper meaning in my sons' nightly requests for some direct personal attention and physical affection of the kind that maintained some connection but clearly indicated they were no longer children. It became a symbol to me of how, even as young teens, they needed me to "be there." I dared not be away from them two nights in a row, because I knew they needed the reassurance that my time, attention, and affection were available and freely given.

Regardless of their anger and other distancing behaviors, our teens need to go through their days with a sense that a loving and committed parent is nearby and available. Sometimes they want explicit advice, whether or not they are able to ask for it. Many times they simply want a friendly ear to listen to them talk out a problem. And they continue to need defenders—as I discovered when supposedly "good" friends left my sons out of plans and activities.

Dealing with the moods of teens can be difficult. I have found that sometimes I have to set limits simply because of my own fatigue level. But we must remember that no matter how difficult they may be, they still need to know they are loved. And no matter how much they may seem to resist our affection, they will never outgrow the need for our love.

Prayer suggestion: In what new and "acceptable" ways can you affirm your teen and show your affection? What are your own social and emotional sources of affection and affirmation?

MAY 15   Read 1 Corinthians 15:58.

TO EXPECT CONSISTENCY IN TEENS is to expect the impossible! Most teens swing between poles of maturity and immaturity, selfishness and compassion, idealism and crass materialism. Even their habits and preferences seem to have little consistency.

One teen cares very little about designer clothes but has to have the best compact disc player available. Another teen doesn't care if his room is an absolute wreck but is very particular about his personal appearance.

What keeps us parents on our toes is that the priorities change—sometimes as often as every month in the early teen years. And this makes us more flexible—whether we value flexibility or not!

This inconsistency in personal preferences, styles, habits, and even values requires us to be consistent in response. Our teens need to know that we don't change our minds about values, appropriate behavior, and good taste. Such consistency requires self-awareness and self-knowledge on our part. After all, if we don't know what we stand for, how can we pass on our values to our teens?

Prayer suggestion: What are the three most crucial values for you? What is God's leading about how you live these out? How can you be a steadfast example for your family?

MAY 16   Read Proverbs 10:10-12.

BEING A MOTHER OF TEENS definitely keeps us acquainted with our human fallibility. We do make mistakes, and our teens—who are feeling new "ego strength"— are cheerfully capable of pointing them out. At some time or another, we all disappoint our teens by our busyness, our impatience, our forgetfulness, or our occasional wrong-headedness. What may seem a small, inconsequential matter to us may have enormous significance to our teens. This is where we need sensitivity and patience and lots of time to listen and be aware.

One Sunday evening I told Michael that we would go to get some supper after I caught up with him at home. I was fairly late getting home, having forgotten the promise, and he was distraught from both hunger and hurt feelings. What he needed was validation that his hurt feelings were justified and that he deserved an apology. He got the apology.

An honest "I'm sorry" to our teens can be one of the strongest anchors for our relationship. They know we are fallible, that we make mistakes. We affirm their maturity when we also recognize our fallibility and acknowledge it to them. Teens whose parents need to be perfect, at least in the parents' own eyes, have trouble trusting adults' words. Instead they focus on adults' actions. For most teens, our actions really do speak louder than our words. Like children, we make ourselves known by our acts (Proverbs 20:11).

We set a good example for our teens when we acknowledge our mistakes and openly apologize. Then they are more likely to do the same—knowing that though they will continue to make mistakes, they will live through their apologies.

Prayer suggestion: What comfort do you need from God about your mistakes as a parent? What reconciliation, if any, do you need to make?

MAY 17   Read 1 John 3:2.

ONE OF THE MOST BELOVED teachers in my community used the image of a caterpillar turning into a butterfly to describe the process of growth that her eighth-grade students would experience during their thirteenth year. In very creative ways, she used the theme throughout the year to convey the significant changes her students were undergoing.

Think about caterpillars. We would seldom name caterpillars as one of the most beautiful creatures in nature. They are slow and ungainly; they usually are dull in color; and, generally speaking, they don't have much "eye appeal."

Whether they ever actually appear awkward of unattractive to others, most teens feel that way for at least a period of time. Unfortunately, this dip in self-esteem usually corresponds with a growth spurt and a desire to appeal to the opposite sex!

During their "caterpillar stage," our teens need encouragement about what the chrysalis represents and where they can find their own "chrysalis." We can help them find the security and protection they need while they await the transformation that is taking place both within and without. What they need more than anything is to know that others believe and trust that the butterfly will appear. Part of our job as mothers is to communicate that belief and trust.

And when it is time for them to emerge from the chrysalis, let us remember that they will be most vulnerable then; for, like the butterfly, they will be weak and will not have tested those bright, beautiful wings.

Prayer suggestion: What promising beauty do you see in your teen? What grace do you need from God in order to believe in and share that beauty?

MAY 18 Read Psalm 139:14*a*.

EACH OF OUR TEENS IS UNIQUE, "fearfully and wonderfully made." Many of them have their own "trademark," so to speak. For Jacob it was duct tape and tools. His nickname in junior high was "gadget man" because he wore a sleeveless denim jacket that had pockets filled with hand tools and other items "he might need." The jacket weighed about fifteen pounds when fully loaded!

For Michael it was baseball caps for his favorite teams, which had to be regularly replaced because washing them would surely ruin them. A request to remove his cap at dinner or even at casual church services was tantamount to insult! Another of Michael's "trademarks" was high-top leather basketball shoes, which had to be a specific style and color. I gave up recommending what seemed sensible to me.

These individual expressions of identity are important to our teens. They need visible, physical symbols of their personality—such as clothes and shoes that prove they know what is "rad" or cool—as well as symbols that set them apart from the crowd, which are expressions of their individual taste and style. As we mothers know, meeting both of these requirements can be expensive! But we can encourage our teens to develop their own earning power by making agreements about what we will pay for and what has to be paid for with their own money. After all, the best consumer lessons are learned with money *they* have earned.

Prayer suggestion: How much tolerance do you have for your teen's individual expression? What do you need from God to grow more tolerant and accepting?

MAY 19   Read Galatians 6:2.

MY PARENTS BELIEVED they were paying for piano lessons. And they were, for the most part. What they didn't know was that they also were paying for informal counseling, for my piano teacher was also my confidant. She listened to my sorrows about social slights made by girlfriends and my crush on an older guy who didn't know I existed. I did a lot of "venting" sitting on a piano bench rather than a psychiatrist's couch.

Many teens need such a person in their lives. We parents cannot always be their confidants, because defining themselves "against us" is part of their emotional growing up. And perhaps they sense that we know too much about them, or that we have already made up our minds and are ready to give advice rather than a listening ear. Sometimes our teens seem to know that they need someone who can "bear their burdens," who can listen with more objectivity than we can have. No matter how we try, it is hard to separate our sense of self as parent from what is going on in their lives.

One of the most freeing things we can give our teens is the right to a confidential relationship with another adult who will listen and perhaps offer advice—but, for the most part, will just listen. Our teens also need to hear the ideas of other adults regarding the decisions they are making—both big and small.

How comfortable are you with the idea of your teen forming a close relationship with an adult friend? What can you do to encourage such a relationship?

Prayer suggestion: Reflect on your own sense of privacy related to your teen's thoughts and feelings. Can you release your son or daughter to talk with someone else as confidant?

MAY 20

WAITING ON THE LORD is the hardest thing in the world to do. There are many scriptural examples and admonitions calling us to do just that, but knowing what an important spiritual ability it is seems to make it even harder.

There may be months, even years, when it is hard to see what God is doing in the lives of our teens. We want to believe in God's purposes for each of them, and we want to teach them how to seek and find those purposes. Perhaps the phrase "let go and let God" applies more to us parents during these years than at any other time. We do have to let go. And if our own trust in God is not flourishing, then we have great difficulty entrusting a not-yet-fully-formed beloved child to God.

So we learn to wait with patience. We learn to be patient with our teens, patient with ourselves, and, most important, patient with what God is doing. We wait on the Lord.

Waiting does not have to be a passive activity. It doesn't mean that we don't order the college catalogues and keep talking with our teen about future dreams and hopes. What waiting on the Lord means is living in the biblical dictum to never worry or be anxious. It may mean that our daily, even hourly, prayer is for the peace that passes understanding, because sometimes we simply do not understand.

Prayer suggestion: What is your prayer today for the ability to wait on the Lord?

MAY 21

ONE DAY WHEN A FRIEND and I went to lunch, we found ourselves talking about the grief of knowing that a son or daughter is in emotional pain and we are unable to help—or worse, we are not allowed "in" to even try. After talking about our own teens, I began to think of other teens I have known who have suffered from depression and have been unable to get the help they needed.

When trying to negotiate the rapids of adolescence, often teens need a point of view other than that of their parents. We parents can be steadfast in standing by and proactive in getting help, but we cannot be our teens' counselors. Sometimes they may need an objective ear for a short period of time, or they may even need professional help. At those times, our best act as parents may be to step out of the way for a while, perhaps until we are asked to participate in a family session.

We also can help our teens by getting to know more about ourselves from their point of view. We can invite them to talk with us openly and honestly, without fear of any repercussions. It may be very uncomfortable for a while, but the assurance that we have clearly heard one another's honesty and the potential for reconciliation or healing are worth the discomfort. And whatever we are required to face, we have the promise that "God is our refuge and strength."

Prayer suggestion: Pray for teens you know who are having a rough time dealing with emotional pain. If one of these is your own, what assurance do you need from God?

MAY 22   Read Psalm 42:5-8.

HAVING GROWN UP IN SMALL TOWNS, I had difficulty entrusting Jacob and Michael to the big city environment once they were driving and staying out late. Perhaps that is because I remember some of my own escapades—mild by most standards, but not by my parents'!

There is something about the late night hours that is exciting to teens. Maybe it is all those years of being told, "Be home by dark." Having wheels and being out late become the recipe for excitement. And in our society it seems that excitement almost always connotes danger of some kind.

Steve and I decided that the best approach was concrete clarity about what our expectations were. Jacob and Michael both agreed to "no alcohol, no drug use" contracts while living at home. We were lucky; the fact that their peer groups were primarily church youth meant that getting drunk or high wasn't the definition of a good time.

We also agreed that they would wake me up when they got in. That way, I would know whether or not they had met their curfew. Somehow I eventually learned to fall asleep when one of them was out with the car.

I knew I had to entrust my sons to God's protection. They needed freedom in order to learn responsibility. And by giving them freedom, I learned to trust God even more.

Prayer suggestion: What kind of trust do you need to extend to your teen? What assurance do you need from God?

MAY 23   Read Luke 8:16-21.

IN THIS READING FROM LUKE 8 there is an enigmatic passage that must have first brought chills to the heart of Mary, Jesus' mother. When Jesus was told that his mother and brothers were outside, waiting to see him, he responded, "My mother and my brothers are those who hear the word of God and do it" (v. 21).

There is no further explanation. We do not know whether the gospel writer edited out further conversation in order to make a point. But there is some significance here for us as Christian mothers of teens, and it is this: If we do a good job, then we work ourselves out of a job. We may never stop being mothers, but there comes a time when the "job description" we've been following for so many years is no longer appropriate.

Our responsibility is to prepare our teens to leave home, not to stay forever young and within our sight. Jesus had to live out God's purpose for him, and so do each of our own children. They need to test themselves against the world's realities. They need to form relationships with people who know them as individuals, not as someone's son or daughter. They need to find their own way within the family of faith beyond their family of origin—so that they can have a faith of their very own, not a borrowed one. And they need us to help get them ready.

Prayer suggestion: What "cover" do you need to remove from the light that shines in your teen's being? What word of God is crucial at this time for growth and development?

MAY 24 Read Romans 8:28.

MY FRIENDS WITH OLDER TEENS and I often ponder with great confusion the phenomenon of our children's reluctance to leave home. We remember our own eager anticipation of our future as young adults, wanting to have our own apartments, regardless of the condition, just because it would be "our space."

There are many reasons why adulthood is not as appealing as it once was. The media predict lower standards of living for the next generation. Our teens have grown up with news on cable television that brings every world trauma and crisis immediately to them. Even if they have not personally experienced it, they have seen stories of AIDS, abuse, and personal and social violence way beyond what we heard of twenty years ago.

One of our responsibilities as parents is to make adulthood appealing. If we are overworked and overstressed for months on end, our teens may decide that adulthood is not very much fun at all. They may even feel a sense of dread about growing up and being on their own, rather than an optimistic anticipation.

Teens are close observers and listeners. They form their opinions of their options as adults by what they see us doing and saying. Do we truly believe that "all things work together for good for those who love God" (Romans 8:28)? Are we a living example of this belief? Modeling is the most powerful form of teaching. As Frederick Buechner puts it, they are "listening to our lives." What message are they hearing?

Prayer suggestion: What message about adulthood do you want your teen to hear? What do you need to offer God to be transformed by God's grace?

MAY 25   Read Ecclesiastes 7:8.

As HARD AS IT IS TO BELIEVE, the fads of adolescence are a necessary evil.

While looking at photo albums together, Jacob and I were reminded of his "break dancing" phase. The right look required nylon pants with multiple zippers and a host of bandanas tied around the legs and arms. In one photo Jacob was dressed this way for a performance, but I remember that for a number of months he hardly wore anything else!

Like all parents before us, we are taking our turn at being appalled at what our teens are putting on their bodies—or not putting on them! Who could have predicted the "grunge" look? But we know that fads of dress and music are part of the establishment of identity. Our teens are just trying on a look and the identity it represents. And if the look gets a horrified response from us, so much the better!

In the middle of what seems like terminal embarrassment at how our sons and daughters present themselves in public, we need to remember that "this too shall pass." A fad, by definition, is not permanent. Otherwise the clothing industry would suffer economic catastrophe.

Sooner or later, the "uniform" required by a job or the negative response of a new boyfriend or girlfriend will put the current form of expression on the shelf. But you might save some of the items for future family get togethers!

Meanwhile, look for what the fad represents. Ask yourself what part of themselves your teens are expressing. And when your patience wears thin, pull out some old photos from your own teen years and have a good laugh!

Prayer suggestion: What is your prayer for patience while dealing with the current fad at your house?

OUR TEENS ARE GROWING UP in a world that doesn't always offer clear definitions. Just what is "grown up"? How will they know when they've made it? To what extent do they get to define it, and to what extent do they have to meet society's expectations?

Part of the process of adolescence is learning to "reality test." As parents, we have a responsibility to provide some of these reality tests. One test at our house has been that if school grades are adequate to obtain the car insurance discount, then we pay the premium. But if grades aren't adequate, then Jacob or Michael has to find a part-time job to earn the money. For each of them, it has been the first literal lesson that you "pay your own way" in this life.

The experience of a part-time or summer job is another reality test that helps to define a teen as more grown up than before. No matter what the responsibilities may be, teens begin to develop maturity when supervisors and others are depending on them and when they are getting paid.

What are your definitions of "grown up"? How are you communicating these to your teen?

Prayer suggestion: What particular wisdom do you need at this time as you instruct and guide your teen to adulthood?

IN HER BOOK NECESSARY LOSSES, Judith Viorst describes one aspect of the teen years: "A normal adolescent (who now is capable of abstract logical thinking) can use this new cognitive skill to contemplate deep philosophical issues but never to remember to take out the garbage."

It is hard for us to remember that a whole lot of confusing things are going on, all at the same time, in the bodies, hearts, and minds of our teens. Some days they really seem to focus, and everything runs smoothly. Other days, you may feel like you are sending signals to someone who lives beyond Jupiter, who says "Huh?" all day long.

One of the hard things about living in a family is that each person gets up in the morning with his or her own mood and attitude about the day. The day seems to be a matter of negotiation between a group of people with very different agendas.

On certain days, we may simply give up on getting through to our teens. Perhaps we need a day off from the tension of their seeming opposition. It has always been my opinion that parents are the ones who need to run away from home!

It is important to give yourself permission to "take a day off" now and then. This might mean finding a place close by where you can be alone for a while, or it might mean literally getting away for a retreat when you need respite and rejuvenation. Wherever you go, use this time to draw closer to God and to replenish your spirit.

Prayer suggestion: Where is the place you can find rest for your spirit and time for communion with God? When can you set aside time to go there?

MAY 28   Read Matthew 18:1-3.

I BELIEVE THERE WILL BE a special place in heaven for middle school teachers. For them, teaching must be somewhat like "riding herd" on human-sized jumping beans. Whether it is hormones or just the energy of being together, young teens seem to have boundless energy!

One of my memories of my own early teen years is crystal clear. A friend and I were excused from our chorus class to drill each other for the Spelling Bee. We got bored and started looking around the empty room next to the gym. There we discovered a dead mouse, and we concocted a scheme to put it in a paper cup and roll it into the science class of a fairly straight-laced and imposing teacher.

We got the reaction from the students that we wanted—

shock and laughter. But the one who was mortified was our chorus teacher, because he saw the misconduct as a reflection of his own supervision.

Like my own episode with the mouse, many teens misbehave because they are bored. They are acutely aware of the world and what it has to offer in terms of excitement, and they want to be part of it—often despite the risks. Our grandmothers were right: Keeping them busy tends to keep them out of mischief. Perhaps we need to focus on channeling all that energy in positive ways. Could it be that we need to channel our own energies in more childlike ways?

Prayer suggestion: What kind of attention do your energetic teens need? How can you retain a reservoir of energy to keep up with them?

May 29   Read Psalm 104.

A FRIEND EXCITEDLY TOLD ME about a wonderful birthday gift for her thirteen-year-old son: a new bicycle that enabled him to get himself to and from friends' homes and activities. Not only was she freed from some of her chauffeur duties, but she also took pleasure in seeing her son's increasing independence and responsibility for his own life.

Independence. It can be a scary prospect because we know our teens can get hurt. And isn't one of the characteristics of youth a belief in their own invincibility? Still, some of the most important lessons in life are taught only by the natural consequences of personal experience.

Another friend used to sometimes make the motion of zipping her lips while talking with her teenage sons. This would remind her of an important lesson she had learned: many times the less said in terms of warning and caution, the better. Sometimes a mother's caution about what seems like risky behaviors only increases a teen's determination to participate.

We have to loosen the apron strings, then untie them, and finally take off the apron. The image is apt. Think how ridiculous the picture is of a nearly grown teen being tied to a mother's apron!

As we begin to take off the apron, perhaps we may find some unexpected benefits, such as more free time and more independence of our own as our teens assume more responsibility for themselves. Despite what some may think, there are days when it is wonderful to be a mother of teens!

Prayer suggestion: What wider world do you dream of for your teen and yourself as you both grow?

MAY 30   Read Psalm 118:5-6.

I DON'T REMEMBER THE GUY'S name, but I do remember the red Ford convertible. My friends and I had met a group of out-of-town guys at the lake near our home. The mutual interest level was high; the excitement was almost palpable. What might happen? Would the handsome one ask me out?

Well, he did invite me to go for a ride later, and he hinted that he might even let me drive the red convertible. So, like any teenager, my girlfriends and I put a good spin on our stories to our parents about our plans for that night. We were just going to the lake for a swim.

I think my dad knew something was up. Chances are, my excitement was just too much for going to the lake with girlfriends. Probably against his better instincts, he said yes.

I remember driving that red convertible. I remember the aura of excitement, the sense of endless possibilities about what might happen. Looking back from the vantage point of parenthood, I'm just grateful I didn't wreck someone else's car!

It's an advantage for us as mothers of teens if we can remember not only the events of our own adolescence but also the feelings that were attached to those events. Then we will be more empathetic to our own teens' desire to seek out thrills and the unknown. And there will be times when we will just have to let them take a chance.

Prayer suggestion: What are your primary fears about your teen and the unknown? How can you release those fears to God?

SOMETIMES THE WELL-BEHAVED CHILD turns into the most defiant teenager. When this happens, we are not only confused but also disappointed and concerned about what kind of adult our child is going to be.

One reason adolescence is hard on us parents is that we not only have to turn our teens loose to face the world but we also have to turn them loose to face themselves. Because all of us, by virtue of our human fallibility, have some undesirable personality traits and know firsthand the pain and disappointment those traits can bring, it is sometimes difficult to watch a beloved son or daughter struggle with shortcomings.

Another reason adolescence is difficult for us is that our children tend to be mirrors, reflecting various patterns of our own personalities and characters. It's not easy for us to see and accept in our teenagers particular qualities we don't like in ourselves or character flaws with which we also struggle. Yet to live with teenagers is to live in the presence of living mirrors of our own characters and behaviors. We cannot afford to ignore the wisdom we gain by reflecting on this phenomenon. Trying to hide our fallibility and mistakes is one of the biggest mistakes we can make—one that risks long-term alienation from those we are closest to.

What can we do? We must be honest with ourselves and one another. Somehow we have to find a way to risk that vulnerability so that we can grow closer, even through our failings.

Prayer suggestion: What particular character or personality trait of your teen worries you? Is it a reflection of you? What is your prayer to God about this?

JUNE

MY INCREDIBLE BLESSING

Pamela Crosby

JUNE 1   **Read Isaiah 53:4-6.**

SINCE HE WAS *11 OR 12*, I've referred to Adriel as my enigma. He's always been special: creative, sensitive, artistic, intuitive, introspective. For some time I've felt that he hasn't forgiven me for divorcing his father. And I know he didn't forgive me for remarrying.

Now that I'm twice divorced and it's just the two of us, I wonder why he's hostile toward me at times. Although I've given him opportunity to talk to me about it, even begged for it, I wonder if he'll ever tell me how I've hurt him, when I've hurt him most or why we're not as close as I want us to be.

I think he doesn't want to bring up "stuff" from the past—because it's the past. And he believes nothing can rectify that. I, however, believe that discussing disappointments and sharing pain can help one understand the past; and, in that way, healing occurs.

Sometimes I look at him and try to see within his heart. I try to imagine what pain he must be hiding, what anguish he still harbors. I remember the way he was before the first divorce, and I think of specific influences that probably shaped him into the young man he is now. What happened during those 14 years—between the 5-year-old and the 19-year-old?

I tell him he doesn't have to endure that pain, that Jesus

endures that for him. The peace I live in was bought with the punishment of Jesus. That's how I have been able to forgive myself for not giving him what every young man needs—a father in his home. Perhaps one day he'll understand.

Regardless of the outcome of all our situations, Jesus is not only able to bear our transgressions; he *chooses* to bear them. Thank God for Jesus' monumental choice, my incredible blessing.

O God, provide our young people with appropriate places to release their pain and grief. May they know the blessing of Jesus' sacrifice for our mistakes.

JUNE 2   Read Colossians 3:15-17.

"*OH, OH HERE SHE COMES.* She's a man-eater."

I remember one day when that Hall and Oates song played on the radio. My son was eight or nine then, and he confidently said to me, "I know what that song is about."

I gulped and asked, "What?"

He said confidently, "It's about Mrs. Pac Man."

I breathed a relieved sigh and said, "You know, I think you're right."

My usually passive child surprised me that day. He was not quiet because he was daydreaming; he was taking in ideas and making intelligent assessments of the songs he heard. I had always tried to be critical of songs I listened to on the radio and felt my own standards for acceptable lyrics were pretty high, but I realized then that I needed to consider what lyrics—any lyrics—would mean for my son.

Music is such a vital part of nearly every teenager's life. Music expresses for teens many unspoken emotions and thoughts at an incredibly deep level, and it also *shapes* their emotions and thoughts. It's unfortunate that some of today's songs have to carry "explicit language" warnings. We aren't winning the battle to keep pure lyrics before our children, but there are positive steps we can take.

One thing we can do is take advantage of opportunities to expose our children to songs that exemplify Christ-like qualities and behaviors, songs that serve as spiritual food for their minds and souls. It's also very important for us to monitor the music they listen to, paying close attention to the words they are hearing, and to discuss and analyze the messages with them. The outcome of such exchanges will reveal much about how our teens think and feel about a variety of subjects; and perhaps more important, these exchanges will give us the opportunity to share our beliefs with them.

Dear Jesus, help us to "teach and admonish" our teens in wisdom as we seek to help them distinguish your messages from the degrading and destructive messages of much of today's music.

JUNE 3   Read Matthew 18:2-5.

WHEN ADRIEL WAS ABOUT 14, his father and stepmother went to New Orleans for the weekend. We kept their two children, Christopher, 5, and Erin, 3.

I was excited about having little guests in our home. Adriel and I went to the grocery store and bought "fun food" for the weekend. Chris and Erin arrived Friday afternoon, and we all got settled.

By Saturday afternoon, our guests were completely acclimated to their new environment. I walked into the den and saw something I didn't expect. I saw my son as a brother.

It took me by surprise. I knew Adriel had a stepbrother and stepsister. They'd come to church with us many times, and he spent nearly every other weekend with them. Yet I'd never seen the three of them relating to one another. Walking into that room and seeing two giggling and screaming little kids piled on top of Adriel was a pleasant and unusual blessing for me. My son was a brother!

They really love him, I thought, and although their personalities are different, the sibling blend is there. And I had been feeling guilty for not having another child as a companion for Adriel. He was doing fine with these two.

I chuckled and thought, *I should thank Christopher and*

Erin's parents for this experience, but they might offer to let us keep them longer!

Gracious God, thank you for the joy and vitality of youth we see in our teens; they bless our paths and remind us of characteristics you desire in us.

JUNE 4   Read Philippians 3:20-21.

LIKE A COMET BLAZING 'cross the evening sky,
Gone too soon.
Like a rainbow fading in the twinkling of an eye,
Gone too soon.
Shiny and sparkling and splendidly bright,
Here one day, gone one night.
Like the loss of sunlight on a cloudy afternoon,
Gone too soon.

Last year my son attended a double funeral—two of his friends, ages seventeen and twenty, victims of a drive-by shooting. I asked him if he felt sad that they were cheated out of their young lives. He said, "No." I sat dumbfounded for a minute and then asked why. He explained, "The way I look at it, they've gone to a better place. Why should I be sad? They should be sad for me."

His reasoning actually made sense. It was, after all, what I'd been teaching him: That Christians go to heaven when they die; and that heaven is definitely a better place than earth. He had a simple peace about him that I could not help but admire.

I know he misses seeing his friends, but more important than missing them is the reality that they are experiencing a better existence—one he hopes to experience.

I learned that my son is not afraid of death. He seems to have the peace that passes understanding, which God wants for each of us—especially while we're here on earth.

Dear Lord, help us teach our teens your promises about life everlasting, so that they may have the peace that passes understanding.

"Gone Too Soon" Music by Larry Grossman-Lyrics by Buz Kohan. One Zoe Music Publishing company, Inc. © 1983.

SOMETIMES IT TAKES ONLY ONE interested teen to spark the others' curiosity in a subject or event. At a recent family reunion, I was amazed at how interested the teens were in learning about family traditions. On a hot Sunday afternoon, they crowded around an older relative while he spun tales of what life was like during the Depression—what they wore, what they ate, how they danced, what they sang. They paid special attention when he revealed information about values and how people treated one another. They grew pensive, asked questions, and seemed to admire the ways of the old days.

The example of those teens restored my resolve to gather and give to them the stories of our family and of the family of God. Giving them this "history" to pass along to others is a precious gift.

I think about how stories of my own parents and other relatives have inspired and strengthened me through the years, and I find myself feeling proud of the family I was born into and happy for the legacy of accomplishments, laughter, and spirituality they have given me. It has been beneficial to know the struggles my family has survived, as well as the celebrations they have shared.

So I have made a commitment to periodically send each teen in our family a story or some information about our family and to solidify in some way the links we have with our Christian family. The heritage of our own family and the heritage of our Christian family are precious gifts, indeed.

Gracious God, may our teens be able to see the faith that lives in us and in other family members. Help us to pass on that faith heritage.

"MOM! WE WANT TO GO TO THE CITY!" My friend's sixteen-year-old son announced and explained in full detail the exciting events planned for a day-long excursion with three other boys. As we listened, I could almost see every motherly bone in her body screaming, "No you're not!" However, her son had worked very hard, successfully managing school projects and assignments and an intense soccer practice schedule. He deserved a break.

"The boys were good drivers; all were insured; the car was in good condition. Except for the anxiety it would cause her, worrying about them every mile of the drive, there was no real reason to deny the request. Here was an opportunity to exercise her faith, to ask God to take care of her son and his friends—and to take care of her, whatever might happen.

It reminded me of the first time I loaned Adriel my car. I remember that I had to relinquish my son and my car to God. Although I'm a single parent, I don't parent alone. God is my partner. Many times I have to take a step of faith and say, "Okay, God. I'm depending on you to handle this, because it's too big for me." Though I may not know the outcome, I do know that God will be with me, sustaining me whatever happens. I'm getting pretty good, because my son grants plenty of opportunities to practice those faith steps!

Teach us again, dear God, that you want us to depend on you. Give us fresh confidence in your power and your peace.

JUNE 7   Read Isaiah 41:9-10.

WHEN MY NOW NINETEEN-YEAR-OLD son was younger, I looked forward to Sunday worship especially because it was one time I could sit next to my son and participate in the worship service with him. No, he didn't sing joyfully or throw back his head in praise. Actually, he barely parted his lips. But he always sat beside me, and we were a family unit. Even when it was popular for the teens to sit in the back, he still sat with me. For as often as I can remember, I would periodically put my arm around Adriel or pat his back while we worshiped.

One Sunday I put my arm around my sixteen-year-old and he quickly pulled away. That response hurt me deeply—so much that later that day I called his father and said, "Please come get Adriel for awhile. I need some time alone today."

I was thankful that his father understood, picked him up, and even kept him overnight. I don't remember much about the rest of the day, other than writing a two-page letter explaining to Adriel how I felt rejected by his response. Though male friends later helped me to see that this may have been a necessary thing for Adriel to do—that he was trying to assert his growing independence as a young man—I still felt he needed to understand that his response hurt me. So often our teens feel the pain of rejection themselves, but sometimes they fail to recognize when others feel rejected by their actions. It was an important lesson for him—and for me. You see, as the pain of rejection pierced me, I began to realize how much I valued Adriel's love and acceptance. And then I had a startling revelation: When I pull away from God, is this how I make God feel?

Almighty God, help us to be aware of the pain we cause one another and you when we withdraw from one another's love of from your love. Help us to remember that we are your chosen servants. You will never reject us or cast us off.

JUNE 8   Read Mark 9:23.

WHEN ADRIEL WAS FIFTEEN, I took him to Atlanta to the Black Arts Festival. For us it was three days of cultural expression: concerts, African dancing and drumming, a play, museums, displays of all kinds, and music everywhere—in addition to Atlanta's booming cultural personality. We went to Greenbriar Mall to look at art exhibits, and the mall stores drew in my son. After we had made our way the length of the mall, he said with surprise, "I've only seen three white people since we've been in this mall."

Though we never discussed it, that incident showed both of us how important it was for Adriel to see African Americans in a variety of roles: entrepreneurs, artists, filmmakers, even mall managers. It was an important experience that helped him to see his people in all parts of life. As I continue to enlighten him about the important contributions that African Americans and other ethnic groups have made to this country, I'm aware that it is another way of saying, "You, too, can do it!"

All teens, regardless of their race, need to have experiences that teach them "You, too, can do it!" So often what we see speaks louder than what we hear. What can you do today to help your teen dream and believe that that dream can become a reality?

Dear God, help us to see the possibilities you set before us and to know that your power is in us, helping us turn the possibilities into realities.

JUNE 9   Read 1 Peter 3:3-4.

I TOOK MY TEENAGE GODDAUGHTER shopping for a swimsuit last spring. Her mother enjoyed the idea of me dealing with her teenager in her natural habitat. Much to my chagrin, I learned that she is a "mall rat" and loves it. She doesn't have to purchase a thing; she's just happy to be in that element.

We looked for an hour, and I was shocked at the selection—which seemed perfect for one of the actresses on *Baywatch*, but not for a fourteen-year-old going to camp! I found myself becoming irked at the prevalence of two-piece suits and string bikinis. (My generation gap was showing, and I didn't mind.) The suits seemed to convey a message to customers: "You *will* wear this style, and there's something wrong with you if you can't fit into me." My mind began to collect questions to ask the store's buyer: "Who do you think you are, encouraging my special girl to embrace this mind-set? Do you think of twelve- to fourteen-year-olds when you select these suits? Do you have a girl this age in your life? Would you like to see her wearing these suits in public?"

When I asked my goddaughter if she would be comfortable in these suits, she said, "Maybe. I just don't think this is how God wants me to dress."

"I know that's right!" I said. "I'm proud of your response."

She asked me to take her to a smaller store, located outside the mall. She had purchased her last swim suit there.

I was happy to see how easily she wore her Christianity. Those suits couldn't and wouldn't fit her personality or her Christ-like spirit.

Thank you, God, for challenges that produce the nature of Christ in us and our teens. We long to be perfected in your image.

JUNE 10   Read Proverbs 2:1-5.

HOW MANY TIMES HAVE YOU asked your teen "What's wrong?" only to hear, "Oh, nothing." I wish I had a penny for the number of times I've heard that response! Since I've heard it so often, I've even come to expect it.

But sometimes I am given a real answer, and what usually follows is a realistic discussion about why people do the things they do—why a teacher says a certain thing to a student, why some kids steal, or why Adriel took $25 to school and what went through his mind when he lost it.

As Adriel grows older, I've noticed we are having fewer conversations like these. There comes a time when we have to trust our teens' ability to process information and act wisely—to trust that everything we've tried to teach them about right and wrong and God's ways has been "stored up" within them. There still will be many opportunities to contribute to their storehouse of wisdom, but we have to trust that the storehouse is there.

Lord, I pray that you will grant our teens discernment and understanding. Help them to seek your treasures of wisdom and to store them up within.

JUNE 11   Read Ephesians 4:29-32.

"WHY DO YOU LET THAT CHILD talk to you like that?" criticized my friend's mother. My friend agreed that her teenage son's remark was uncalled for. That's why she sent him to his room to think about what he had said. But her mother's response bothered her as well.

We talked about it, and we recognized how her son's remark must have sounded to her mother's ears. When she was growing up, things were so different from the way they are now. Unfortunately, good manners sometimes seem to be a thing of the past. I could write a book about the telephone manners of Adriel's friends! I know that my mother and her eleven brothers and sisters were more polite to their parents than Adriel is to me. Yes, times have changed. But I have to remind myself that the changes are not all bad.

Our parents were raised with the "children are to be seen and not heard" philosophy. Boys were treated very differently than girls. Life was more rigid then.

Today we raise our children in a less autocratic way. We explain to them *why* we set rules; they are privy to the reasoning behind our decisions. We value what our children have to say and encourage them to share their views and opinions. When a child is treated with that kind of respect and knows that he or she can speak openly, smart remarks are bound to surface in the heat of conflict from time to time.

What hasn't changed is our responsibility as parents to model the importance of respect—our respect for our children and their respect for us. Certainly we have to discipline our children when they are disrespectful. But more and more we are learning that discipline involves much more than punishment; it is a way of parenting that recognizes how important it is to praise our children, to accentuate their accomplishments, and to make them feel loved and appreciated.

Another constant is the long-lasting effect of good parenting. As we model positive examples for our children, we are influencing the values of future generations. God commands that we treat one another with kindness and compassion, as we would want to be treated. In the process, it's possible to raise God-fearing, respectful individuals for the benefit of ourselves, our children, and our children's children.

God, help us to be positive examples for our children, demonstrating the importance of respecting one another and building one another up in love. It's not easy, and we need continual guidance. Please hear our cry and intervene in our examples of living.

JUNE 12   Read Colossians 3:8-10, 12-13.

ONE EVENING MY FRIEND'S FAMILY was enjoying dinner, casually reliving the events of the day, when more than once for no apparent reason, her son snapped at her. She simply asked him a few questions; yet, regardless of the subject matter, he spat out his response.

"Why do you have to talk to me that way?" she demanded. "Your manners are so good with everyone else. You're so nice to them; why can't you be that way with me?"

He answered plainly, "Because I've run out of good manners."

I was struck by what that means. At the end of a long day, most of us have been through a good deal emotionally and mentally. Maybe what her son said was really true. I don't condone or excuse his behavior. Yet, somehow, it reveals a new insight. Perhaps he was not intentionally being mean to his mother. He had been putting his best foot forward all day for everyone else and had "run out" of good manner reserves. Now that he was home, he felt that he should be able to act like he felt without having to put on a facade.

The phrase "we always hurt the ones we love" rang in my head. Maybe we hurt those we love because we do feel relaxed with our loved ones and don't feel the need to pretend or masquerade ourselves.

Where does our true heart, the reality of our true selves, remain in all of this? Where do we fit in as "God's chosen people, holy and dearly loved"? We all have our limits, our last nerve, our breaking point. And when we reach it, we need to be able to rely on Christ in us. The glory of the Lord can take up our slack. It makes up for our fallible side.

It's not an easy lesson for teens to learn. Perhaps the best place to start is with our own example.

Help us, dear Lord, to be tuned in to you so that we reflect you, your spirit, your best—especially when we are at our worst.

JUNE 13   Read Matthew 11:28-29.

SOMETIMES THE BEST GIFT you can give your family is a day away from them—time away to rest, to contemplate decisions, to pray. How often do you give yourself permission to have a long nap, to eat a leisurely meal, to stare at the moon, to be alone with yourself? Sounds nice, huh?

With our hectic schedules and people constantly asking for assistance, our minds are already programmed to think for other people, anticipate needs and questions, foresee conflicts and concerns. Even though we may get a good night's sleep, the repetition of the previous day's demands seldom brings the distance we need to achieve complete rest.

This is evident when we do take a break from activities and find our minds are still working at the same break-neck pace. The time to disengage takes longer than we expected. (Remember this when you do "get away" and you're waiting for the anxiety to pass.)

Before you take your break, plan to make maximum use of it. Decide what you'd like to achieve—whether it's maintaining quiet for more than an hour, reading a good book, working through a tough problem, watching a ladybug, whatever. Do you know where to go to find rest?

Dear Jesus, be with us as we seek to find solace in our complicated, convoluted lives. Grant us your peace, your gentle spirit. Amen.

JUNE 14   Read Psalm 139:13-16.

I LIKE LOTS OF ACTIVITY at home and interaction with family. That sometimes poses a problem because I'm a single mother with one child who could live comfortably with little activity or interaction. I sometimes envy my friends whose children pounce on them at the front door with requests, news, and even problems to solve.

My son, like some teens, rarely shares things about himself with his mother. Consequently, I ask a lot of questions. And, in his typical teenage way, he hates a lot of questions. As he gets older, I find myself worrying that he won't have the communication skills necessary to make it in this competitive world. And although Adriel and God continue to remind me that Adriel's personality is not and does not have to be as I think it should be, I still worry.

I know I shouldn't worry. When I worry I make a mistake many mothers make: forgetting that our children are works in progress—"fearfully and wonderfully made," yet not fully formed into what God intends them to be. That will happen in its own time—not according to my schedule for my child.

My son is still God's work in progress. My work is to admire and praise the work, to support and nurture, to wait and see.

I know I sound like a broken record, Lord, but please help me be patient. Help me to nurture and love my child with my eyes on you.

JUNE 15　　　　　　　　　Read Galatians 6:2.

ONE OF THE BEST BLESSINGS I have received is participating in a group at our church for mothers of teens. The group meets once a week and is a confidential setting in which mothers can say, "I'm having trouble with this," or "I've tried this, and it worked for me," or "I have to tell you what happened this week!" For me, the group is like a cold glass of water on a hot summer day. It is wonderful to talk to other mothers who understand when I say, "Sometimes my son just doesn't think," or when I ask, "Why would my child say that to me?" or when I gush, "I'm so proud of my son for . . . ."

Our group is led by a woman who has raised several teens and still has one teen at home. Her own willingness to admit that her life isn't perfect, that she has problems, makes the rest of us feel safer, saner; and somehow it enables us to go on.

It is such a relief to be able to share our concerns and problems with other mothers who understand and care. And it is so revitalizing to celebrate our joys together. When someone expresses a need, concern, or joy, it seems to open the mouths of other mothers. Hearing others share their problems makes each of us feel less alone, less helpless. Part of the wonder of the group is that it is one of the few places in our world where we're allowed to be vulnerable. We also benefit from one another by sharing suggestions, encouragement, and valuable, specific prayers. Knowing that others will lift us up in prayer and mention our specific needs, we can leave the group feeling hopeful, even confident that we can do the job God has given us.

God does not intend for us to bear our burdens alone. Whether you choose to join a group for mothers of teens at church, have coffee with several friends who also have teens, or talk to one understanding friend on the phone, you can find ways to give and receive the support, encouragement, and understanding that are so important to all mothers—especially mothers of teens.

Generous God, thank you for bringing women into our lives who give us your support and love and show us how to say, "I need help."

JUNE 16   Read 1 Samuel 2:10.

ADRIEL AND I HAVE BEEN fortunate to be part of two mission teams to Belize, Central America. Before our first trip when he was nine years old, I remember saying to a friend, "This will be a great experience for him. He'll see how other people live and he'll surely be cured of `toy lust.'"

Seeing the children in Belize who had less than he did was good for him. He learned how to adapt in unusual surroundings and how to be gracious to people who share with him out of their poverty. He saw how blessed he is to have a wonderful home, plenty of food, variety in nearly every product he considers buying, and a comfortable night's sleep.

During the second trip, when Adriel was thirteen, he was able to participate more with the team and have responsibilities of his own. Since then we've been able to participate in many situations where he has seen God using us to help others. He knows how good it feels to be used by God.

Participating in ministry with your child is one of the most wonderful gifts you can give. The teen years are especially ripe for this kind of experience, because it is during this time that an individual's beliefs, views, and lifetime interests are beginning to take shape. As your teen serves others, he or she receives validation and respect that can only be given by the recipient of the service your teen provides. What a wonderful way to learn that he or she is needed and, in fact, is *necessary* in God's kingdom!

God, I pray that you will present opportunities for service to our family. May we quickly and eagerly answer and obey.

JUNE 17   Read Isaiah 46:9-11.

WHEN ADRIEL WAS VERY YOUNG, I planned all the fun things we would do together: go to museums, parks, and concerts; discover things; take rollerblading and sign language classes. According to my plan, he would allow me into his space and would let me do things for him and enjoy him—in the ways that I wanted to.

But things haven't turned out quite like I planned. We have done some of those fun things together, but the mother-son connection I envisioned hasn't come to be. I thought that since it was just the two of us, we'd be closer, more of a team. Instead, Adriel is very independent—and very different from me. He's just not interested in doing the things I like to do, and he offers no suggestions of things he'd like us to do together. Sometimes I manage to "persuade" him to go on one of my planned excursions—assuring him that one day he will thank me for it—but later I usually say to myself, *We should be having fun. Why isn't he enjoying this?*

Perhaps this is God's way of sending me a message. I can clearly see that when I withdraw or am negligent in communicating with God, God cannot provide for me as God wants to. When I resist, I make God do all the work in the relationship. Yet God never gives up on me. God never abandons me. God continues to provide all that I need.

A friend whose children are a few years older than Adriel said something wonderfully freeing to me one day: "Have you ever considered that God may not have created Adriel for you, but you for Adriel?" That stunning query opened my eyes. I realized then that my "mom and son duo" scenario is my plan, not God's.

This passage from Isaiah reminds us that God's purpose, God's plan, will stand. I need to focus on God's plan. That I am Adriel's mother is part of that plan. Therefore, I will be a blessed mother to him and support him in ways that others have supported me, regardless of his response. I must not worry about what I receive from this relationship. I must be patient and trust that my efforts to provide for Adriel, however he receives my gifts, are not being wasted.

Help me, dear God, to be the best gift of a mother that I can be. Thank you for the pleasure of having this child in my life and for trusting this child to my care.

JUNE 18   Read Proverbs 29:23.

RECENTLY LARRY KING, IN REFERENCE to political positioning, asked a guest, "Why is it so important to save face?" I've asked this question myself. Many political positions and even judicial decisions seem to be designed only to cover someone's missteps. Why this incredible fear of not being perceived "appropriately"? Pride is an awesome thing.

Why is it easier to cover up painful problems? So many families today are afraid to let others know when mistakes have been made or to admit when someone has a problem because of pride or an attempt to save face. The family members become pros at "keeping it in the closet." Our society seems to encourage an unwritten rule that says it's a terrible thing to admit that we have problems, that we're wrong, or that we have not behaved correctly in a particular situation.

Just as many financial advisors encourage us to include our children as we make decisions about day-to-day household finances, so we need to let our children know about some of our personal struggles. When we do, they have some understanding of how to deal with similar problems. When we allow them into our process of solving a difficult problem, we are able to model how to go to God in prayer, how to deal with disappointment and betrayal, how to forgive—even when we are hurt.

Today I challenge myself and you to be a "superwoman" when it comes to admitting our faults and being vulnerable. Accept the challenge, because Jesus is really the one who offers it. When there is something wrong in your family, be the first to admit it. Face the pain with your hand in God's hand.

Precious Lord, help us to remember how you accepted fault when you were faultless, how you forgave when you were innocent, how you apologized when you deserved the apology. We long to lean on you for support.

JUNE 19   Read Joshua 24:15.

WHEN ADRIEL AND I MADE our second mission trip to Belize, Central America, we went with about seventeen teens and eight adults. Adriel, then thirteen, was soft-spoken compared to most of the young people, but he formed special friendships with a few of them.

One night an eighteen-year-old girl told me about an incident involving Adriel. Earlier that night she was talking with two young men from the town where we were working, and one of them tried to get closer to her than she wanted. Adriel was nearby, but not close enough to be considered part of their group. However, he seemed to pick up on the negative vibes, and he moved closer. He just sat near them, and immediately the conversation of the young men changed to a more platonic tone. As that happened, she made the change work for her and soon exited.

She told me how smart Adriel was for picking up on the situation and being there for her. In his quiet manner, he made a strong statement that let the young men know she was his friend and that he cared how she was treated.

I was glad she told me about the incident, because it gave me new respect for my son. From time to time as others have shared similar compliments of Adriel, I have done the only thing I know to do—and that is to thank God for giving me such a wise, intuitive son. That kind of information about my son gives me a glimpse of what his life and relationships are like when I'm not around. It also gives me reason to beam, because I admire the young man those glimpses reveal.

One of the greatest joys a mother can have is witnessing her child growing into a faithful servant of the Lord.

Precious God, help us to teach our children what it means to be a servant of the Lord, and help us to support them with your tools, your attitude, and your love.

JUNE 20   Read Micah 6:8.

As I'm WRITING THIS, the murder rate in my city has doubled since this time last year. All across America violence is on the rise. Every day we read about robberies, gang activities, domestic disputes, and simple mistakes resulting in tragedy. Weapons of mass destruction are being manufactured continuously. Wars continue around the world; the life of the enemy is of little consequence. Debate about genetic engineering, physician-assisted suicide, abortion, AIDS, rationed health care, and other life and death issues continues to increase. Refugees around the world are crying for help. Even the relatively new electronic frontier carries contamination; already there are warnings of pornography on the information highway.

What is our responsibility in all of this? I am ashamed of the messages we are sending our children. Our jaded response to statistics and the continual decline of our society is the pitiful legacy we offer them. As they come into adulthood, the risk is great that they may take on our malaise toward these traumatic issues.

As mothers of "the next generation," our responsibility in all of this is not to remain silent or apathetic. We must take up the battle and fight, trusting in God to give us the victory. Our weapons include lessons from the Word of God, the guidance and strength of the Holy Spirit, prayer, and the strength and support of our faith community. We must stand with new courage, allowing God to work through us to bring help and hope to those who live in fear. We must show our young people what it means to do justice, to love kindness, and to walk humbly with our God.

Dear God, forgive us for not being more involved in the life and death matters of your world. Help us to make someone's life more comfortable, more peaceful, and to do justice for all. We pray that as we do this, our children will follow our example.

JUNE 21   Read 2 Timothy 3:14-15.

ON SOME DAYS GUILT and motherhood seem to go together like syrup and pancakes! One day I asked Adriel what his favorite Bible story was, and he said, "I don't have one." I couldn't help feeling responsible—and guilty.

Have you ever felt guilty because your teenager doesn't read or depend on the Bible like you wish he or she would? Have you ever thought it's your fault that your teenager collects more information about singers or sports figures or movie stars than food for his or her spiritual journey? At one time or another, we've all experienced a similar kind of guilt.

I've encouraged Adriel to read books and other materials to broaden his literary appetite, and this is good. Yet I must admit that sometimes I'm more enthusiastic about works of literature than I am about passages of Scripture. What kind of example am I setting?

Most teenagers—and most adults, for that matter—don't know the Bible well. The books, magazines, and computer programs we read are entertaining, but in the long run these alone are not enough to feed our souls and provide the direction we need as we journey down life's road. Inspirational books and other materials that provide spiritual nourishment and direction are helpful; but without the foundation of the Word of God, we are like lost sheep in the wilderness.

When I was growing up, reading and even memorizing scripture was an important part of my life. When we took long road trips, my mother insisted that we memorize Bible verses. And even though I sometimes hated the process, those verses are still with me, carrying me through the stresses in my life at just the right times.

Sometimes I worry that because Adriel is reluctant to read the Bible, he may never turn wholly to God. But my faith reminds me not to give up, and to be a good example for him. My patient and incessant prayer is that one day, with God's help, Adriel will know the joy of being in the Word.

How can we begin to share the joy of God's Word with our teens? Get together with one or more friends this week and brainstorm as many creative ways to share God's Word as you can. Who says getting into the Word can't be fun?

Holy God, help us to keep your Word at the center of our lives, making it a natural, familiar part of our family.

JUNE 22   Read Luke 6:27–36;10:25–37.

"IT'S JUST ONE OF THEM DAYS, when I want to be all alone," sings Monica, a popular R&B singer. "Don't take it personal."

Monica may be referring to a romantic relationship, but her attitude accurately typifies the moods and sensitive natures of teens.

Sometimes teens seem to drown in an emotional pit or a "blue funk"; at other times they just want to be left alone. It's a definite sign of growing pains.

When things are going wrong, it's often difficult for teens to deal constructively with emotions such as depression, frustration, and anger—especially when such extremely intense feelings seem to conflict with their basic natures. They see so many examples—on television and in everyday life—of people exploding or getting even or hurting themselves when things don't go their way. Our teens need more positive examples. I'd like to create a cartoon character who knows how to handle anger and how to react positively when things go wrong. That's probably not going to happen anytime soon, but I can begin to work on my own example.

One of my strongest intuitions is that when we're suffering—especially when we're suffering emotionally—we need to find some way to give ourselves to another. If it's someone we know, good; if it's a stranger, better; if it's an enemy, even better still. That way our gift is all the more precious. So many of us fail to remember that when we're struggling, we are in a prime position to learn. We minimize our struggle by thinking that all we can do is survive it. We can do much more than that; we can actually learn and grow through it. It is in the struggle that we learn about ourselves, because we see ourselves in our most vulnerable state. Unfortunately, because we seldom conceive of helping someone when we ourselves are helpless and vulnerable, the idea of serving escapes us.

We need to help our teens—and perhaps ourselves—learn that when we give despite our own suffering, we are able to forget our pain because we are concentrating on fulfilling someone else's need. Focusing on another's need takes the spotlight off our own need. Jesus set the example for us again and again. He asks us to be kind to a stranger, even an enemy.

The magnitude of this truth isn't learned overnight—for teens or for adults. But what a profound and helpful lesson to teach our children!

Lord, only through your power can we give others your generosity, your love. Bless us as we strive to be imitators of you, and help us teach our children how to look beyond their own needs to the needs of others.

JUNE 23   Read Galatians 5:25.

ONE OF MY FAVORITE STORIES about Adriel involves a formula my mother passed along to me: *Never give up. There's always more than one solution. When an obstacle comes along, jump over it, walk around it, go under it, whatever. Just don't let it impede your program.*

It was about four days before Christmas. I walked into the room to see Adriel sitting on the sofa, cheeks in hand, looking like the last person on earth.

"What's wrong?" I asked.

"Nothing," he sulked.

"I know something must be wrong. What is it?" I demanded.

"I washed my check," he said dryly.

"Well, don't worry. We can get it back," I said assuredly.

"No, you can't," he moaned.

"Yes, you can," I held my conviction.

"No, you can't. You don't know those people," he said firmly.

"Where's the telephone book?" I asked.

I called the people at the auto emissions testing company and told them the situation. The clerk said the main office was in Baltimore, but she felt sure the check would be traced and a replacement check could be in Nashville by the next afternoon. It could be sent by express mail.

"Boom!" I gave a regrettable, I-told-you-so smile. "Problem solved while you wait."

In three minutes, Adriel's gloom had changed. I was so proud of the network of positive people who worked at the company. The clerk seemed to take this as a challenge and wanted to produce a check almost as much as Adriel wanted to have his Christmas money.

Sure enough, by the next afternoon, he had a replacement check. We put his washed check, which could now fit on a nickel, in a baggie and exchanged it. We took the clerk some Christmas goodies and thanked her profusely. Everyone in that office seemed to have been rooting for Adriel's check to make it in on time. The positive people in that office gave Adriel a new perspective of his colleagues at work. I felt like we had a little story of hope to get us through the hectic season.

When we live by the Spirit, we live by hope. We never give up. Are you passing along this faith formula to your children?

Gracious God, increase our faith and help us live in your Spirit and in the light of your power.

JUNE 24   Read 1 Corinthians 10:23.

WELL, THIS TIME HE'S DONE IT, God. He purchased a *snake*! I can't believe it. He brought a three-foot boa constrictor into my home and is looking at me like I'm crazy because I told him to keep the receipt!

We had discussed the possibility of having a lizard for a pet, but I had asked him to do more research before I would give him an answer. Now he says that he has done the research; and, without checking with me, he purchased this snake.

We've discussed my feelings, and he has apologized for disrespecting my space. I haven't demanded that he take it back . . . yet. With this snake have come some interesting developments. I can see that Adriel is using the snake as an attention-getter, though I must admit that I'm suspect of persons who are attracted to a snake just as much as I'm suspect of the snake! Another development is the change in his room. It's immaculate. A person can actually move around in there without stepping on anything. Of course, now that there's room to get in there, I don't want to go in!

I'm letting him keep the snake for two reasons. One, he so rarely asks for anything that when he does, it's pretty hard to say no. And two, because he is meticulous about most things, I'm sure he'll take good care of the snake. Even though I have a problem with keeping a creature like that in captivity, I'll allow it for now.

This, too, may be a fad—albeit an unpleasant one to me—but it is an opportunity for Adriel to show that he is responsible and can use good judgment. I'm not sure what the snake will get out of this, but I do know this: If it should happen to turn out to be bad judgment to keep the snake, Adriel will learn something, and we both will be wiser for it.

God, be with us and our teens as we learn from new experiences and exercise judgment and leniency in our lives.

JUNE 25   Read James 1:17.

ADRIEL IS MY ONE AND ONLY beloved son, in whom I am pleased. As I've mentioned, I often call him my enigma. He is a gentle, creative, intuitive spirit. I, on the other hand, am a rowdy, spiritual creature, given to primal screams and other spontaneous noises.

In spite of our differences, at times our personas complement each other very well. Surprisingly, this happens when I least expect it. It has happened quickly, when I've been too busy and preoccupied to notice. And quietly, when I've been too harried and worried to care.

Once, I was very busy with a group of singers I direct. We were singing at a place where the sound technicians were not accustomed to miking our group. I didn't know until the concert was over that Adriel provided the sound technicians with valuable information about the group and how to distribute microphones and sound projection. This assistance helped our performance come off smoothly and profession-ally. The sound technician who complimented my son thought Adriel worked in that capacity all the time.

If I had been asked about Adriel's ability to do that job, I might not have given him such flying colors. It often seems that he would like to have as little as possible to do with my interests. What I've learned is that many times, when we are in public, my son and I bond together as a one-for-all, all-for-one unit. We are in each other's corner. We support each other and anticipate each other's needs. We've not made any pact or commitment toward this effort; it just happens natu-rally.

So I thank God for sending me my enigma. Were I able to figure out this young man, I might miss out on the blessings of his presence in my life.

Gracious Father of lights, thank you for my child. Help me to celebrate my child's gifts in your name.

JUNE 26   Read 1 Peter 1:14-15.

A VERY SPECIAL FRIEND TOLD ME that whenever her children would go on a date or on a special outing, she'd say to them, "Don't forget who and whose you are!" I've imagined what effect those words must have had on her children—especially later in the evening when temptations of all sorts might have presented themselves.

That's a good saying for all Christians as we traverse this world. So many times we are confused because our inner and outer selves are at war with each other. Should we answer a mis-guided person who assumes something false about us? Should we respond to the person who cut in front of us in traffic? Should we set straight the salesperson who speaks negatively to us?

We know the answer. It is simple. It's just that our strong wills can turn a simple solution into an irresistible con-frontation. We yield to the weaker side because it's so satisfying setting someone straight. Why is it so easy to do the negative thing? Why do we get such satisfaction in revealing someone's faults? Why does the urge to speak harshly come so easily?

Because we've lost the right perspective—that holy perspective we received when we chose to follow Christ. When we see the other person as Jesus, then the urge to tell that person off isn't nearly as appealing. When we choose to excuse our offender, the desire to correct that person isn't as strong.

Remembering whose we are helps us through many difficulties. We can hold our heads up and be proud of our behavior, because we know we are children of the most high God. We are bought with a price. We are precious in God's sight.

What powerful mothers we can be when our children see that we carry ourselves as though we are bought with the precious blood of Jesus. Let's live it!

Precious Lord, help us in the midst of conflicts and confusion to remember we belong to you and that our actions reflect your power in our lives; and help us to teach our children to remember who and whose they are.

JUNE 27   Read James 1:5-6.

HOW TERRIBLE IT FEELS WHEN you know you've made a stupid mistake that includes your child. I just made one. I let Adriel go out with someone I hardly know. I trust the people who introduced me to this person, but I really don't know this individual. If something bad happens while they are out, I'll never forgive myself. What if something happens that Adriel doesn't feel comfortable telling me about?

I can't worry about that now. What I've got to do is ask God to give me a generous supply of wisdom. I know God empathizes with my mistakes. I must remember how God has helped me through other burdens. I must remember that God cares about how things affect me. God wants me to be content, to be at peace. I must savor the thought that God loves me and is pleased with me—most of the time.

When I nurture those thoughts, I can ask for wisdom in faith, never doubting. I know that conflict in this life is inevitable. I know that struggles and disappointments will come, but God's promise to give me wisdom is the power that helps me face the future. I may be a single mother, but I am not alone.

Holy Father, thank you for your promise to give me wisdom. Fill my heart with your wisdom, and help me to live my life never doubting that you care for me and those I love.

JUNE 28   Read Proverbs 3:5-6.

EVERY MOTHER HAS BEEN ON the receiving end of a pair of rolling eyes! A teenager can say so much by rolling his or her eyes. That unspoken statement can convey disgust, impatience, disbelief, or incredulousness at the utter absurdity of a comment or suggestion.

I remember how I felt the first time Adriel rolled his eyes at me. I was shocked and saddened. *He's grown up*, I thought later. Gone was my sweet little innocent boy. Not only was he willing to go against my authority, but he was also questioning it.

Foolishly, I, too have questioned authority—God's authority. I have leaned only on my own understanding, treating God as a stand-by consultant. Yet in spite of it all, God comes through for me. God takes my mistakes and turns them into clever opportunities, changing my mourning into gladness. The only sensible response I have is to acknowledge, once again, that God has saved me, rescued me, provided for me, healed me, and forgiven me. How reassuring it is to know that God is sovereign. God is infallible. God is.

O glorious God, your outstretched arms are my salvation. Thank you for receiving my selfish soul again and again. And help me to be just as understanding and forgiving.

WHEN I WAS PART OF A TEAM of yokefellows (a group of Christians who regularly visit the penitentiary for fellowship and Bible study), I took Adriel to meet some of the men in prison. Many of them were glad I brought my son to one of the meetings. They were eager to warn any young man about how easy it is to end up in prison and about how to avoid the pitfalls that brought them there.

At first, I thought Adriel's response was too casual. He seemed to have a glorified view of prison—as if being in prison was a rite of passage or a badge proving virility. He even asked one of the prisoners to give him a shirt—one of the hottest fashion fads. I called it an "ambiguity preference." Young people Adriel's age like to wear prison clothes, but they don't want to be in prison; they wear fake eyeglasses, but they can see; they use canes, but they can walk; they wear work clothes, but they detest work.

Then Adriel had a rude awakening. One of the prisoners actually recognized him. During my visit the previous week, I had noticed this new prisoner in the group. When we met, we smiled and silently noticed a familiarity between us. But it wasn't until Adriel went with me that this familiarity was named. His name was Gary, and he remembered Adriel from Bible classes and camp. We had picked him up on our church bus for worship and Bible classes many times. Now here we was in prison. That sad reunion brought the harsh reality of prison home to Adriel. Suddenly prison was intense, real. Prison had a face and a name.

I hope Adriel will make another visit with me sometime. Providing our teenagers opportunities to sympathize with those who are hurting and to reach out in love can be extremely valuable and fulfilling—for them as well as for us.

Heavenly Father, lift up our eyes to see our world. Help us and our families to respond as you would respond to those who are hurting around us.

O LORD, I KNOW YOU MUST SAY, "Oh no! Another last minute request." I know you must ask, "Why can't she pray about something different? Why doesn't she get the message? Why can't she be creative this time?"

I am creative, Lord—when I'm happy, when I'm focused, when I'm driven, when I'm passionate. But when I'm torn and confused, I can only pray one prayer. I get stuck with this same prayer because I can't seem to grow beyond the faith step. Lord, have mercy.

- Help my son to reach out to you, to recognize your work in his life.
- Assist my child through this world; help her make the right choices.
- Help my child to stay on your path and not be drawn away by individuals who don't know you.
- Correct my daughter; help her to control her temper.
- Encourage my son to study your word and find the treasures and promises you've given him.
- Create in me a pure heart, O God, and renew a right spirit in me.
- O Lord, use our family for your service. Trust us to carry out your will.
- Empower me with your strength so that I, like you, can constantly assure my children that no matter how grave the sin, how traumatic the mistake, or how severe the error, they always can come home to love and forgiveness.
- Help me to be the mother you created for these children.

Lord have mercy on me. In your name and spirit, Amen.

$\mathscr{J}$ULY

A TIME TO MOURN
AND A TIME TO DANCE

Mary Catharine Neal

JULY 1
To everything there is a season . . . (Ecclesiastes 3:1a)

ALL OF US, AS MOTHERS, NO MATTER what the climate in which
we live, witness the changing of seasons as we participate in
the lives of our children. It may not be winter into spring
exactly, but the changes in young people are no less dramatic than ice and snow giving way to tender plants emerging
magically from mud and dirt. However, as the mother of a
biological son, a foster daughter, two stepsons, and an
adopted son, all of whom have reached or passed their
teens, I know that the changes in the teen years may seem
more like the beautiful and fragrant roses of summer giving
way to the eventually barren landscape of fall washed by
occasional harsh wintry blasts.

Sometimes, when they are in the midst of a particularly
difficult stage, it is hard to remember that these changes are
cyclical—that with no given change will they, or we, remain
that way forever. As with the seasons, there will always follow another time to mourn, and another time to dance.
They struggle for freedom while we strive to teach responsibility. The dance is not easy for either parent or child. It is
very important to remember at these times that they are
doing exactly what they need to be doing to grow up, and

that we are honored to be witnesses to and participants in their growth.

Gracious God, you have been so patient with us; please help us to be as patient with the children you have entrusted to us.

JULY 2
and a time to every purpose . . . (Ecclesiastes 3:1*b*)

SOMETIMES WE ARE UNSURE about what to do next; our purpose is unclear, or even if it shines like the sun, we don't know how to bring it about. It is that way for our teenagers too. They are being driven towards the goal of independence without the benefit of having a clear understanding of the process they are going through. For the first dozen years, their identities have been tied up in the identities of those who parented them. That may have been us, or it may have been someone else. In any event, we have the responsibility and privilege of parenting them now.

Whether we are just walking into this process or have been with them since the beginning, the advent of adolescence brings with it a special problem: they are trying to differentiate themselves from us, their parents, even as we struggle to continue parenting them. Our purpose is at odds with theirs. It is just as important that we continue to set limits—even if those limits are in a period of flux—as it is for our children to test those limits and struggle against them. Neither of our purposes is more important than the others'.

Please, God, help us to trust the process as it is unfolding.

JULY 3
under the heaven . . . (Ecclesiastes 3:1*b*)

IT IS EASY WHEN WE ARE in the midst of struggles over curfew, friends, the car, homework, and social activities to lose sight of the larger picture. No matter how much it feels like we are caught in a "Twilight Zone" episode with an angry teenager between us and the door, or like we are trapped in the living room talking with a young person who keeps saying over and over, "But my real mom would have let me do that," we will eventually escape the perimeter of the house and get out into the world again. And so will they.

It is out there—in God's world—that they belong. Our job from the time we begin to parent is to prepare them for leaving our care. However, we are free do derive all the pleasure we can from the process, and at this point there's not much time left. We must hurry to enjoy to our children. Just as we would take a walk in the park, we must indulge ourselves in listening to their dreams, bask in the glow of their pride at their own accomplishments, and make time to listen to their despair. Each of the feelings so familiar to us is still new to them, so we must be gentle. Our children are no less God's children than the best of our friends.

Loving Parent, please help us to appreciate and treat with respect all of your children, even if—especially if—they are also our own.

JULY 4
a time to be born . . . (Ecclesiastes 3:2a)

NEAL IS THE ONLY ONE of my children whose birth I was present for. Mary came to live with me as a foster child when she was thirteen, John and Alex were nine and eleven when their dad and I married, and Shane was a day short of ten when I adopted him.

Because of the circumstances of our meeting, I missed the day each of the others made their grand entrance into the world, and sometimes I am sad I was not able to know and love them and be a part of their lives from the beginning. Yet, I have witnessed births in each of them. The birth of integrity, of humor, of love of art and music, of finding self, of maternal instinct—all are births no less than the other, the biological birth.

Each of you, too, has been a witness to some birth in the next generation, whether or not it was the one you dreamed of. Think of when some idea first glimmered in your child's eye and you struggled to bring it to life. Think of how you have nurtured compassion and honorable action. Mothers are midwives; midwives are mothers, too.

You who labored to give birth to the world, guide us in our calling to bring forth new life within it.

JULY 5
and a time to die . . . (Ecclesiastes 3:2*b*)

WHEN ANGELA DIED, she was the sixth of our good friends to die within two years and one week. Three of them died of AIDS, one had a heart attack, one died of alcoholism, and another of cancer. Angela held a different place in our lives than the others because, when she could no longer take care of herself, we moved her to our house, where she lived her last weeks until she went to the hospital a few days before she died.

The boys and I had talked it over before I invited her, but I never expected them to be so gracious. Neal could hardly bear to come upstairs and see her wasting away, yet he did, day after day. Shane brought her gifts and shared me with her when I expected him to be demanding of my attention. The confusion of our lives being turned upside down was never so overwhelming that it got in the way of tender care for our friend.

The young men I live with have learned to accept death as a part of life; they have seen much of it in their short lives, and so have all our teens. Their generation has grown up with death in movies, on television, and in the news, in addition to the deaths we all encounter in our daily lives. As the AIDS epidemic spreads (in my state it is already the fourth leading cause of death among 20- to 29-year-olds), they will continue to become more and more familiar with loss. We must struggle to give words to their grief and to our own so that the silence does not overwhelm either us or them.

Life-giving God, please grant that we might understand and accept death as a part of life, and be as willing to give back to you as we are to receive from you.

JULY 6
a time to plant . . . (Ecclesiastes 3:2*c*)

IN THIS *"INSTANT EVERYTHING"* society, we are encouraged to be impatient. If we want food, we have been taught to want it right now, without any effort on our parts. Everything else follows suit. As mothers, on the other hand, we have been forced to learn patience; and our children are our teachers.

With children, there is hardly any instant anything. Almost every request is answered with "later." Just as we once waited for them to sleep through the night, we now wait for them to clean up their rooms, take out the trash, get ready for school—you know the routine. It is easy to get impatient about things like that, but it helps if we think of what we are doing as planting. We plant ideas. We plant good habits. We plant courtesy. We plant punctuality. Perhaps Paul was thinking of mothers when he said we do the planting, other people do the watering, and God receives the harvest.

Planting is not reaping. We may never see the results. But without planting, we can be sure there will never be results. We plant in faith; God tends the garden.

O Keeper of the world's garden, it is with great difficulty that we entrust to you our precious ones. Give us courage to trust you and your world to bring them to full fruit.

JULY 7
and a time to pluck up that which is planted . . . (Ecclesiastes 3:2*d*)

EVERY ONCE IN A WHILE, we get glimpses of the adults our teenagers are becoming. I experience that sometimes when I teach confirmation class each year. At our small church, we encourage everyone to make the decision about church membership carefully, and the decision that one is not ready is honored just as much as the decision for commitment. It is not uncommon for an adult to join the church after years of faithful participation in the life of the congregation, or for young people to go through confirmation classes a couple of times and then come back later wanting to connect themselves to the congregation. We rejoice in the process. We rejoice in their growth. We don't just rejoice in their making the same choices we have made.

One year, on the retreat that ends each year's class, one of the teens who decided to be confirmed was one of my own children. I was surprised. It was not the first time he had been through the process, and I certainly had not expected him to make the choice he did at that time. For me it was a glimmer of the kingdom and the continuity of faith—and of hope for the adult to come.

Thank you, Creator God, for the signs you give us that there is reason to help, reason to be encouraged that life will go on, and that we—all of us, adults and children—continue to be in your hands.

JULY 8
a time to kill . . . (Ecclesiastes 3:3a)

LAST YEAR, ON MY BIRTHDAY, the puppy Shane found ate my lovebird. I wasn't happy, but the puppy seemed delighted. I could just imagine how excited she must have been to discover a "throw toy" that threw itself! She had no idea that the bird was alive, or that she had killed it. She was just playing with it, doing what puppies do. The death was neither good nor evil; it just was.

When humans consciously make a decision to kill, however, the decision takes on moral value; and there is rarely a consensus as to what that value is. Philosophers and theologians have debated as long as there has been moral thought over whether or not and under what circumstances it is morally appropriate to kill. We often carry on that debate within ourselves.

Whether I think in any situation that it was either right *or* wrong, I still feel horrified when I read or hear about one human being purposefully killing another; yet I know without a doubt that if my children were in danger, I would do anything I could to protect them. That is the curious dilemma we are in as parents. We know the world is not always safe, yet we must trust our children to it. We want *our* children to be protected from harm; yet in order to keep them safe, most of us would, if necessary, be willing to harm others to protect them. Each of us needs God's guidance and the community of faith to keep to the path.

Forgive me, O God, for believing we ought not to kill each other while knowing I might, if I thought doing so would protect the ones I love. Please lead me in your loving way.

JULY 9
and a time to heal . . . (Ecclesiastes 3:3*b*)

SHANE LIES SLEEPING, SPRAWLED across the couch. He got home from the hospital today. Again. It was his fourth time there since I adopted him—the third time within two months. The first time was over two years ago. He was hurt so badly before he came to live with us that he has posttraumatic stress disorder, and his overwhelming emotions and reactions make it necessary for changes in medication to be done at the hospital, "inpatient." Neal, for his part, is still waiting to get off crutches (after three months). He went too long saying, "It's only shin splints," when really it was a stress fracture. There is nothing quite like living with an adolescent athlete—used to two hours of swimming *and* two hours of running each day—who is suddenly sidelined just as his little brother gets particularly hard to deal with.

Understanding teenagers is not the same as living with them, especially when it is *our* children who are in need of being healed. It takes time to heal. Knowing that those we love are going through a normal process, and even understanding the process, does not necessarily make it any easier for them—or for us—to wait.

Have pity on us, God, and grant us patience that we may be healed even as we wait and pray for healing in the lives of our children.

July 10
a time to break down . . . (Ecclesiastes 3:3c)

I HAD BEEN DELIBERATING for quite some time about how to rearrange things so the child I was waiting to adopt could have his or her own bedroom, when my friend Ingrid and her son, Isaac, came for Thanksgiving dinner. While we were eating, she and I talked about the child, as yet unknown, who would be coming. We had enjoyed the kitchen in its sunny new location on the back porch while cooking, and our talk turned to the construction project of building the coming child's room. Ingrid suggested I tear out a wall, opening up the living room in a different direction. That would make it possible to close off the end of the room where the table stood to make another bedroom. It was an ideal solution. I thought about it all through the meal.

After dinner she asked if I would like to take a walk. I replied that what I would really like to do was to tear out the wall! We got out our hammers and, while the boys sat in the next room playing games, knocked the wall out. Before Ingrid and Isaac went home that evening, we discovered underneath the drywall a brick archway exactly where I wanted the opening! Tearing down the wall revealed a door that was already there, a door that became for me a symbol of getting rid of the things that keep me from doing God's will—in this case welcoming home another of God's children.

Sometimes, God, we have to be willing to break down the walls that separate us from doing your will. Help us in the midst of the chaos to believe that when they are out of the way, your way will be clear.

July 11
and a time to build up . . . (Ecclesiastes 3:3d)

BY THE TIME I HAD GOTTEN FAR enough into the reconstruction project to be building the wall and closet for Shane's room, I knew that it was he who was coming, and I knew that making him feel safe was going to be a major issue.

The room, as I worked on it, was becoming *his* room. For his walls I had photographs made of his biological siblings. I bought a Lambourghini bed because that was his favorite kind of car. I asked about and used his favorite colors. I wanted it to be filled with things he was already familiar with that made him comfortable.

We do that same kind of building up when we interact with these young people of ours everyday. We offer them continuity, security, familiarity, comfort. We try to design the aspects of their lives to help them feel safe enough to change and grow. We put limits on their freedom and work as containers to hold their frustration, anger, and rebellion. Every day, our patience is put to the test as they try out their new independence from us. We know a lot about them by the time they reach this stage, and yet, each day it can be almost like meeting someone new.

Give us fortitude, Lord, to weather the storms that come with parenting teens. Help us build strong walls to contain them, and help us put the doors in the right places, too.

JULY 12
a time to weep . . . (Ecclesiastes 3:4a)

SEVERAL YEARS AGO, one of the boys came into my room late one night and asked if he could talk to me. He blurted out, "I have a really bad drug problem, and I can't stop, and I'm really scared, and I need help." He said it like he had practiced it a million times. I had been asleep and wasn't quite sure how to take this news, so the first thing I asked was if it was a joke. It wasn't.

I had sent a number of young people to drug treatment in the time I had been a high school counselor, but knowing where to take him and whom to talk to the next day did not ease the grieving in my heart. All I could think was that he was going to have to live with this the rest of his life. I had told him long before that if he was ever anywhere and was in trouble, I would come get him, no questions asked; and he had promised to call me if such a situation arose. I felt he had betrayed my trust. It was months before I could accept that as soon as *he* knew he was in trouble, he did tell me. He just didn't know that he was in trouble until he had tried to stop three times on his own.

I spent the night weeping, as well as many days in the weeks that followed. I wept because I was powerless to protect him. I wept because my life had changed with the words he spoke. I wept because while he was in treatment I missed him. I wept because I felt betrayed. I wept because I love him. And so we all weep, when for one reason or another we have similar feelings for the teenagers that we love.

Comfort us, O God, when we weep for ourselves and for those we love. Hold us in your arms as we hold a little child, and let us know your love.

JULY 13
and a time to laugh . . . (Ecclesiastes 3:4*b*)

LAUGHTER IS A WONDERFUL GIFT that God has given us all, but for mothers of teenagers it is often a lifesaver. Numberless are the times it relieves tension or disperses anger. It can also be a valuable teaching tool; things we would never want to hear from someone who was lecturing us can be a delight to learn under the right conditions. For instance, one night at dinner we were role playing: Shane was pretending to be me, I played Neal, and Neal was, for the length of the meal, Shane. "Mom" kept holding "Neal" responsible for things "Shane" kept doing and blaming on "Neal." Dinner took a long time, because "Mom" kept sending "the kids" to their rooms or time out. We each learned things about the way *we* were relating to each other, as we pretended to be each other—and we laughed.

Laughter can also perform one of the most valuable of all functions: It can help us keep things in perspective. It certainly did so one night, when Alex was at the house of our friends, Marnie and Gene, and the car we had bought for him to drive wouldn't start. Fortunately, they live on a steep hill, so he and Marnie pushed the car from where he had parked it at the top of the hill, to roll start it. As it started rolling, Alex realized he couldn't get the door open to get into the car, and they started trying to pull it to a stop. The car escaped, rolled downward through the orchard, through the fence, and crashed into the woods at the bottom of the hill, at which point, for some absolutely unknown reason, it started. As he told me about it, on the verge of tears, I already knew he was safe; and in my mind it played like a Charlie Chaplin movie. The car was a complete wreck, but sometimes you just have to laugh.

God of Abraham and Sarah, give us the gift of laughter to help us through our days.

JULY 14
a time to mourn . . . (Ecclesiastes 3:4c)

WHEN BILL AND I DECIDED to divorce, it was a time of great sadness. It was important to us not only for our own friendship, but also for the relationship the kids had with each of us, that we not become enemies in the process. We negotiated all the particulars between ourselves, and a friend of ours did the paperwork. There were no fighting lawyers. No long-lasting animosity. Only grief.

The boys did well with it, I hope. We worked hard to be sure they knew that neither of us was right nor the other wrong. We tried to make sure they were not put in a position of having to take sides. Although it was winter when we decided, we chose not to tell them until school was out for the summer. When we finally did tell them, they thought we were kidding. As far as they could tell, nothing had changed.

The hardest thing was separating them from each other.

Although the three of them had been together for six years at that point, John and Alex, who were Bill's children before we married, were both in high school and stayed at the farm with their dad, while Neal moved into town with me. It felt as though my heart was being ripped apart.

Tender God, you know what it is like to lose your Child. Comfort us whenever we mourn and help us to love each other.

JULY 15
and a time to dance . . . (Ecclesiastes 3:4*d*)

I NEVER KNEW UNTIL I started working as a high-school guidance counselor that there was such a thing as a father-daughter or mother-son dance. It seemed a very strange notion. I could not imagine having gone to such an affair with my own father, who died when I was twelve. I couldn't even imagine wanting to.

When Neal began to attend the school where I worked, we went the first year with great misgiving, reassuring each other that we could leave any time we wanted to. We ended up having a blast, staying till the end, and winning the dance contest. For the next four years, it was one of our favorite things to do together.

We anticipate the dance eagerly each year, but winning the contest is not what we remember most. What we remember about that first year is an older student named Doug who came up to talk to Neal, who at the time was hanging out and being silly with his friends. Doug's mother had a prosthesis for one leg; for some reason her bone was not healing, and her prognosis was not good. That wasn't stopping the two of them from dancing the night away. Doug, who knew well that his mother might be dying, told Neal to dance with me while he could, because he never knew if he'd ever get another chance to dance with his own mother. Neal did dance with me that night, and we have remembered Doug's words whenever we have danced since then.

Lord of the Dance, just as we remind our children to do things they may not get another chance for, remind us to take time to dance with them before we don't have another chance either.

JULY 16
a time to cast away stones . . . (Ecclesiastes 3:5a)

IN THE YEARS WHEN ALEX and John and their friends from church—Josh, Trey, Brook, Andy, Christopher, George, and Akosua—were graduating from high school, I got a lot of practice watching young people I love and admire leave the homes that have nurtured them and set out on their own into the larger world. I did not, however, have any illusions that the practice of those separations would make Neal's leaving any easier.

As I've mentioned, Neal is my only biological child. I have witnessed other births—I was there when my friends Nancy and Janet gave birth to their children, Jonathan and Benjamin, and when my foster-daughter, Mary, gave birth to Christopher—but I never stayed awake at night with those children. I never walked the floor with them. They have never known what I would say before I said it. They have not lived with me for almost half my years, nor did they come to life inside my frame. This one, I know, will be harder.

When Neal leaves home at the end of the summer, I will be losing one of my best friends. I will be saying good-bye to the young adult who, as an infant, taught me how to love unconditionally; who, as a child, taught me more about patience than I have ever wanted to know. He made me want to take care of myself so I could care for him. It will be very hard to watch him go, but it is time.

From the time we first left one of our children at day care, to the time we first trusted one to drive the car alone; each time the risk is a little greater; each time they reach greater independence. It is hard to remember that it is just as hard for our children to take each step as it is for us to let go.

Loving Parent, guide us both through each daily separation so each of us grows in your love and care.

July 17
and a time to gather stones together . . . (Ecclesiastes 3:5b)

ONE WEEKEND LAST YEAR I experienced the delight of having all the young men in my life together in my home at one time. Those of you who have at least one child who has already left home know what a rare occurrence that is, and how hard it is to orchestrate. It was the first time all four of them had been together at the same time since Shane had come, and though he had already fallen asleep by the time the older guys got there, it was for me a wonderful moment. I could reach out and touch them all at once, and know they were safe.

For many families, moments like that are rare after the children leave high school. They happen at graduations, in hospital waiting rooms, and maybe, if you're lucky, on a birthday or at a wedding. Maybe, if you're not so lucky, at a funeral. But even while our teens are still at home, it may be just as difficult to orchestrate a time when they can all be together. It is hard to compete with the pull of friends, sports activities, band, clubs—adolescence is not a time when "the family" is at the top of the list.

I never knew until recently why the older generation wants the younger one to gather round them, why they think it is so important to try to at least be civil to each other for the meal, or the day. Knowing has changed the way I've related to my family of origin. It is always amazing to me how parenting my children helps me to grow.

Gracious God, forgive us for wanting others to change when we are so reluctant to do so ourselves. Be with us when we gather together, and help us to love each other too.

July 18
a time to embrace . . . (Ecclesiastes 3:5c)

WITHIN TWO YEARS, NEAL AND I experienced the death of three good friends from AIDS. Each death was different:

Arthur died quickly, and kept his personality and sense of humor to the end. David, and later Angela, grew weak as their bodies wasted away until dementia set in. Neal took David's death hardest. At a movie one night in which the main character dies of AIDS, the accumulated grief of David's death, Moses' death, and the others he had experienced since then was overwhelming; he leaned his head over onto my shoulder and began to weep. I put my arms around him and held him there in the dark while he cried.

Sometimes we hold each other for joy, and other times it is for sadness. Touch is a way we communicate instinctively with infants and small children, but sometimes it is even easier to reach out to strangers than to our own teenagers. Sexuality gets confused in it. We don't want to give any wrong messages. We don't want our touch to be taken the wrong way. But touch is a mode of communication that nothing else can replace.

Infants who are not touched do not thrive; their physical growth is stunted, and they do not develop normally. Teenagers who are not touched may continue to eat and grow physically, but often they do not continue to grow emotionally without touch. Though their bodies are quickly becoming adult, their emotions during adolescence swing widely. Often they feel like children. Without sufficient nonsexual touch, they tend to think that sexual touch is the only kind. It is up to us to teach them differently.

Help us remember, Lord, that you have no hands, no arms on earth except our own.

July 19
and a time to refrain from embracing . . . (Ecclesiastes 3:5d)

SOMETIMES WE DON'T WANT our teenagers to touch us; sometimes, our teenagers don't want us to touch them. It is hard to know exactly when it is the thing to do and when it is not. If they are in front of their friends, the answer is usually never. If they want you to, the answer is usually always. In between lies considerable confusion.

There are times we can best show our affection for our teenagers by some other act than physical contact. It was often hard to tell just what to do with John, who wasn't particularly physically demonstrative. Sometimes, after his dad and I divorced, it seemed I touched him most when I showed up with food at band contests. Or food anytime, for that matter. Food always got a wonderful smile. Just being there at those times and listening to what was important to him was, I think, the closest we were during his high school years.

It was often hard to restrain myself from giving him an enormous hug in front of his friends. It was not always easy to relate to him on his own terms. One thing that helped was remembering how I would feel when I had children hanging on me and I just wanted to get them OFF! Somehow I think that must be a little like how it is for our adolescents when the roles are reversed. They may not be as exhausted as a mother of young children, but I can easily see how they could be no less exasperated with our wanting to hang on them.

Help us, God, know how to meet our children's needs.

JULY 20
a time to get . . . (Ecclesiastes 3:6a)

WHEN JOHN AND ALEX'S MOM decided to let them stay with us, for the boys it meant permanence—they knew where they would be when school started the next year. For Bill and me, it meant happily settling in for the long haul.

I was excited. I had been given a great gift: the opportunity to spend the next several years with two young men I had come to love. I was immensely grateful to their mother for the decision she made, and at the same time was struck by how poignant was the moment. Her decision to let them live with us meant a great loss for her. I knew that to make that choice, she must have loved them very much.

After hearing the news, I went to the grocery about seven miles from our farm. It was raining when I left, but it started clearing on the way home. As I rounded the last hilltop before the farm, I saw, for the only time in my life, a *complete* rainbow, the sign of God's promise. It was nestled around the house Bill and I built with our own hammers and saws over a two-year period, the home in which we all would live.

We do not always get a sign, Lord, to tell us if we are headed in the right direction. But we are oh, so grateful, for the ones that remind us you are present with us every day.

JULY 21
and a time to lose . . . (Ecclesiastes 3:6*b*)

THE MYSTERIOUS WAYS OF child welfare agencies are puzzling and exasperating to many who have worked with them. They can move children at will. Foster parents have no rights to speak of in the decisions concerning the children in their care.

When Neal was eighteen months old, I decided, as a single parent, to accept as a foster child a young woman whose worker introduced her with these words: "Would you be willing to take a thirteen-year-old, sexually active, behaviorally disordered, mentally retarded female? No foster home in the county will take her, and we think you would be just the right placement for her."

In spite of my misgivings, I agreed to meet with Mary and her worker to discuss it. In the end, I took her home. She was in a residential program four days a week and with me the other three days and holidays. When I wasn't tearing my hair out, I was crazy about her. She was with me almost exactly one year. On the day we had been looking forward to, when she was to graduate from her program and come to live with me full time, the decision was made to move her. There was nothing I could do.

I felt I would die from grief. I had no warning. I was powerless to change things, and I was angry. You may have felt those things too, initially, some time when your hopes and plans for your children were dashed. Hold fast to the knowledge that Jesus' parent can see you through your parenting loss.

Loving Parent of us all, we believe that each time we grieve, you suffer with us. Comfort us, we pray, when the wounding is more than we can bear.

JULY 22
a time to keep . . . (Ecclesiastes 3:6c)

SHANE HAS DEVELOPED A delightful sense of humor; but when he first came to live with us, he had not had a lot of practice with it. He kept everything close to himself. He was guarded in what he said, just as he guarded everything he owned. And he had reason to hold on.

When he came, he had no reason to believe I would keep him. Until that point, through twenty placements, no one else had. His wanting to keep everything he had ever possessed and had carried with him from placement to placement seemed symbolic of keeping himself. So we kept it all, stored in the closet in his room. Frequently, he would want to get everything out and look at it. Mostly, though, he just kept it.

Time went on, with me keeping Shane and Shane keeping his stuff. Every once in a while, we'd be going through the boxes when he would say we could put something in the give-away pile, that it was too small for him anymore. Sometimes, if his little brothers, Ronnie and Donnie, or his little sister, Tasha, wanted an outgrown toy when they were visiting, he would let them have it; but he was allowed to keep things as long as he needed to.

As mothers, we know well the need to keep things—mementos, souvenirs, drawings and letters our children have made for us—and we long to keep our children close as well. With God's help, we can honor their needs as well as our own, without losing our sanity in the chaos.

Keep us faithful to our children, God, that we might let them hold on for as long as they need us to.

JULY 23
and a time to cast away . . . (Ecclesiastes 3:6d)

NEAL WENT THROUGH A DIFFICULT time around the time he started high school. He was not feeling good about himself or the things he was doing. His choice to have his room painted dark gray seemed to be shouting out how he was feeling on the inside. It was dark and gloomy, but he said he liked it that way. Fifteen had definitely been the worst time for both John and Alex, but Neal was especially morose.

With the help of counseling, encouragement, patience, and prayers, he gradually began to work his way out of it. He started running every day and changed the way he ate. He pushed himself to be involved in the activities that had seemed far out of reach. He began acting like the people he wanted to be like, even when he didn't feel that way. He started waking up an hour earlier so he could read and pray before school. I was amazed at the effort he put into changing into the person he wanted to be.

Finally, towards the end of his seventeenth summer, he decided to purge everything remaining from his bitter years. He completely gutted his room, painted it the lightest of blues, and put back in only the things appropriate to who he was becoming. His letting go was complete. His transformation was inspiring for all those who watched.

It is hard, I know, to hold on to the promise of conversion and new life when we—or our children—are overwhelmed with the present. But it is the promise God gives us for them, and for us, also.

Remind us, O God, that just as there are times to keep, there are also times to let go of old things, old habits, to make room for new life.

July 24
a time to rend . . . (Ecclesiastes 3:7*a*)

ONE MORNING WHEN WE were all in the car getting ready to go to school, I did the regular litany: "Seat belts? Homework? Lunches? Money?" I usually asked everything I could think of, because we lived almost fifteen miles from the boys' schools, and it was terrible to have to go back to get anything. When I finally asked, "Everybody ready?" they all replied in the affirmative. I started to back out of the driveway when suddenly, with a loud thump and a ripping sound, I tore Alex's door off the hinges on one of the posts holding up the carport. We were late and there was nothing I could do about the door at that point, so I just told them all to get out of the car and into the jeep, and off we went. I didn't say a word about the door.

Alex, who was rarely in trouble, was expecting me to kill him, I think, as he sat in the back seat saying over and over again, "I just don't know what I was thinking about." Golly, I didn't know what I was thinking about, either; it had never occurred to me in all those years to ask about the doors.

Sometimes, accidents like that just happen. Things get broken. Sometimes it's our fault; sometimes it's theirs. It would be so easy for us as mothers to get angry or cast blame, but the truth is that accidents are just accidents; things that are broken are just things, after all. And while things can be fixed or replaced, the words we might say in anger could cause wounds that might never heal.

Remind us, O Lord, that material things are just things, and that our children are more precious to us than any thing at all—no matter what they do or don't do, or what gets broken as a result.

July 25
and a time to sew . . . (Ecclesiastes 3:7*b*)

MY FRIEND SUSAN WILTSHIRE writes and talks about women's lives being like patchwork, sewn together from bits and pieces in a pattern representing the parts of our lives. When new additions are made, whether by acquaintance, birth, adoption, marriage, or fostering, sometimes the pieces added to the quilt may be of an entirely different type of fabric, a different weight, a different color, a different feel, than anything that has been part of the quilt before.

When we are the mothers of such a family, we sometimes feel as though we are not just trying to piece *our* lives together, but the lives of everyone else in the family too. Conflicts can become glaring clashes. We may feel like we're running around with thread and needle trying to mend holes as fast as rips are made.

Sometimes, we can derive more delight from our lives if we rearrange the pieces. Maybe some parts have served their purpose and no longer need to be part of your quilt. The bits might harmonize differently—maybe even better— if parts were moved around, so that they got more, or less, attention or wear. The pieces that make up our lives may not always be of our choosing, but the patterns we make are up to us.

Creator God, you have woven together a world of colors, sounds, tastes, smells, and feelings and made it good. Help us to do the same.

JULY 26
a time to keep silence . . . (Ecclesiastes 3:7c)

EVERY YEAR ON THE NIGHT BEFORE Neal's birthday, I used to tell him the story of the night before he was born. I told him about my friend Annette, who was working in Memphis that summer, showing up the afternoon of July 26, 1977, because she was sure he was going to be born that day. I told him about visiting various friends that evening, telling each to be ready in case he was born in the night. I told him about waking up every hour or so all night long, looking at my watch, and thinking, "Nothing is happening. Annette is going to be so disappointed," and of how the next morning she kept saying "That's OK, because when you get to the doctor for your check-up this morning, you're going to be in labor." I told him about the doctor's being late, and how by the time he got there, I *was* in labor. I described the walk to the hospital, visiting friends on the way, the very short wait for him to come, and the nurse's asking if it was my birthday when my mother and friends sang "Happy Birthday" as she wheeled me out. I told him every year because I needed to tell the story. Every year, that is, until the night before his sixteenth birthday when Neal decided he didn't want to hear it.

There are so many times, Lord, when we have things we want to tell our children. Please, God, help us to honor silence when it is time to.

JULY 27
and a time to speak . . . (Ecclesiastes 3:7*d*)

ONCE, I AGREED TO PARTICIPATE in a Victims' Speak Out in spite of the fact that since no more than a handful of people knew about what had once happened to me, I was completely overwhelmed by the idea of speaking about it in public. In spite of my terror, I decided to speak in order to represent all those who could not speak. I asked other victims what they would like the public to know. I spoke about the long-term effects of that particular crime. I talked about statistics, about what happened to us, and why it was kept silent. In the end, the result of my speaking was that a program was started in my community to help survivors of that crime. I was glad for that reason that I had done it.

The greatest thing that happened for me, however, was my personal experience of Neal standing guard over me that night. All his life I had supported and protected him, as you have done for children of your own, but that night it was he who was proudly supporting and protecting me. When several people rushed up to talk to me as I was trying to leave, he was for the first time a man speaking, telling my friends to take me to the car, and that he would take care of those who wanted to talk to me. Although he was only fifteen, it was the first time I had experienced him in that way, as the adult who would someday take care of me.

God calls us to speak the truth in spite of our fear, and the good that may come of it may be something totally unexpected. Sometimes it is even in what our children say to us.

Loving God, you have called us to be prophets in spite of our reluctance. Please help us to speak the truth in love, trusting in you that good may come of it.

JULY 28
a time to love . . . (Ecclesiastes 3:8a)

EVEN THOUGH IT IS ALWAYS TIME to love, it is *most important* to love when love is the hardest thing of all to do. Funny how it works that way.

When they don't call and come home hours late. When they take the car without asking—or even worse, wreck it—and you don't know where they were. When you find out the unexpected and unwanted news. When they announce they are eighteen and no longer have to live by your rules. When you find out your child's been doing drugs at school. When you find out your child hasn't *been* at school. Those are the times to love.

When you've been yelled at for the fiftieth time that day. When everyone in the family wants something, but no two people want the same thing. When your kids think you're the only person in the world who still treats them as children. When everyone else's parents let them do it. When you know that "no" really is the right thing to say, and your resistance is almost worn down. When they do things that wound you and you'd like to strike back. It is always time to love.

God, I believe you suffered when your Child suffered, and that you also grieve when I am wounded. Help me at those times to act lovingly in spite of my pain and anguish.

JULY 29
and a time to hate . . . (Ecclesiastes 3:8*b*)

HATING IS NOT SOMETHING I am proud of. There have, however, been people I have hated, always ones who would do others harm.

People are capable of unspeakable horror. Sometimes, parents prey on their own children. Sometimes, abusers are teachers, coaches, scout masters, friends of the family, siblings. It is rarely the stranger in the overcoat hiding in the woods. Abusers are usually known by the victim, making it even harder for the victim to tell. Sometimes, the things children tell are so horrible that they are not believed once they have told.

In such a world we grow into motherhood, trying to protect our children. We know (usually) that even when we want to strangle our kids, we are being melodramatic, and will not actually do it. We aren't always so generous when it comes to someone we think might have harmed them.

The time I found out a pedophile was "grooming" one of my children for abuse, I wanted someone else to kill him so I wouldn't have to feel guilty about wanting him dead. I still want him never to get out of jail. There has never been, nor do I ever anticipate, any type of reconciliation. Sometimes, we hate; how hard the commandment is to love our enemies.

God of the sinner, God of mine, forgiving me for hating when you would have me sow love.

JULY 30
a time of war . . . (Ecclesiastes 3:8*c*)

ONE DAY, WHEN NEAL was small, I heard a pronouncement on the radio that I have never forgotten. I have no idea who the speaker was, or the topic, but what was said was this: "Every mother wants her daughter to grow up to be Miss America, and her son to grow up to be President." I remember that I was in the car when I heard it, and that as I drove I prayed, "Please, God, I don't want my child to be President; I just want my child not to die in someone else's war."

Now Neal is no longer a child, but almost an adult. He is a leader at many things: president of his senior class, captain of the cross country, swimming and track teams, life guard. He is also fiercely protective of those he loves. I cannot imagine him passively resisting if he believed those he loved were in danger. I know that if there were a war, he would fight in it to protect his brothers, and to protect me. And the thought of his fighting and possibly dying is something I try to avoid.

That possibility is something mothers have lived with always. There are times when we, as a nation, have gone to war, and will go to war, and in every war there have been mothers who have lost their daughters and sons. We each pray that God will keep our children safe, but every other mother prays the same. When we are not in a war, we pray that we and our children will be spared, knowing the decisions are not up to us. It is hard, at those times, to trust in God. But that is exactly what we are called to do.

Help us, O God, to be true to our convictions, even when our feelings get in the way.

JULY 31
and a time of peace . . . (Ecclesiastes 3:8*d*)

IN THE CALM OF THE EVENING, all is quiet. The boys are asleep. It is my time to read, to think, to listen, and to pray.

Mothering is hard work, and we all need restorative time. Time to rest, to regroup, to replenish our resources. For some of us, that time is found in the early morning. For others, it's a walk in the park at noon. Some may go into a valley. Others may climb a mountain. A quiet place of worship may be just what we are looking for, or it may be the comforting arms and reassuring words of an older woman who has already been through the stage of parenting we are in the midst of. Sometimes, it may be just looking in on our children and watching them while they sleep.

Wherever you find peace, hold fast to it. Tomorrow they will likely think you are completely unreasonable—again. They may yell at you or stomp around and slam their doors—again. They may try their hardest to bluff their way into being your equal—again.

Whatever you do in response, love them. Love them as your God loves you even when you rebel and think you know what's right. Love them like the eagle who pushes her young out of the nest when it is time for them to fly. Love them with all your heart.

Give us grace, O Lord, so to entrust our young into your loving care, and grant us peace.

$\mathscr{A}$UGUST

BEGINNINGS AND CHANGES

Lisa Flinn

AUGUST 1   **Read Isaiah 66:13.**

MY JOURNEY INTO MOTHERHOOD began in August, with the birth of my first daughter, Emily. Ever since, this month has meant a time of beginnings and changes: the first day of school, the long-awaited thirteenth birthday, the day she received her driver's license, and her entrance to college life. Over the years both smiles and tears have mingled on our faces under the hazy August sun.

As a new mother, I soon realized that my baby had different cries to signal differing needs. The sobs and the tears were calls for food, comfort, help, or company. After a lot of practice, I responded more appropriately to her crying.

Later, as the mother of a teen, I entered a new time of crying. Before long I learned about the tears of anger and embarrassment, the tears of frustration and of a broken heart. I quickly discovered that comforting a teen is not as simple as comforting a baby!

My first impulse was to fix the problem; however, I learned that some teenage problems were out of a mother's control. Still others were best left for my daughter to work through. My next inclination was to offer advice. This was occasionally helpful, but frequently caused more tears.

Joking around never worked unless the story had been told and the tears had stopped. Ignoring the crying was impossible for me. After stumbling on this new path of mothering, I finally accepted the idea that I could just sit with Emily, give her a comforting hug, and listen as she cried. Wonder of wonders, that is all she really wanted.

In what ways does your teen need to be comforted today?

God of Consolation, I am comforted when you listen to me and hold me in your love. Prepare me to comfort my child at any age.

AUGUST 2   Read 1 Corinthians 13:4-7.

I THINK IT WOULD BE GREAT to be a mother on a situation comedy show. My house would be spacious, well-decorated, and always clean. If I were a sitcom mom, I'd look casual but attractive. I'd be witty and wise, ready for any situation. My kids would be adorable, even when misbehaving. The problem at the heart of each episode would be resolved with love and laughter. Best of all, I'd be paid to be a mother!

Of course, TV land is largely a fantasyland, but I can learn a thing or two from "the neighborhood of make-believe." When I listen to my favorite sitcom moms, I hear them discipline the kids and overcome strife without condemnation. They teach lessons and share insight with an easy grace. Somehow they stand firm amidst the chaos of family life, creating a positive influence for all.

If I had these qualities, I'm sure I'd be a better mom. Now, what steps can I take toward this goal?

First, I can remember this goal in my prayers. For inspiration, I'll read 1 Corinthians 13:4-7. As a refresher, I'll tune in to next week's show.

What steps can you take?

Gracious God, when I'm tired or busy, I sometimes fall short of the mother I want to be. Help me to have the focus, the energy, and the willpower to be my better self.

MY FRIENDS AND I HAVE always discussed our children.

With parenting guides at hand and each other's children to use as measuring sticks, we watch our children grow and mature, acquire skills and expertise, and develop personalities and identities. As time goes on, the differences between our children become more distinct. As we listen to each other, we learn. By comparison and contrast, we begin to have some perspective on our children as individuals.

We discovered that early days of mothering are only a warm-up for the adolescent years! Then dramatic physical changes, demanding social changes, and definite emotional and behavioral changes make for turbulent times. Networking with other parents seems essential for keeping up with all that's happening in the lives of our kids.

Some of the wisest and most helpful words have come from my friend Lois. Her insights help me see my daughter from a new perspective. She has a genuine interest in Emily and offers her thoughts on a variety of topics. I trust Lois because she always discusses people and situations with the hope of understanding and harmony.

Having a friend who really knows me and my teen and sincerely cares about our relationship is a blessing from God.

Think about the friends who have blessed your life. How can you be a blessing to another mother of teens?

Understanding Lord, I am most thankful for friends who listen to my concerns and offer their support. Open my ears and my heart to those who need to talk with me.

AUGUST 4   Read 1 Samuel 16:7.

EMILY CAME HOME FROM SCHOOL with a colorful account of a friend's latest driving calamity. While it was a good story, I knew she was driving home a more personal point: "I'm a more responsible driver." The message was not lost on me! I commented on the story and then complimented Emily on her good judgment behind the wheel.

Not all unspoken messages are quite so obvious. Over the years she has communicated many, usually at a sub-conscious level. Her conversations have implied "I'm trustworthy"; "My feelings are hurt"; "I tried my best, but I'm worried"; and even, "You were right, Mom."

Teens, like Emily, who are inclined to be open and conversational, offer their mothers greater opportunities to figure out what's going on in their lives. However, some teens are very private and protective of their thoughts and feelings, which presents a real challenge to their mothers or stepmothers.

Body language, tone of voice, facial expression, hesitation when speaking, or even the willingness to be in the same room are the outward signs that help me to truly listen to my daughter and discover her unspoken messages. These messages are important to me because I want to know what is in my child's heart. Yet no matter how diligently I seek this understanding, I simply see the outward appearance of my child. Only God can see in her heart.

Look for the unspoken messages your teen communicates. What do they reveal? How can you respond?

Lord, I seek to be in touch with my child's heart. Help me to understand the spoken and unspoken messages so that my responses will be most beneficial.

AUGUST 5   Read Psalms 133:1-3.

EVERY FAMILY HAS ITS OWN definition of an argument.

In some families it is a competitive sport: boisterous, loud, and good-natured. These arguing athletes enjoy defending their ideas; and no matter who wins, they most likely feel they have fought a good fight.

With other families, quite the opposite is true. No disagreements are allowed. As soon as someone says "but . . ." in a conversation, the argument line has been crossed. Arguing is considered disrespectful and disruptive.

Many families permit arguing, but the tone is as serious as a college debate; while in other households the arguing is incessant and seemingly over nothing at all.

The first definition of arguing according to *Webster's New World Dictionary* is "to give reasons (for and against)." When I have an argument with my kids, I want to hear their reasons and their logic. I believe that I can learn a lot about their intellectual, emotional, and spiritual development by listening to them argue through their issues.

Arguing with Emily has given me the opportunities to hear her define her values, defend her choices, explain her motivations, and grapple with my concerns. Better than half of our arguments have been positive, with each of us learning more about ourselves and each other.

What can you do to make the inevitable "arguments" with your teen more constructive?

Lord, when I argue with my teen, remind me to be a good listener. Guide my words so that my child will hear the concerns I have.

AUGUST 6   Read Psalm 126:2-3.

THERE IS NO SWEETER SOUND to my ears than peals of laughter ringing in my home.

As a child, I can remember getting in trouble for laughing at the dinner table. Perhaps it's selective memory, but I still don't recall why!

Today at my family's table, laughter is frequent and welcome. Our teenager is a spontaneous mirth-maker, telling the news of the day with drama and wit. She entertains us with impersonations, puns, and pantomimes until we're weak with laughter. Louise and Harrison, our younger ones, follow her lead. Their comments, tales, and turns of phrase are very funny too.

I love to hear my children laugh. I know it is because I appreciate their sense of humor. Their humor is not mean-spirited or derogatory. Rather, the humor comes from word play and their observations of the world around them.

Best of all, our mealtime amusements have given us all the opportunity to laugh at ourselves. It is easy, especially for teens, to take things too seriously. Taking a humorous look at a situation can often lighten the heart.

Laughter releases the stress of the day, relaxes family tensions, and looses the emotional knots. I occasionally laugh so hard that I cry. My children wonder at this, but I find it a cleansing experience.

Have you taken time to laugh with your teen today?

Lord, I am grateful for the simple joys of laughter. Encourage me to use my sense of humor with my family.

AUGUST 7   Read Ephesians 5:15-16.

WHEN EMILY WAS SIX YEARS OLD, my second daughter was born. One day at the Children's Clinic, Dr. Neal said, "Miss Ems has spent several years being your only child. This new baby is going to demand a lot of your time. Be sure to give Emily at least fifteen minutes a day of your undivided attention."

I took these words to heart, but I thought, "I can do better than fifteen minutes a day!" I soon found out that I often talked with Emily while doing something else, such as folding clothes or rocking the baby. Undivided attention meant special one-on-one time, and I had to make an effort to provide it.

Sooner than I thought possible another baby arrived. Things became chaotic. Finding special time for Emily was even harder. When we missed a day, Emily seemed to suffer the loss.

Years later, Emily started living with her father part of the time. On those days our mother-daughter time would take place on the telephone. We missed each other, and these phone calls meant the world to us.

Through Emily's teenage years, I've continued to give her this undivided attention. Funny thing is, though, now it's her life that's so busy.

How can you "make the most of the time" with your teen today?

Timeless and Eternal Lord, time seems to pass so quickly. Now that my child is a teenager, I know our time under the same roof is limited. Help me find precious moments with my child every day.

AUGUST 8   Read Luke 6:31.

I WANT TO BE A GOOD LISTENER, but when a conversation becomes unproductive and negative, it's time to stop.

Emily, despite her ability to be reasonable, sometimes has a fit of teenage ranting and raving. The outbreak of temper is predictably over clothes or hair. It will begin mildly enough: "Mama, what do you think of this?" No matter what my answer is, it is not what she wants to hear. When Emily is in this mood, she seems combustible.

I used to think it was a test of my patience to weather her stormy temper. My husband, Bill, believed I was teaching her that her behavior was acceptable. He was right.

My input in the clothes or hair decisions is not what she wants when she is in a bad mood. What she wants is someone on whom she can vent her fiery frustrations. Patiently waiting for her temper to spend itself did not send her a message of love or strength. Instead, it told her that it is okay to yell at others. Now at the first hint of an outburst, I excuse myself and walk away.

What limits do you need to set on your own patience with your teen?

Lord, teach me the difference between patience with my teen and being shortsighted. I want my child to learn to treat others, even me, as she would like to be treated.

AUGUST 9   Read 1 Chronicles 22:12*a*.

BASKETBALLS BOUNCING, OUTBURSTS of laughter, hushed phone conversations, music reverberating through the house, the whisper of the refrigerator door opening again and again, car horns beeping—all are sounds of teenage friends spending time together.

What do teens want from friendships?

Of course they want to have a friend to go places with them. They also need a confidant who can be trusted. Teens want a friend who can lift their spirits and a buddy who will just be there. Often they like the "wild child" for a while; then they turn to someone a little more predictable. Teens want to keep some friends from their childhood while seeking the adventure of knowing someone new.

Ask adults if they would be willing to be teenagers again and most will answer with an emphatic "no!" Those who say "yes" qualify by adding "only if I knew what I know now." They're not referring to book knowledge either; they mean social know-how.

Adults recognize that teen relationships are the un-official course of study in school. There are daily tests and lots of outside work, and the only grade that matters is the one that teens give themselves. Parents can sometimes offer tutorials, but their most important function is to listen to the oral reports.

Think about your own friends. Are you setting a good example for your teen of exercising discernment and wisdom?

Creator God, we are created in your image, but not with your wisdom and insight. I pray that my child will have discernment when choosing friends.

AUGUST 10   Read Matthew 14:23.

WHAT DOES IT MEAN TO BE ALONE?

Various pictures come to my mind: a person sitting on a park bench looking bereft; another strolling on a beautiful beach, enjoying the solitude; a child lost in a crowd; a gardener absorbed with a task; Jesus praying on the mountain.

Erin, a friend of Emily's, relishes her alone time. She recharges her social batteries and works on creative projects. She enjoys reading and is devoted to her studies.

Meanwhile, Emily prefers to read or study in the living room with people and the accompanying background noises. She does her projects in the kitchen, and her room is more like a closet than a haven. When Emily chooses to be alone, I listen in the direction of her room for clues. If there's no music, no TV, no sounds of conversation, I know something must be troubling her.

Soon Erin and Emily will be leaving home. Until now, their aloneness has been in the context of a loving home. When they're on their own, being alone will feel different. I hope they remember that God is with them always, and that their mothers' hearts are with them too.

When does your teen need time to be alone? How can you encourage your teen to spend time alone with God?

Lord of our Solitude, help my child always to adjust to new surroundings and encourage my child to use time alone to draw closer to you.

AUGUST 11   Read Proverbs 17:17.

WE KNOW HOW IMPORTANT FRIENDS are in the lives of our teens. Maintaining our own friendships is equally important for us mothers.

I talk to Barbara almost every day. We work together, so our conversations are part business and part pleasure. Even though I do household chores while talking on the phone, I consider my telephone time a limited luxury. I'm just too busy to be on the phone very much.

My conversations with Barbara have become important in my day-to-day living. We know the details and the smaller problems in each other's lives. This is valuable for me because I'm not quick to discuss my problems and concerns. In fact, I'm more likely to be the listener in my relationships. With Barbara, I can speak of these things because she's familiar with my everyday life and actually interested in it.

I'm remembering how I benefit by having a close friend who is a part of my daily life. Barbara listens for what I say and what I don't say. She asks me questions ranging from the hilariously hypothetical to the earnestly serious.

I wish I had this relationship with God. My prayer life is erratic at times. I usually pray for people or a specific concern. I don't spend enough time in dialogue with God, as with a friend. Talking and listening on a daily basis make for a close relationship. When I remember that Jesus called us "friends," I realize that I could be a better friend.

What wishes do you have for your friendship with God? How can you be a better friend?

Listening Lord, I seek to have a stronger relationship with you. I thank you for the friends who walk this life with me.

AUGUST 12   Read Genesis 2:24.

WHILE MINGLING AMONG UNFAMILIAR faces at an open house, I introduced myself to a woman standing nearby.

As we exchanged names and the usual information, she asked the ages of my children. I replied, "10, 11, and 17." With raised eyebrows, she inquired, "How do you feel about your teen graduating and leaving the nest?"

My answer came quickly: "It's time for my oldest to fly."

Her smile broadened, and she leaned forward and spoke confidently: "My two daughters have been out of the house for several years. At first I missed them a lot because we were close. However, the most wonderful thing has happened since they left. My husband and I have renewed our friendship with each other." Then she slipped her arm around her husband and said, "We have the best time together." As my husband joined the group, she added, "It is truly something to look forward to."

How bittersweet to realize that the years of raising my children are better than half over. Sooner than I expect, my baby will be at the threshold of independence. She will be ready to leave her home, her family, as God intended. Making the transition to this stage of motherhood may be challenging. Yet I am reminded that there *are* things to look forward to, including refreshing my friendship with the father of our family. After all, "This is my beloved and this is my friend" (Song of Solomon 5:16).

In what ways do you need to prepare to let go of your teen? What things do you have to look forward to?

God of Creation, through your blessings I became a mother. With each passage of motherhood I learn more about love and life. Thank you for bringing children into my life; now help me to let go.

AUGUST 13   Read Psalm 19:14.

AS I LISTEN TO THE VOWS of baptism for a child at our church, the congregation promises to care for the child, individually and as a group. This sounds like a sweet responsibility as I gaze upon the infant in our pastor's arms. I can picture rocking the baby in the nursery or teaching the child in Sunday school or mentoring the youth for confirmation class.

But what about the difficult times? What if a teenager is slipping away to "make out" and I'm the chaperon? How about the rumors that a teen I know has picked up a drug habit? What about the reckless driving I witnessed?

It's not easy to be responsible when the babies become teens. They are testing the waters of life. I want them to "get their feet wet," and even learn to swim against the current, but I don't want the kids to venture too far into dangerous waters.

Questions ring in my ears: Is this an isolated incident or a glimpse of the bigger picture? Do I speak to the teen first or the parents? Do I wait and watch or do I act immediately?

No matter what I decide, I take a risk. I may alienate the teen. Whether my concern is just or not, the parents may not welcome my interest. Other teens might steer clear of me, believing that I'm very uncool. And what if my speaking up really makes things worse for the teen in a way I could never predict? Fortunately, I don't have to decide alone. I can ask God for wisdom.

What wisdom do you need from God today regarding the teens in your life?

Lord, give me wisdom for the sake of these kids.

211

AUGUST 14   Read Phillipians 1:27.

LISTENING TO OTHER MOTHERS talk of their busy lives, I hear echoes of their family values.

Karoline speaks of scouting, foster children, soccer coaching, foreign exchange students, teaching autistic children, and Sunday school. I know her family places value on children and child advocacy.

I hear that Lois was chosen to go to NASA space camp. She and her husband are always taking interesting classes. Their daughter teaches a unique summer camp program. A visit to their home reveals books and paints and musical instruments; they are invested in education and the arts.

When I speak with Robin or Cathy, I hear of their families' interests in community activities and community service. These energetic mothers are role models for the rest of us.

In talking to these mothers and hearing about their activities, I am certain that family values aren't learned from a lecture at the dinner table. They are modeled by parents and experienced through family participation.

Over the years, church life has been an important aspect of my family's life. To my children, God's house is a comfortable place to be; and they take time to participate in church life. Emily will often drive twenty-five miles from her father's house to come to church. She sets a good example.

What values are you passing on to your family?

Father of All Families, I am thankful Jesus was a model of love and faith for all of humankind. I ask your guidance in being a good model of faith and love to my children.

AUGUST 15   Read Proverbs 8:32-33.

THROUGH MY TEENAGE YEARS, my mother and I stood side by side almost every evening to wash the supper dishes. We talked as steadily as we worked. Besides learning good kitchen habits, I absorbed little tidbits of wisdom from my mother. In this easy-going atmosphere, I was also able to share what was on my mind.

Following in my mother's steps, I have always had chores for my children to do. A great many of these tasks I do with them, intending to make the work as pleasant as possible.

As Emily and I tend the plants in our sprawling gardens, we become avid gardeners. When preparing a meal, we put on our chef's hats to transform ourselves from good cooks to great chefs. Give us a creative project, from feather masks to hand-painted ornaments, and we take on the air of inspired artists. Whatever the task, if we tackle it as a team, we are enthusiastic. Of course, while we work, we talk; and these conversations bring us closer.

My relationships with my children are strengthened through our chore and project times together. We have fun, tell stories, share skills, discuss problems, and feel a sense of accomplishment. Perhaps I'm teaching them to make the most of life's small tasks. Hopefully, I'm helping them to sort through their feelings and to be comfortable expressing them.

In what ways do you spend time alone with your teen? How can you make the most of this time?

Holy One, I give thanks for the opportunities to work with my children.

AUGUST 16   Read Matthew 18:20.

A FEW YEARS AGO I BECAME the youth leader at our church. I told Emily that it was something I wanted to do, because some of my fondest high school memories were of times spent with my own youth group. No matter what cliques any of us belonged to at school, our youth group met as one.

Our leader, Reverend Boatwright, usually called "Boats," led us in challenging discussions of faith, folk singing, genuine fellowship, and even cross-country adventures. One of the most exciting adventures we had was a trip out west. We began our journey in Indiana and rode by bus to link up with another group in Wisconsin. On the way to Montana, we met other youth groups as we stayed overnight in their churches. Finally in Montana, we bunked at an old camp in the foothills of the Rockies. Our mission was to paint a church and work at an Indian Reservation. We had adventures in friendship, travel, faith, and service.

Now that I have some knowledge about youth ministries, it occurs to me that my youth group had an exceptional experience. Yet I know that any circle of Christian friends can have a significant and lasting impact on a teen's life. I want each of my children to have the opportunity to experience the joys and the growth that such a group can bring.

What needs does your teen have related to a circle of Christian friends? In what ways can you help?

Heavenly Provider, joy fills my heart when I think of the wonderful times I have had with Christian friends. Please show my teen how meaningful a treasured circle of Christian friends can be.

AUGUST 17   Read 1 Corinthians 12:4-7.

I CONTINUE TO BE AMAZED at the interesting combinations of traits that children inherit from their parents. Each parent's talents and attributes, as well as temperament and personality, are mingled unpredictably with the other's to create a surprise-package child.

As the child matures, the wonder of individuality is slowly revealed. There is pleasure and frustration for child and parent, especially in the teenage years.

One friend told me, "I'm such a klutz! I never imagined that I'd have a child who could dance so well." Another friend said that her daughter inherited a beautiful voice, but she doesn't like to sing.

Emily, my own teenager, has many interests, and it is taking her a while to discover her true gifts. We've spent considerable time discussing her abilities as she signed up for high school courses, applied for special workshops, and chose a college.

The Bible says that we have different gifts according to the grace given us, and I believe it! I want Emily to realize that in finding her gifts, she will be discovering how she can serve the Lord. The path of self-knowledge and personal fulfillment can also be a journey in faith.

My friends and I are still learning about ourselves and about ways we can serve God. I became an author at age forty, and I'm still listening for the next call to serve!

What gifts do you see in your teen? How can you help your teen to discover yet realized gifts? What gift(s) of your own have you been neglecting?

Great Gift Giver, I pray my child will discover the gifts you've so generously given.

AUGUST 18   Read Ephesians 6:18.

LATE ONE EVENING THE FROGS were peeping and raindrops were spilling out of the clouds onto the rooftop. The house was quiet. My husband and younger children were on a canoeing trip. Emily and I sat listening to the nocturnal symphony.

The scripture "Be still, and know that I am God!" came to mind (Psalm 46:10). Then I began to think about prayer. I said to Emily, "I'm not sure that I've expressed to you how important prayer is." I began sharing with her that I pray for her several times a day. I talked about some research that has been done to test the effectiveness of prayer and the affirming results.

Emily listened, and I continued: "Jesus said, 'Ask, and it will be given you; search, and you will find; knock, and the door will be opened for you.'" (Matthew 7:7). The more I turn to God in prayer with my questions and concerns, the more I see God's hand in my life. Things don't always come about as I expect them, but I've learned to be open to the possibilities."

After a long moment, filled with frogs and raindrops, Emily said, "Well, Mom, don't worry; I do pray."

What do you need to share with your teen about your own prayer life?

Lord of Light, I know my own faith, but I wonder if my children know how strong it is. They see some outward signs as I teach, pray, or worship, but do they see its importance in my daily life? Help me to talk more openly about my faith and especially about the power of prayer.

AUGUST 19 — Read Colossians 3:13-14.

AS I LISTEN TO MY CHILDREN'S conversations, I hear that one of their chief concerns in life is fairness. Bill and I have taken many opportunities to explain that in our home, they will be treated fairly.

It seems to be a challenge for young adolescents to grasp that the circumstances of fairness are not always parallel or equal. Older adolescents, however, can incorporate differing circumstances, values, needs, and outcomes in their definition of fairness. This ability to understand how or why things happen as they do often relieves some of a teenager's concern about fairness. However, it does not eliminate it.

Competition for first chair, the first string, the homecoming court, club officers, or honors nominations can stir the issue. Struggles over friendships, romantic interests, or homework assignments are daily tests of fairness.

These teenage judges of right and wrong may begin to say "life isn't fair." In order to deal with the perceived unfairness in a healthy way, they will need to learn to forgive their classmates, teammates, teachers, friends, or parents. Forgiving others is one of the most challenging things for any of us to do. It calls for reason over emotion, generosity over self-interest, and trust in God over worldly uncertainty. Forgiveness is a learned ability guided by faith and gained through practice. Forgiveness is a facet of love.

What opportunities do you have to both demonstrate and teach lessons in forgiveness?

Forgiving Lord, open doors to understanding and hearts to love, so all may have the capacity to forgive.

THOREAU WROTE: "IF YOU BUILD castles in the air, your work will not be lost. That is where they should be. Now put a foundation under them."

Many teenagers have sky-high hopes and starry-eyed dreams about their futures. Emily's castle has a familiar address: Sesame Street. Yes, one day she hopes to work for the Children's Television Workshop. Bill and I support her dream.

I'm sure there are castles in the air that parents never hear about; but if a teen starts talking, it's time to listen. While some dreams inspire parental involvement, others may seem unrealistic and not worth the time. Either way, a teenager's self-esteem will be increased through a parent's sincere interest.

Building a foundation for any teen's castle is a process. It begins with the belief that the dream is possible. The next step is to discuss the cornerstone skills—knowledge or experience that the realization of the dream will require. The third step is to create those necessary building blocks.

If the entire foundation is not built or the castle disappears, a teenager will still learn much in the process. Most of all, the teenager will know that he or she had parental support. And that makes all the difference.

How can you help to build the foundation of your teen's castle?

Lord, help me to listen to my teen's dreams. Give me guidance so I may support my child as the castle's foundation is built.

AUGUST 21   Read Romans 12:15.

THE DAY BEFORE THE PROM, Emily and I created a beautiful rose garland for her hair and did the final fitting of her satin dress. As we gathered the accessories and talked over plans, her excitement grew. Little did I realize that soon I'd be listening to a story of disappointment.

"How was your evening? Tell me everything!" I said.

Emily replied, "I knew it was a bad sign when he refused to wear his boutonniere." She went on to say that her date had decided he liked another girl. Instead of behaving like a gentleman, he was distant and rude. They didn't dance even once. Later, he met up with his new girlfriend at the after-prom party. Emily and her date were friends, she thought. She hadn't expected romance, but she had counted on having fun.

No mother wants to hear that her child was hurt and embarrassed in this way. Even though I didn't worry about her self-esteem—I know she receives her sense of worth from sources other than boys and social events—I knew how important it was for me to be there for her, to share in her sorrow. And that's just what I did.

As I reflected on Emily's disastrous evening, I hoped that this incident would stretch her heart, making her more aware of others' feelings, more able to sympathize with others, and more grateful for happy times.

In what ways do you rejoice and weep with your teen?

God Who Hears And Sees All, help my child to grow wiser and stronger through the disappointing experiences in life. May my love and your love give my teen courage and support.

AUGUST 22   Read Exodus 20:12.

MY MOTHER AND I ARE SEPARATED by more than 500 miles and tend to be a bit conservative with our telephone calls. For these reasons, we have missed countless opportunities to discuss problems, issues, and concerns we've had in our mothering experiences.

Many times when I have asked a question or sought advice, my mother has paused to think and then said, "What would Mother say?" My mother greatly treasures her mother's wisdom—so much so, that she will think of her mother's advice before offering her own.

When I was a new bride, this surprised me. I considered

my mother quite experienced in her role as wife, mother, and working woman. Why did she tell me what Grandma would say?

In my increasing maturity, I now understand. My mother was showing her deep love and respect, and sharing her mother's legacy of wisdom with me.

My grandmother, Audrey Spear, was known only in her own neighborhood; but her sweet, energetic, generous, and optimistic life made her a heroine to my mother and to me. Both my grandmother and my mother have taught me much as I have listened to their wisdom and their life's stories.

What is your legacy of wisdom?

Lord of the Ages, I still have much I can learn. Remind me to open my ears and listen to the wisdom of the generations.

August 23   Read 1 Corinthians 13:11.

IN THE BEGINNING EMILY FOUND high school exciting and wonderful. It was a whole new world of opportunity. However, by the end of her third year, she found the high school world to be tarnished and tiresome. That's when I began to tell her my stories about going to college and beginning life on my own. It was time for her to hear there is life beyond high school.

High school is a high-pressure microcosm where standards are rigid and the judgment is swift. Many teens cluster into cliques, each pledging allegiance to the group's identity. At first it's great to belong; later it can feel claustrophobic. Often teens are ready and eager to move on.

Of course, there are teens for whom high school is a paradise of popularity and recognition. These captains and queens who have lived the ultimate experience may have a hard time letting go.

Life beyond high school means life beyond childhood. It can mean enrolling in college and choosing majors, starting real jobs and getting engaged, finding first apartments and establishing credit, taking trips abroad and visiting home to see Mom and Dad. It's the threshold of adulthood, which can be both exciting and frightening.

Part of our responsibilities as parents is to help prepare our teens for the adventure.

What do you need to do to help your teen begin to "put away childish things"?

Lord God, as I watch my child become an adult, exploring life in the world, I am reminded of my own years as a teen. I pray my teenager will learn from mistakes, have courage to persevere, grow in faith, and find happiness.

AUGUST 24   Read Psalm 79:13.

EMILY HAS HAD MUCH to be thankful for through her teenage years. One afternoon I asked her to think of the people in her life and something for which she might thank each of them.

Without hesitation she said, "I thank my dad for making sure I had all that orthodontic work. I really appreciate how Bill is always there to help me out of various predicaments. When Stephanie became my stepmother, I'm glad she didn't try to exert too much control. I'm thankful to my seminar English teacher for her encouragement. Mom, I'm grateful that you're so easy to talk to."

As we discussed the topic further, she spoke of other friends, employers, folks at church, and teachers. When she mentioned experiences for which she was thankful, I interjected, "What about thanking God?"

"But of course," she laughed, "I thank God for all the wonderful things that happen, like winning a contest, or having a spectacular day. Also I thank God for those really scary things that have not happened. For example, the car accident could have been worse! I'm sure I should thank God every day for things I don't even know about. I do have a lot to be thankful for."

It's important to remind our teens to give thanks. It's also important to remind *ourselves* to give thanks for the many blessings we so often take for granted.

What can you give thanks for today?

Lord, hear my thanksgiving for all the blessings and challenges in life. May my teen always know your presence and be thankful.

AUGUST 25   Read James 2:12-13.

LIZA IS THE LEAST JUDGMENTAL of all my daughter's friends. When Emily is completely out of patience with someone, Liza is accepting. If one of the group is being difficult, Liza is tolerant. If everyone is mouthing off, Liza doesn't say anything. Emily admires yet is baffled by Liza's patience with people and her non-critical approach.

Does nothing bother her or does she simply keep her thoughts to herself? Does she work to maintain her calm acceptance or does it come naturally? Could it mean she's slightly detached from her friends or full of love and mercy?

For most of us, it is difficult not to judge others. When we hear neighborhood gossip, the latest buzz at work, the news from church, or the rumors from school, we have opinions or concerns. It's so easy to be critical.

Teenagers are especially likely to sit in judgment or feel the hurt of being judged. Their limited life experience often makes them quick to criticize and less merciful than their elders.

Regardless of age or experience, we all must heed Jesus' words: "Do not judge, so that you may not be judged. For with the judgment you make you will be judged, and the measure you give will be the measure you get" (Matthew 7:1-2). Let us remember that our teens are watching.

How can you show mercy today?

Merciful Lord, your forgiveness surpasses our understanding. You ask adults and teens to be merciful; we do otherwise. Help us to believe in the power of mercy and change our ways.

AUGUST 26   Read Psalm 118:24.

MY FRIEND BARBARA AND I were browsing in The Owl's Nest, a gift shop specializing in bird paraphernalia. I mentioned that I enjoyed the random melodies of wind chimes. Barbara spotted onyx dove chimes and said, "How about an early birthday present?" With surprise and delight, I accepted the lovely gift.

Returning home, I announced to my family that I wished to collect wind chimes. Soon after, my husband created a large, free-standing set of tubular bells with oriental styling.

One afternoon Emily and I listened to the tinkling of the doves and the deep resonating tones of the bells. As a wind tugged at our clothes and pulled at our hair, a verse from one of the psalms came to mind: "You [God] make the winds your messengers" (Psalm 104:4*a*).

I said to Emily, "If the winds are God's messages, I wonder what this breeze is whispering to us?"

Stretching her arms skyward, she replied: "It is telling us to enjoy this beautiful day." Then she ran into the yard to play with Bay Boy, our retriever.

Sometimes it is our teens who teach us. As I enjoyed watching them romp, I thanked God for the pleasure of the moment.

What can you do to enjoy the gift of this day? Will you ask your teen to join you?

Lord of My Days, thank you for wind and wind chimes, teenagers and old dogs, time with my family and the possibilities of each day.

AUGUST 27   Read Matthew 11:28-30.

I CLOSED MY EYES AND LEANED back into the porch rocker. Listening to the gulls cry, the waves break, and the wind rustle through the tall sea oats, I contemplated the decisions of the day. What kind of sand castle will I build? Shall I swim at high tide or low tide? Who will I invite to go shelling with me?

As I mused over these decisions, it occurred to me that Emily wouldn't understand the simple pleasures of such small decisions. This appreciation comes from carrying the weight of many decisions. My child is nearly an adult. Her time to know the yoke of reasonability is coming.

However, there are numerous teens, far younger than she, who face tough decisions every day: the girl who becomes pregnant; the boy who runs away from home; the one who considers suicide; or the abused who will choose anything to escape the misery.

When I hear of these troubled teens and of parents who are struggling with difficult decisions, I think of Jesus' words: "Come to me, all you that are weary and are carrying heavy burdens, and I will give you rest" (Matthew 11:28). And I pray that there are persons in their lives—parents, other family members, teachers, church friends—who will share the message and help them find that rest.

What worries about your teen or others do you need to give to God? How can you help to share Christ's yoke with others?

Lord, I pray that the young and the experienced alike will turn to you with their troubled hearts. May they learn from you and find rest.

AUGUST 28   Read 1 John 1:8-9.

A FRIEND RECENTLY SAID TO me, "As I look back on raising my teenager, I do not regret anything I have done. I only regret the things I haven't done."

I told her that I knew exactly what she meant. We commiserated with each other, reviewing situations we didn't straighten out; issues we hadn't pushed; questions we left unasked; and words we never voiced.

For many of us, our oldest children, our teenagers, have suffered from our inexperience as parents. With hindsight, we recognize our weaknesses in childrearing and the mistakes we've made along the way.

Mulling over the conversation later, my heart ached. I thought of the many things I regret. These painful sins of omission make me feel angry and upset with myself. Yet, troubling about the past will not change it. Scripture says, "Love covers all offenses" (Proverbs 10:12), and that will be my consolation. I hope and trust that Emily and Bill love me enough to forgive me, as I know the Lord does.

What regrets do you need to let go of today?

Lord, I confess to you that I have not done my best as a parent. My sins range from stubbornness to laziness, from timidity to poor judgment. When I ponder the effects of my sins on my child, I am ashamed. Please forgive me, Lord, for all I have done without your guidance.

AUGUST 29   Read 1 Thessalonians 2:19-20.

I PUSHED MY HEAD BETWEEN a flannel shirt and a tweed jacket, to retrieve a sweater from the floor. As I grabbed the sweater, cascades of laughter filtered through the clothes carousel to my muffled ears.

Standing up, I spotted Emily and Cathy putting the finishing touches on a mannequin's beach ensemble. The formerly bald, woolen-clad "lady" was transformed into a picture of spring.

My church women's group was volunteering at the local thrift store, operated by the congregations of our county. Emily had asked to join us, saying, "Mom, I'm almost eighteen. May I help out tonight?"

Upon our arrival, Judy welcomed Emily, and Robin got her started redoing the displays. Brenda offered her help and snapped photos of the work in progress. Throughout the evening Emily talked, laughed, and worked as a woman among her peers.

Suddenly I had a glimpse of my teenager as a young woman. For a moment I saw her, not as my child, but as a member of the group, in service to others. My heart was filled with joy.

Have you had a similar experience when you have glimpsed your teen as a young adult? What hopes and joys can you rejoice in today?

Gracious Lord, thank you for allowing me to know this person who is my child. Today I am full of hope and joy as I picture the adult that is to come.

AUGUST 30   Read 1 John 4:19-21.

THE FOUR OF US WERE TOURING college campuses. Jessica, seventeen, was driving; and Emily was the front seat "disc jockey." The mothers were the picture of trust and tranquillity in the back seat. Miriam and I discussed the topic of her devotional for church the next day.

I enjoy listening to Miriam talk about church activities. I'm always interested in hearing about churches of different denominations. As a writer, my view of the Christian faith is enriched. As a Christian, my understanding of fellow believers is expanded. Speaking as a parent, I want my children to be familiar with the church universal.

Emily has attended Jessica's church for worship and youth activities. Likewise, Jessica has participated at our church. Both are quite active in their respective congregations—and pleased with their ecumenical experiences.

Often teens, especially middle schoolers, like to invite their friends to church activities. I think this informal, interdenominational exchange is wonderful. It's an energizing way to build faith and religious tolerance at the same time.

How can you encourage your teen to be more accepting of his or her "brothers and sisters"?

Lord of the Church, I pray that Christians within the community, the country, and the world will seek to understand and respect one another. Help us to see our relationship to one another through your eyes. May the fellowship of Jesus Christ bear fruitful experiences for all.

AUGUST 31   Red Luke 8:11-15.

SOME MAY THINK IT ODD, but I collect all sorts of interesting clothing and accessories to stock a family costume closet. I have everything from uniforms to grass skirts.

Last spring, Mrs. Wade led her drama students in a revival of *Godspell*. Emily, my teenage thespian, volunteered to costume the entire cast! She pulled out all the old hippie clothes in the collection.

At the opening curtain, I had to chuckle when I saw all those teenagers flitting around in vintage bell bottoms and peasant dresses! However, I was soon drawn into the play and absorbed with its message.

One of my favorite parts was the parable of the seeds. The actors and actresses became the seeds on the path, the seeds on the rock, the seeds that fell among the thorns, and the seeds in good soil. Listening to the parable, I wondered where the seeds of God's word fell upon those teens. Every one of them looked like "good soil." Their voices sounded honest and pure. Yet I knew that, statistically speaking, some of them would be like a path, a rock, or thorns to God's word—even to the very words they were singing and speaking.

The production was marvelous. As the curtain fell, the audience was on its feet. When the students appeared for their encore, they were glowing with the experience.

I hoped and prayed that a seed would take root in each of them.

In what creative ways can you encourage your teen to explore God's word? How can you nurture your teen's own creativity?

Lord, hallelujah for creative people and the joyous ways they lift up your word.

$\mathscr{S}$EPTEMBER

LOOKING BACK AND LOOKING AHEAD

Margaret Anne Huffman

SEPTEMBER 1 **Read Deuteronomy 28:6.**

OUR DOG NUTMEG BARKS at the window, telling me "The school bus is here!" The first day of school: Can there be a time more filled with hope and resolve to make this the best time ever? It's as clean and promising as a new notebook!

"Where are the kids? They're going to be late," Nutmeg seems to be saying as she looks at me. Neither she nor I can quite adjust to the fact that "our kids," Lynn, Rob, and Beth, have graduated from riding the bus. They got off one day, and it seemed that the next day our grandson, Aaron, was getting on! Aaron, who's thirteen, connects me to teen years I savor from a distance. Every grey hair, every wrinkle, every creaky joint has a name, date, time, and place written on it from days when Nutmeg, my husband, and I lived with three teenagers.

On each first day of school I stood at the window where I am standing now, watching the school bus and praying it would usher in the best year ever. It requires a leap of faith to move into the teen years, for they are "first days" for us mothers, too. We've never mothered teens before. There's so much to learn—which I confess I often did the hard way. Kids have "school work"; we have "home work" to help them as we can.

Join me at the window as I look back and look ahead. Feel God's companionship as we explore days of drama, laughter, tears, worry, discovery, and stretching. What a rich time of growth!

Creator God, you are alpha and omega, encompassing all our days.

SEPTEMBER 2   Read Matthew 6:34.

AS I'M LOOKING BACK, I see my son dancing around the kitchen table. We're about to have our first "teen party," and he, the host, is nervous. I am frantic. Are all teen parties disasters? Will this be one too? Will there be party-crashers? Troublemakers? What will I do if . . . ? My worry list is endless.

Sometimes we worry and generalize about our teens to the exclusion of common sense and enjoyment. My worrying has this party in trouble before the first teens have arrived! I remind myself that there's a difference between preparedness and anxiety! And I confess to the latter; sometimes my faith in our teens, myself, and a watchful Creator are more abstract than down-to-earth!

Yet we can only travel by the light we have at the time. That's true for looking ahead and looking back. We mothered little tykes as best we knew how; we are doing the same with our teens.

Take this minute by minute, I tell myself, recalling the wisdom of ancient nomads who traveled the desert in the cool of night. Tiny candles in holders sewn to the fronts of their shoes gave just enough light for the next step. Do I need more than that? Like wearing a seatbelt, I can be as prepared as possible and then enjoy the ride—even as hair-raising as it may sometimes be with teens at the wheel. My alternative? Keep us stuck at home, wallflowers in the party of life.

Still our anxieties, Lord, as we learn to live one step—one dance—at a time.

SEPTEMBER 3   Read Psalm 127:1.

IN A HOME OCCUPIED BY TEENS, *furniture is best arranged in a circle,* I thought one day as I paused for morning prayer. *Eye-to-eye conversation is more important than designer decor,* I continued—as if the Creator who gave us this round globe to call home didn't already know!

Did you laugh, Lord, watching me with my crowbar in hand as I knocked out a wall last month to gain an even bigger circle—one without barriers to block conversation or corners to get backed into? It was a funny sight.

It was past time to redo our kitchen. The "bottom line" of the new design was determined by family gatherings as much as by budget. We needed room for more people, including three teenagers.

The proud centerpiece is a round oak table where we gather to laugh, cry, renegotiate, swap ideas and support, pray, ponder life, debate issues, share goals and fears, and break daily bread. Thanks to my crowbar, it is a spacious room that says "Welcome" with kid-proof textures and eye-to-eye seating. Soon we will light fall's first fire, adding warmth to a family circle that can grow chilly in challenging times. Thank God, it's hard to stay upset in a circle.

We feel you scoot among us, Companion God. Welcome. You are our honored guest, peacemaker, and teacher. Stay for dessert; the best is yet to come as we renew our family circle, with you at its center.

SEPTEMBER 4   Read Isaiah 40:29*a*.

I CHECKED MY RIPENING GOURDS today; soon it will be harvest. And then it will be a year before I can make them into birdhouses. It takes patience to raise gourds.

A friend came by while I was puttering in the dirt. She's ready to "give up" at the hand of her teens: missed curfews, smart mouths, outrageous clothes. Been some of those places; felt some of that. Sometimes it can be painful raising teens, and I confess to many errors. But am I a failure when I make mistakes parenting my teens? Are they failures when they make wrong choices?

No way. Giving up is failure, and it sends kids the wrong message: that there is no redemption. Besides, is there ever sufficient evidence to prove once and for all that someone is a "failure"? No. There is always hope; there is always energy to press forward. There is always a way for God to redeem even the worse scenario. Anyway, now is too early to tell what is failing and what is not. This might be a single barren season—all vine and no gourd.

Raising teens is like planting a garden: You don't keep digging up the plant to see if its roots are growing! There are seasons of stunted growth just as there are seasons of blossoms and fruit. Even then—gourd to kid—it takes a while for them to ripen and become useful.

Help us, Loving Parent, to treat our kids with the same strengthening patience you extend us.

SEPTEMBER 5   Read Matthew 7:1-5; 12.

HOW MUCH "LIP" IS TOO MUCH? How much disagreement is okay? We've created a dilemma by raising independent children. Who could have guessed they would live in a world so different from ours that we'd do battle at the drop of a thought? We used to applaud each time they walked and "talked back."

Yet, stop and listen now: Is that *our* voice outshouting them? At what age do *disrespectful* and *opinionated* become okay? Mothers are fixers of everything from broken crayons to hurt feelings and skinned knees. Might we fix *our* mouths and attitudes first? Of course, teens are sometimes mistaken. It's part of the job description. Yet where will they learn listening and negotiating skills if not by our side? Would we rather they not talk?

No wonder many teens reject God. Perhaps they've learned from us that parents don't listen. And if their earthly parents don't listen, they reason, then why would their heavenly Parent listen?

May we do better; there's power in simply saying, "I never thought of it that way. Tell me more." Isn't that how we want to be treated?

Candid, respectful conversation. We forget, ever-listening Lord, to respect our kids' opinions. We may disagree, but we can listen. With you as guide, we might discover a new world our kids are eager to show us.

SEPTEMBER 6   Read Proverbs 13:4*a*; 17:22.

"I'M SIXTEEN! GIVE ME your keys, give me the credit card, and get out of my way!" I sighed when I saw the T-shirt in a catalog. Where did such arrogance come from? After much soul-searching, I concluded that neither I nor my kids "owned" this problem except by default: Everyone's kids are touched by the few who get what they demand. Some parents give it, and I've been tempted. Perhaps they feel blackmailed by guilt or simply desire to avert a teenage tantrum—and who wants that?

My own strategy was to nip the selfishness flower in its greedy, whiney little bud. One day when it began to surface, I recalled the words "Laughter is good medicine" from Proverbs (17:22, adapted), and I had my own tantrum—oh, a gentle, belly-laughing one, to be sure—poking fun at tantrums in general and selfishness in particular. Kidding took the edge off my first impulse, which was to lash out and deflate the kids' trial balloon to see if I was a pushover. I wasn't—nor was my sense of humor going to be taken hostage by kids with an attitude!

What could they do but laugh at my pantomime of their "gimmie, gimmie"? What could I do but acknowledge their efforts to get what they wanted? We all do that. The issue is the *way* we do it—a topic for further conversation.

Thank you for funny bones, wise Creator; we need to use them more often when our teens test our limits. Help us to deal creatively and effectively with our teens' selfish demands.

SEPTEMBER 7   Read Joshua 1:9.

IT'S DIFFICULT TO KNOW HOW to teach our teens caution without instilling a crippling fear. This is seldom truer than when we're teaching them to drive. Buckle your seatbelt; don't speed; don't cruise; slow down; speed up; turn your blinker on; watch out. Nag, nag, nag. The kids tuned me out.

I wrote myself a note: "Have your say, make reasons and concerns clear, and then let it go." With God's grace and much tongue-biting, I did—sort of. Nagging is hard to give up.

When one of my teen's classmates was arrested for speeding, I almost started nagging again. The boy's father berated the police for "picking on teens who are just having fun." Some time later the boy was killed—speeding. A month later, another teen was killed in a car accident—this one a child of nagging parents. *How could either teen's parents survive?* I wondered. How could I?

What are we to do when we are pushed to the wall by teens who can't see far enough down the road to understand no-margin-for-error consequences? I asked myself which parent I would rather be: the one who nags a bit too much or the one who excuses? As I strove for balance and caution—not fear—I reread my note: "Have your say, make reasons and concerns clear, and then let it go."

With all fearsome issues and choices, may we have the courage to treat our kids this way, as God does us. May we be worthy of this trust, this gracious gift of free-will. Some days it's a heavy burden.

Give us the strength and courage we need, Lord, to protect our kids without scaring them to death with awful possibilities. Comfort us when we do the best we can and it backfires.

SEPTEMBER 8   Read Psalm 21:11; 34:4.

A STATE TROOPER WHO HAPPENED along helped my daughter to get the car out of the ditch. "Accidents happen," he said; we echoed his assurance as we held her hand. Accidents happen. Though it was an accident, the worst accident of all was avoided—my daughter wasn't harmed.

It's those near misses that cause me to shudder and shake, like the day I drove across railroad tracks only to look up and see a freight train in my rearview mirror! A corn field had hidden the train from my view when I stopped and looked—but obviously not well enough. I shook then like I shook at the ditch incident with my daughter—and a zillion more near misses that have come my mothering way.

At first I was quick to criticize my daughter; I missed the point: nothing happened. She was okay. Then I realized that making speeches wouldn't accomplish anything except perhaps to make her more reluctant to admit a mistake or to ask for help the next time. After all, I blow it many times too, and criticism has the same effect on me.

From then on, when disaster was averted and I found myself wanting to say, "Told you so" or bad-mouth the behavior, friend, or event, I recalled the train in *my* mirror. Then I hugged my reprieved kid and uttered a prayer of gratitude.

Hold us, Lord. Thank you for second and even third chances. Help us to be grateful.

SEPTEMBER 9   Read Isaiah 41:6.

AS I UNPACK MY SUITCASE from a visit with friends who have three teens the same stair-step ages that mine were, I remember the scene with a smile. Their driveway looked like a parking lot; their kitchen, a restaurant as their kids' friends "just stopped by." Home sweet home away from home.

Lord, bless this mess, I had whispered as I surveyed the sprawl of kids, homework, keys, food, music, and yes, safety. How wonderful to provide a home away from home for other kids. We fried up some burgers and unearthed some foods to go with them, promising ice cream for dessert.

In some cultures, parents send their teenagers to live with other people in the village for a period of time. The next best thing is to share the parenting job with other caring, available adults. Kids need a place to hang out, talk, and play—a place where the pressure is off to conform, posture, and bluff; a place like my friends' yard, where thirty high school seniors played "Capture the Flag." For a brief moment, it was okay for them to be children again, to relax and play, knowing that adults were there to keep them safe, fry burgers, and listen.

Like a dove flying over a rainbow, teen laughter was a gift of hope landing on the front step of a family willing to open their door.

Fortify us to take in "stray" teens, Lord. Our laps, like yours, are spacious enough for the privilege.

SEPTEMBER 10   Read Isaiah 58:11.

SOMETIMES I TOOK A BUM RAP as "meanest mother in the high school if not the whole world." It was, however, a reputation I encouraged and offered to my kids. "Hey, I have broad shoulders," I told them. "I don't care if people think I'm wrong or mean. I'm not in a popularity contest." It had worked for a friend who passed the idea along to me.

It's hard to know how to support teens who want to believe they don't need it. It is equally hard to know they need sturdy boundaries, but not battle lines. Learning the difference grows grey hairs!

I came to the conclusion that this arrangement was divinely inspired and practically needed as the kids and I negotiated and rehearsed how to handle inevitable situations. "Can't do that; my mom will ground me for life." "Drink at my party, and my mom will call the cops and throw you out." "Mom will . . ." threats worked whenever the kids needed a prop to lean on—until the day came when the security of their own convictions and their discovery of God's intentional will for them enabled them to say to friends, "I don't want to go drinking," or to themselves, "I'd rather fail a test than rely on stolen answers."

I'm thankful that God gives us broad shoulders.

Thank you, Lord, for enabling us to help guide and protect our kids. They need our broad shoulders.

SEPTEMBER 11   Read 1 Corinthians 15:58; Romans 12:2.

"IT'S NOT ME!" WAILED my high school senior. Homecoming was in a couple of weeks; and as a homecoming queen nominee, Lynn needed something special to wear. Nothing worked; nothing "was her," we agreed as we traipsed from store to store. Of course, we had different ideas about "who" she was!

As teens hesitate before a multitude of choices, image peddlers hurry in to fill the void. Sometimes teens take a "self" from one-kid-does-all racks instead of claiming a unique self—despite the latest fad. Sometimes they let us help "dress" them; always, they struggle to discover who they know themselves to be deep within and how they want the world to see them. It's like playing dress-up all over again.

Relax, I told myself at the umpteenth store, *she'll find it*. I kept my fingers crossed that it wouldn't blow either my mind or my billfold! And it didn't. She chose an outfit that showcased her God-given individuality—what we both valued far more than color, length, or trendiness. She returned my grin in the mirror, looking neither like stereotyped teen nor mama's girl.

Later when she was selected as homecoming queen, we both knew it was not because she was trying to be or look like everyone else, but because she was herself—a self I'd glimpsed in a three-way mirror and knew I would enjoy in years ahead.

Character is not something we wear, Lord, so help us to lighten up about our kids' outward appearance. Help us hold mirrors that show who you see them to be.

SEPTEMBER 12   Read Isaiah 45:3*a*.

ONCE IT HAD BEEN STYLISH, that vintage black cashmere overcoat an elderly church member gave my husband. Before it hit the closet, one of our teens adopted it. It drooped from young shoulders and dragged the ground like teens' spirits sometimes do. It hid pride and optimism, which parents sometimes worry their teens have lost. By the time the second teen found it in the back of the older sibling's closet, the coat was frayed but still serviceable enough to wear for a while.

I loathed that coat and all it represented: fear, doubt, darkness, low self-esteem, anonymity—the dregs of teen years. Feeling a guiding, shushing Hand gently across my mouth, however, I resisted making an issue of the coat. After all, the kids did wear other coats; they did talk in roundabout ways of why they wore it; they did outgrow its somber, floor-dragging cloak of angst.

In time, I came to respect the coat and its brief appearance in our otherwise sunny, busy home as yielding "treasures of darkness" (Isaiah 45:3*a*); for together we had shared new reasons for hope, grief for unfixable troubles, options for coping, and a deepening faith.

My teens were trying on a cloak of pain, tentatively acquiring the adult garb of compassion, grief, and mortality. The black coat was mourning clothes to wear after the loss of childhood. The experience, like the coat itself, has taken its place in a sequence of life-affirming events—interludes along the way.

God, guide our teens through the dark valleys that beckon; the dark thoughts that distort; the dark moments of self-doubt. Shine your light bright these days.

SEPTEMBER 13

Read Ecclesiastes 3:1-8; Numbers 6:24.

"How LONG," I ASKED the waitress, "have you been growing that braid?" The braid in question swung like a pendulum down her back as she thought. About eighteen years.

About eighteen years, I mused, rechecking the math of motherhood that had brought me to that restaurant on the way to visit prospective colleges. I mashed my potato soft enough to swallow with my tears. About eighteen years—the amount of time it takes to grow a high school senior. As quickly as a snip of the scissors could detach the braid, so would graduation the following spring remove our daughter Beth from our nest.

What a wonderful time we had this summer with Beth, the last fledgling to leave, I thought to myself. The summer had begun wonderful rituals of Sunday brunch after church, drives in the country, and working jigsaw puzzles—things she had had to "wait her turn" for with a mom who was pulled in two other directions.

Going, going, gone—that's what teens do just when we get used to having them around. Gone, as Beth would soon be. Gone, as Lynn and Rob had already done.

Better make the most of this year, I reminded myself as we drive home later that weekend from the college of her choice. *It's going to be a brief one.*

Help us to savor the time we have with our growing teens, Lord. One day we must "graduate" to a new stage, too. Help us to get good grades in letting go—not our best subject.

Through the years I have been asked that we not eat tuna if the tuna industry is harming dolphins, that we not use disposable products unless they are recyclable, that we not drive if we can walk. I also have been asked to request that the girls at the high school be given computer time equal to the guys. Teen crusaders. I bow in humility at their vision even as I dread their encounters with foes. Adults aren't always big on change.

Yet here come our teens, fueled for saving refugees, oceans, and worlds; lobbying for fair hiring, human dignity, and peace. And here we sit, ready to talk them out of it! We don't want them to get discouraged as perhaps we have; we don't want them to get hurt. I've so often wondered if Mary said to Jesus, "Oh, Son, why did you have to make the Pharisees so angry?" I think so. Any mother would. We're torn between pride and the need to protect them—even from their own good works.

Their concerns are real—perhaps even responses to a call to faith; they deserve respect. Ecology? Get them involved as volunteers. Homelessness? Suggest they serve meals at a shelter. AIDS? Arrange for them to run an errand or do a chore for an AIDS victim. In the wake of our teenagers' inspiring examples, we might discover that our "get-involved" days are not over. God can use middle-aged crusaders too.

Give us energy and courage, Lord, to accompany our teens into a better world.

September 15   Read Titus 2:11-12;
                          Matthew 7:16.

We sat around the supper table. The news was about one of my teen's classmates. That year she brought more than new pencils to school; she brought pregnancy. Her baby would be born around the time of graduation.

Our teens are torn between curiosity, fear of "getting caught," worry, and support. But as my husband and I later worried, are they also informed? Are they prepared to make *their* decisions? And in this day of disease, are they protected if they choose other than our choices for them? Do we dare offer?

Yet who dares gamble with the answer? When we multiply the statistics related to AIDS and sexually transmitted diseases by the number of sexually active kids, the tally is a grim bottom line. Is ignorance moral? Preparedness immoral? What's a mother to do—especially when our teens are in love, their young bodies primed and ready for one of God's best gifts that needs to wait?

Teen sexual activity indicts us and asks where we, a generation with one foot in the sexual revolution and the other in a reactive backlash, can take a stand. *Answer:* beside them as they hear tunes and tales that ignite the body's passion before the mind has caught up; beside them, unshockable, approachable, and anchored in faith that offers solid guidance and compassion; beside them with facts and opinions; beside them, so that no matter which way they turn, our arms are there for support in decisions that put them at odds with peers, and our arms are there for comfort if consequences come home to nest.

What's a mother to do? Hold out her hand. We offer the safest loving around.

Help us to protect our young and morality—and to know in what order.

SEPTEMBER 16   Read 2 Corinthians 5:7.

IT IS SEPTEMBER 16, SEVERAL years ago. Our trees are alive with fluttering, fall-colored mystery: the Monarch butterflies are back. They stop each year during migration in time for our son, Rob's, birthday, which we'll celebrate later today—if we are speaking. *Can a butterfly go back into its cocoon?* I wonder as I watch him leave for school. From an assured, laughing pre-teen, he has gone backwards to the "terrible twos"! Haven't we already done this?

Here we go again. Now it's the "terrifying teens." It's not just kids who muddle through this stage; moms do, too. Sometimes we feel as if *we* are two years old! Tempers flare; lips pout. There's defiance on both sides. Yet now the stakes are higher on a bad day. The dangers are greater than hurt feelings or skinned knees. Time-outs and cradling on a lap are off limits, but we want to help.

We need to remember that if a cocoon is slit from the outside, the creature inside cannot survive. The butterfly needs the beating of its own wings as it makes an opening to make it strong enough to fly. We can only support, cheer.

Like two-year-olds, teens *are* in cocoons. They are not finished creatures. Are any of us? I think how long it took the birthday Monarchs to get to my trees—a long, difficult trek not yet complete—and I realize it is no different for my birthday teen. We are the plants where they grow, the trees where they rest before flying on. We are the roots; they are the wings.

Help us see past this unattractive but essential stage, Lord. Our kids are exquisite creatures within their cocoons. Give us patience for their seasons.

SEPTEMBER 17   Read Philippians 4:13.

SITTING IN THE BLEACHERS WITH a headache; standing in the rain on the soccer field; burning in the sun on the tennis court sidelines; applauding from first row in the audience: Mom, the cheerleader, a divine calling.

It's what we do best from the first days of our children's lives. It gets less convenient, though, by the time they're teens—especially if there's more than one to cheer on!

There was a time when I lived in my car and threatened to install a toothbrush holder for life between events. Once we were at an event, I confess I often debated: Would she notice if I left early? Would he realize if I were gone before the match ended? Would she miss me in the horde of fans? *Leave*, a voice inside me sometimes urged. *You've had a long day; the kids know you love them.* Then a wiser voice always said, *Stay, your presence is an "assumption" in lives where few things can be counted on.*

Besides being tiring, watching from this distance is hard. Not everyone plays fair with our kids; not everyone is as tolerant as we over missed balls, notes, or steps. How much easier it would be to run the plays, sing the lyrics, recite the lines for them! It is in the audience, in the cheering sections, were we realize—perhaps for the first time—that they must stand alone. What we teach from our spot is perseverance, rooted in a faith that says, "I can do all things through him who strengthens me" (Philippians 4:13)—even staying to the end. No matter the outcome or the score, they will see or hear us cheering their efforts.

Aren't our kids great, Lord? We hear you cheering with us. Help them to turn losing into learning, mistakes into experience.

SEPTEMBER 18   Read Colossians 3:20-21.

DON'T THINK OF AN ELEPHANT! Bet you did. *Don't think of a freshly cut lemon.* Bet your mouth watered.

Don't do this; *don't* do that. Say *don't* to kids—or to adults, for that matter—and so often they can't help but do whatever it is you don't want them to do. *Don't* simply doesn't compute in our wondrously made brains. Our loving Creator means us to find better ways to mold behavior than "thou shalt nots." Besides, look what happened in the garden of Eden!

As a writer, I love words—deciding which ones to choose, understanding what they mean, learning where they came from. Jesus' words, my favorites, are a model for parenting. He tells us to do something instead of saying *don't* do something else. For example, he said, "Go and sin no more," not *Don't* sin anymore." There's a big difference. And our words make a big, BIG difference when dealing with teens and issues such as cars, drugs, alcohol, sex, gangs, fashion, safety, and curfews. "Don't" draws a battle line in the sand, pitting us against them instead of against the issues.

Yet I confess I often preferred to say "Don't . . . " to my teens. It made me think I was in control of their choices, their safety. But my good motives in saying "Don't do this or that" always erected barriers that no simple apology could dismantle. We would find ourselves locked in a contest of wills where no one could win—that is, until I was led into finding the "do's" of life by One who understands how contrary teens can be when told "Don't."

Lord, help us to draw boundaries, not battle lines with our teens. May your words be our model.

SEPTEMBER 19   Read Song of Solomon 5:16*b*.

I WAS DRIVING LYNN HOME from gymnastics. My husband was en route with Rob to basketball and Beth to band. I squinted as I looked ahead. Yes, that was his car. We blinked our headlights at each other and then passed like ships in the night. Whether we blinked "SOS" or "I LOVE YOU" was hard to tell.

Few marriages are prepared for what happens when children "molt" into teens. Having been a single mother to this trio, I was worried even as I was grateful for this mate who gulped, shook himself like a wet dog, and then got on with life when my trio overflowed into *our* space. They required—and deserved—our time, cars, cash, energy, and focus. "What happened to the union that fuels this chaos of schedules and boomeranging personalities?" we seemed to be saying to each other as we blinked our headlights in passing.

Where was the "us"? Still there—waiting for a turn at the car, bathroom, hair dryer. Still there—waiting for a night out when we would agree not to utter our teens' names or concerns or do anything other than enjoy being the roots of the family tree.

Are you wondering where your "us" is? How about Saturday night? Blink once for "Yes."

Help us to retrieve the"us" that supports this family, God of love. As we cope with a "full" house, remind us of the empty nest ahead, a time to rebuild a love-nest just for us.

SEPTEMBER 20   Read Ephesians 4:28.

TWO WEEKEND PARTIES WERE raided. Some of the older teens were arrested; the young ones were released to parents for punishment. Fortunately, my trio was elsewhere.

My little temptations do not seem like temptations at all when compared with those facing teens. Even though the stakes are higher and graver for them than they ever were for us, sometimes they "blow it," yielding to peer pressure and temptation. We feel betrayed and frightened. Punishments leap to mind and anger spews from our mouths, proving we are more powerful than they—but not necessarily smarter.

Sometimes we need to be reminded that the punishment needs to fit the crime. Vandalism? Enlist them to do community service or clean up roadsides. Drinking and partying? Have them volunteer at rehab centers or shelters. Whatever the offense, we can provide a living consequence so that they see what can be done if their energy is refocused.

Doing something worthwhile as a consequence might last longer than spending angry days rebelling against an artificial punishment until its "sentence" runs out. Teens need to take the truths of consequences into the rest of their lives; may God inspire us to teach them.

Protect our teens from life-threatening consequences, Lord. Give us the skills to help them learn and the wisdom to help them bear their results.

SEPTEMBER 21 Read Colossians 1:9-10.

TO SNOOP OR NOT TO SNOOP? Hard question. Ditto eavesdropping. And are their rooms off limits? Did you know that some parents actually hire private detectives to trail their teenagers?

Our kids walk through treacherous times. Some days we are torn between fear and admiration. So, hey, anything goes, we reason. We should be able to do whatever it takes to keep our teens safe from hormonal gyrations, the seduction of chemicals, and the lure of "easy answers" or protection in gangs or cults. We have the right to pry into every nook and cranny of their rooms and lives, right? Hard question. One kid whose parents do pry asked me how I would feel if I were always searched, mistrusted, and spied upon. No question: I would feel violated.

Is ignorance bliss? I asked myself one day as I stood in the doorway to one of my teen's rooms. *Do I really want to know what thoughts are hidden in that journal? Am I willing to risk losing a mutual trust that has survived disagreements, tempers, and opinions? Not now*, I decided. I reserved the right to change my mind if I had "just cause" to snoop—which I didn't at the time.

Vague worries about teens in general didn't give me license to snoop on mine. Instead, I confessed my temptation to the kids and pledged my continued restraint. We talked again about why I worry; I heard again why I shouldn't worry. We sealed "boundary negotiations" over popcorn and rootbeer floats.

I knew my vigilance was needed as much as my trust, and my hair turned gray trying to balance them!

Keep us honest and trusting, Lord. Inspire our kids to be worthy of our trust.

SEPTEMBER 22 Read Matthew 7:20.

IN MY MEMORY I SEE A RAINBOW of confusion that spills from my laundry basket, littering the floor with mismatched personalities and tangled identities as I toil at my midnight task. Bright T-shirts wrestle with fading sports jerseys naming our aspirations, if not our accomplishments. *We wear ourselves on our sleeves,* I muse.

As the shirt goes, so goes the day with clues hidden between the lines, I think to myself. Earlier today, SAT test day, a wealth of "borrowed education" was represented on Rob's shoulders. "Princeton," it said—his stepdad's alma mater. The worn shirt inspires with the assurance of previous success: "If he did it, so can I."

"Children Should Be Heard *and* Believed" was the message that Lynn, an abused-children's advocate, wore last week.

Laundry's done; finally bedtime. I leave my youngest one's "Nobody's Perfect" shirt on top of the pile. Its message should be standard issue for all of us—both confession and assurance on a shirt!

Tomorrow I plan to nudge the kids closer to "perfection," I tell myself, *by reminding them of their promise to help more around the house.* After many more days of doing the laundry without any help, I'll be wearing the shirt they got me last Mother's Day: "When Mom Ain't Happy, Ain't Nobody Happy!" All of them can get that message. And if I let my shirt say it with a smile, all the better!

Lord, like our closets full of messages-on-shirts, we have a lot of choices—a lot to think about—as we decide who you call us to be. May our fruits be evidence of our wise choices.

SEPTEMBER 23　　　　Read Deuteronomy 30:15-20.

ONE OF ROB'S FRIENDS wouldn't come back to our house after one Friday night's discussion. What about? Smoking. You see, we are non-smokers; he was not. He thought he should be able to chain smoke any time, anywhere, despite our request that he smoke outdoors.

Like so many teens who believe they are exempt from the consequences of smoking, driving, driving crazy—you name it—he couldn't see what all the fuss was about. Standing on the porch with my angry, embarrassed son staunchly at his side, he was young enough to think smoking was a statement of his independence. I was old enough to see it as Russian roulette.

I never intended to be hard-nosed about "no smoking" in the house, and I never considered myself a "crusader," one of this young man's accusations. It just happened. It happened as I stood watching a tell-tale wisp of cigarette smoke rise from the graves of seven loved ones who literally suffocated—and left me. He couldn't yet understand what that is like.

How painful it is to honor others' right to choose—especially teens who are so sure and so intense about being sure—when we know their choices may lead to death rather than life.

You can't put an old head on young shoulders, Wise Counselor, but we would if we could—to spare them first-hand harm and second-hand grief. Help us find ways that won't alienate our independent teens.

SEPTEMBER 24   Read Ephesians 4:20-24.

IT WAS BILL-PAYING DAY. Anchoring the bills was the paperweight the kids and I had made years before when the hermit crab in our aquarium died.

I recalled the day as if it were yesterday. The kids were so young. As I plucked the lifeless body out of the water, antennae waved at me from a large shell on the "ocean" floor. It was our hermit; I was holding only his skin. Crabs, we learned, must move into larger shells to accommodate the growth of new skin or be suffocated. We plasticized the shed skin to make a paperweight as a reminder of God's wise provision.

My thoughts returned to the present as I turned the paperweight over in my hands. Its message never seemed more true than then, when I was scampering to keep up with three teens: change is good; change is necessary. *Dear crab,* I said to myself, *you did naturally what I fight: change or else.*

Our kids do it naturally too. They are compelled to go on

or suffocate—even from our love and worry, which also can suffocate us! Like the crab, clad only in new skin as he left his too-small shell to seek algae, they too are vulnerable to "sea creatures." Do we want them to be immobile like a paperweight, or growing as God intends? Maybe we can let go of worry by moving into new shells ourselves. Sometimes we are the ones running out of breathing room.

Remind us moms, creator Lord, that you are not finished with us either. Give us the courage to move on in response to your call.

SEPTEMBER 25   Read Philippians 2:1-5.

MY IRRITATION ROSE IN CRESCENDO to the music dancing through Rob's door. I knocked, then went in. After growing tired of waiting for me to do "one more thing" before coming in to chat and say good night, as was our custom, he had fallen asleep. The slumber erased all signs of his earlier tension. Lately stress seemed to be growing at the same rate as the barely visible fuzz that crisscrossed his upper lip. I sat for a minute in the creaky rocker I had refinished when I was pregnant with him. We had rocked through many a night since. Too bad we couldn't do it now, with the early teen years stretching if not severing our bond.

"You don't understand," he had shouted earlier in a voice sliding up and down the emotional scale. Suddenly I was stung as I recalled those were the very words I had flung at my own parents. My son was beginning *his* journey toward independence—not just "away from me."

Somewhere there's balance for us, I promised him silently, determined not to erect roadblocks in his path with mother-love gone sour. I realized the final distance needed between us would be shortened by the space I gave now. *What a leap of faith that will require*, I thought, *but surely no greater than when I first "rocked" him in this chair as a mother-in-waiting.*

Help us to step back, Lord, and give our teens space to breathe; help us to think more of their best interests than of our own selfish desires to hold on.

September 26   Read James 2:8.

A GLUM REFLECTION RETURNED my gaze in the mirror. Dark circles under my eyes; worry lines around my mouth. I looked like a bad caricature of who I wanted to be, who I knew God had created me to be. Where was the "real" Margaret Anne? Buried beneath dailiness that revolved around three busy teenagers. I was as misplaced as a stray sock under a bed.

"What shall I do?" I cried through tears during prayers that night. "Do something for yourself," was the answer; it came in a dream in which I was skiing down a mountain of laundry.

Wouldn't it be selfish of me to take my time and energy away from the others? No. Did I have an idea of who that "self" might be? Yes. So I took a night class in writing. Later I learned to make wreaths, bake bread, and weave baskets. Out of that valuing of myself came more than a few handmade items: My career as a writer evolved; my enjoyment as a mother returned; my sense of being a delightful child of God resurfaced; my ideas for outreach re-emerged. The kids surprised me: They loved seeing me do new things, and they helped it to happen! I was becoming more interesting, more outwardly focused.

Nurturing the roots ensures the greatest possibility for blossoms and fruit; so it is with us.

Remind us, Creator, that loving ourselves before we love others is a package deal.

September 27   Read Philippians 3:12-16.

THE FACE TELLS US BEFORE WORDS can: "No, I didn't make the team, get elected, win the prize." Bummer. Turning our teens' rejection into anything else seems impossible. They are so difficult to console: part little kid, part blustering, bluffing adolescent. Rejection slows them down like stones along a path, especially in these popularity-driven years. How fickle fame is, we long to explain; yet we know words can't ease the pain when our kids try and falter, if not fail.

"Try" is the triumph we need to help them see they've achieved. By trying, they've entered the race. Baseball hitters who make the most home runs also strike out a lot. Babe Ruth struck out 1,330 times, but he hit 714 home runs! Rejection and success is often a package deal, for God is so good at redemption—taking something useless and making it useful.

Perhaps we can help turn our teens' stumbling blocks into foundations for future success by asking, "You put forth great effort; how can that help you next time?"

Our kids are great even if they don't win, place, or show, aren't they, Lord? Help us to be supportive of their efforts, and keep us from overreacting when those efforts do not bring success. Help us to encourage our kids and ease the sting of rejection.

SEPTEMBER 28   Read Matthew 7:15-20.

CARDINALS ARE HARVESTING sunflower seeds from my gourd plants. How can this be? I stop writing to look closer. True or false: Gourds do not grow on sunflower stalks, and teens who misbehave do not come from good homes? *False.* Gourds twine up sunflower stalks—and even look like the same plant—and teens who misbehave often come from seemingly good homes.

Is the fault in the "soil"? Are our lives as confusing to our teens as gourds on sunflower stalks? Double standards confuse them just as my crazy plants confuse me. "Do as I say, not as I do," we sometimes say. Are we the "white-washed tombs" Jesus was speaking about (Matthew 23:25-28)? How many parents tell "little white lies" yet get angry when their teens do the same? How many parents fudge just a little on their taxes yet are accusative when their teens buy or "borrow" test answers? How many parents drink too much yet are shocked when their teens sneak booze? How many parents voice bigotry yet are horrified when their teens bash those who are different?

What role do we play in who our kids become? What effects do our choices have on the ones they make? When is life their responsibility? Two thoughts exist in my mind side by side, like gourds and sunflowers: "Each is accountable for his or her actions," and "Fruit does not fall far from the tree."

As we raise our teens to be responsible for their actions, we can scrutinize our own lives for contradictory messages—like gourds on sunflower stalks.

God of truth, make us worthy of being role models for our teens, who are looking for reasons not to falter. Keep us honest, for our teens can spot frauds a mile away.

SEPTEMBER 29   Read Romans 8:28.

6 ounces rose petals
1 ounce each lemon verbena leaves, crumbled bay leaves, dried orange peel, orris root
2 drops rose oil
2 drops lemon oil
6-inch cinnamon stick, crushed
Mix petals, leaves, and dry spices; add oils one drop at a time, mixing well. Seal in plastic bag for six weeks, shaking every other day.

TYPING WITH A BANDAGED THUMB is a challenge, but I've had other challenges—like raising three teens, working full time, and enjoying a busy marriage. I couldn't let the early frost tint my prize rose a faded brown; so I snipped it off, getting stabbed in the process. I added the petals to a basket of potpourri—"God's plenty," my thesaurus says. This rose and the potpourri I make from it are God's assurance to me of resiliency, and I sniff deeply from it each day.

A lanky tendril was the only plant thriving in my garden beside the home we built on a river bank—once a homestead and later a campground. Each time I saw it, I snipped it away. The weeds finally won, and for several years I never even noticed the plant. Then it bloomed: It was an old-fashioned rose, planted decades earlier. A bulldozer couldn't dislodge it; our house couldn't squash its roots; my clippers couldn't thwart it. Silly rose. Didn't it count the odds against its blooming? *Silly?* whispered a still, small Voice carried on the rose's fragrance. *See how it bends without breaking? See my hand always tending?*

No matter how stormy the days with our teens may be, God's hands blends them into a potpourri of enduring possibilities.

Thank you, God, for resiliency; for your steadying, stubborn hand on ours.

SEPTEMBER 30   Read Proverbs 11:1; 14:29.

I TRIP OVER MY TEENAGE GRANDSON'S baseball bat. Another of Aaron's items, his backpack, is on the table. B*eautiful, beautiful,* I say to myself as I survey the crowd of family gathered for our annual reunion. Despite my "neat-nik" tendencies I was led by a grace-giving God to raise kids practicing "healthy neglect"! As I eavesdrop on their adult conversations, I'm down-on-my-knees grateful that I learned to close the door on their teen messiness.

For the moment, ignore the present teen-driven chaos and imagine a family reunion ten years from now. What are your adult kids talking about? What are they remembering? Clothes piled on bedroom floors? Dining tables overflowing with papers and notebooks? Not likely. They may, however, recall wars fought *about* those things; they still may feel uneasy about Mom's rigid rules. Is this a memory worth making?

What do we have to gain by drawing battle lines over messy rooms when we could be building bridges over talk, activity, or play? It's not that chronic messiness is okay; tidiness just needs to be re-prioritized. We moms get to choose which we'd rather have ten years hence: "Housekeeper of the Year" award or memories of conversation shared with a suddenly talkative teen over cold pizza and warm soda—never mind dishes congealing in the sink and clothes mildewing in a corner.

Seize the moment, not the laundry basket or "duty roster." Messy rooms take care of themselves; it's our kids who need a mom's hand.

Teach us about priorities, Lord. Sometimes we're confused.

OCTOBER

LEARNING AND GROWING TOGETHER

Kay C. Gray

OCTOBER 1   **Read Isaiah 40:11-12; 66:6-13.**

EVERY CHILD NEEDS A MOTHER and father, not just for the conception but for all the growing up years. My sons, Hunter and Aaron, have grown up without the presence of a father; and I am so aware of what they have missed. I am also aware of what a unique part a mother offers her children.

In Isaiah 66:6-13, we read of God who loves us like a mother. For the Hebrews, Jerusalem was not just a city; it was the place of being with God. And from God, one would be nursed and satisfied, dandied on the knee, comforted. Fathers nurture their children, to be sure; but for mothers, nurturing is second nature. For us, it is painful *not* to nurture.

I'm not one to let the Bible fall open to a page and then search for a message, but one day I was delighted to find the message of Isaiah 40:11-12 in just that manner. In a time of great anxiety for Aaron, my youngest who's still at home, I happened on these words, taking special comfort from the last part: "and [God will] gently lead the mother sheep." Our God who mothers understands the needs of a mother.

God who mothers me, comfort me in the days when my "lamb" is beyond my holding. I do trust that you gather all your lambs in your arms. I claim this promise that you will also lead the mother sheep.

253

OCTOBER 2   Read Mark 13:32-37.

IF OUR HOUSE EVER CAUGHT on fire, I would grab the baby books. Not for the pictures of the locks of hair, but for the little quotes and comments I recorded when Hunter and Aaron were little. Why can't I remember them in my head? Why does Aaron recall experiences that I cannot even vaguely bring to mind? Perhaps part of the problem is that I wasn't really paying attention.

Distraction is one of my worst enemies. I treasure times when I can sit and talk with Aaron, who is so busy with his own life now. Yet often when he begins to relate an incident, I let my mind wander to the "to do" list or let my ear listen for the washing machine to quit running. I have amnesia about past experiences because many times I wasn't really there!

In this passage from Mark, Jesus admonishes us to be watchful. I firmly believe that Jesus comes to us in our neighbor, and sometimes our child is our neighbor. I believe I have missed Jesus many times by not paying attention to the moment. The slogans that promote "one day at a time" capture this same truth: God is only present in the present moment.

If we want to have the treasured memories of these days once they are past, we better start paying attention now!

God, there are so many wonderful experiences in the ordinary moments of my "nows." Teach me to let go of my habit of being distracted; teach me to focus, to watch, to be alert.

OCTOBER 3   Read Matthew 8:18-27.

UNDENIABLY, MOTHERING TEENAGERS keeps us confronted with change. In these verses from Matthew, Jesus describes his followers as people who are willing to stay with him in the midst of change. He describes change as "homelessness," having nowhere to lay your head; as having to move on even when there are loose ends to tie up, such as burying the dead; and as surviving the storm. Each of these descriptions is a metaphor for the feelings of crisis that adolescence brings as both mother and teen endure the changes.

With amazing timing, my first teenager, Hunter, was experiencing hormonal changes at the same time I was! Unexplained emotionalism and physical fluctuations were happening to both of us. We had the feeling of not being "at home" in our bodies! Our "loose ends" came in many forms: at school there were educational requirements, social adjustments, and transportation needs; at home there were schedule demands and new ways of relating to siblings. The storms were short but intense. Through the storms it was tempting to follow child psychologists or other parents of teens rather than follow Jesus—whom I wanted and needed to follow.

"Stay with me through all the changes," Jesus calls to us. Whatever those changes may be, Jesus promises us that he goes ahead of us to prepare a home (in a mansion!), that the loose ends will take care of themselves, and that the storms will be stilled.

Lord, the tempo of change seems to be increasing was I grow older. Sometimes it is frightening to be caught up in the changes of my child, who is now becoming an adult. Please, Jesus, still the storms.

OCTOBER 4   Read Ezekiel 36:26.

OUR EXPRESSIONS ABOUT HAVING A "hard heart" or being "softhearted" have some ancient foreshadowings in this passage from Ezekiel. Once when I endured a great loss, God changed my heart of stone to a heart of flesh.

When I was young, the news of a family whose baby had died made me reflect on this foolish question: How can *this* be such a loss? After all, they really didn't get to know that child. The grief of miscarriage was even more difficult for me to understand. I had no "heart" for their loss.

Then, in my twenty-sixth year of stony-hearted living, God gave me a heart of flesh. Six hours after I delivered a child following a normal, full-term pregnancy, he died. The loss was devastating. I wondered many times in the dark hole of grief if I would go crazy. Because he had a genetic flaw that affected almost every organ, life for him would have been agony. We really had more cause to feel grateful than sad, but it took a long time to feel that way.

From that day until now, my heart aches for the loss of any child, any miscarriage, any broken dream a parent had for a child who could not live. I understand now, with this heart of flesh, that a mother *needs* a child as much as she is needed by her child.

That same need for a child that we mothers have is behind the grief we feel when our teens pull away. We would not deny them growth, but it is still painful. The only way we can avoid the pain is with a heart of stone—and I never want that again. I'm grateful for my heart of flesh.

Thank you, God, for the lessons that are sometimes "heart breaking," because in due time they seem to give us more loving hearts. Give us strength that comes not from hardness, but from endurance as we rely on you.

OCTOBER 5   Read John 3:11-21.

"GOD SO LOVED THE WORLD that he gave his only Son" (John 3:16). It's a familiar passage, yet I really didn't "get it" until I found out that I couldn't sacrifice our dog, let alone my son, for a higher good.

We used to have a sheltie named Foxie. It was Hunter's job to feed Foxie and attend to her needs. It was important, I felt, for Hunter to learn responsibility. Once when Hunter stopped caring for Foxie's needs, I decided the way for him to learn the critical nature of fulfilling responsibilities was simply not to do the job for him. I announced that if he did not feed and water Foxie, she would die; and I would not intervene.

I wasn't able to stick to my resolve for more than a day. I loved that wise little critter as much as anybody. She "spoke" to me of her neglect with questioning eyes, and I just couldn't do it. I gave her what she needed to live.

As I read my Bible later that night, the words about God

loving the world so much and wanting to rescue us from our own failure to be "response-able" haunted me. If it broke my heart to see Foxie suffer from neglect, just imagine the grief that God must have felt when Jesus suffered and died. Yet God's love for us is great that he "gave his only Son" so that we might have everlasting life. I may have difficulty comprehending it, but I will never forget it!

God, the idea that you love us so much that you gave Jesus is so hard to take in. Let me never neglect the responsibilities you give me, lest Jesus somehow suffer all over again on my account.

OCTOBER 6   Read 1 Thessalonians 4:13-18.

THAT WE DO NOT "GRIEVE AS OTHERS do who have no hope" (1 Thessalonians 4:13) is a lesson I was reminded of when Foxie died. Foxie was a part of our life for ten years before she died. She was more than a pet to Hunter, who was then seventeen, because she had been the "new thing" God did in Hunter's life when he was dealing with the death of a baby brother. Though he didn't always take care of her as he should have, when she was dying, he was always there for her.

One morning before school, Hunter came through the kitchen with Foxie wrapped in a towel. She was limp, and her eyes had a vacant look. Hunter was taking her to the vet to conclude her life, which would have ended naturally if she had been living in the wild. I saw then how grown up Hunter had become. In the days to come, I also saw that the love Hunter had shared with Foxie did not end with her death. It lived on.

You see, Hunter has another dog now. His name is Simon, and Hunter says to him, "My bawddy," with a tenderness I know is a legacy of Foxie. As I watch Hunter with Simon, I am reminded of the unending nature of love. We who learn to love from Jesus do not grieve as others because we have the hope of this promise.

God of resurrection hope, thank you for your presence in the many losses of our lives and for the lasting gift of the "Foxies" who live on in us. Teach us to love even in the face of death, so that in those moments hope may over-come the fear that would rob us of love.

OCTOBER 7   Read Isaiah 52:7-12.

"*HOW BEAUTIFUL . . . ARE THE FEET* of the messenger . . . who brings good news" (Isaiah 52:7).

He left his shoes by the front door of our living room. Usually there are *two* pairs of shoes. I used to place them side-by-side neatly, but now I don't fuss anymore. The "good news" is that Aaron's feet have come home on time. The good news is that he has healthy feet (and all the rest too). Isn't it amazing that we bronze our children's shoes when they are little and then nag them when they are teenagers because they leave their shoes "lying around"?

Isaiah finds the messenger's feet beautiful because the people have been through a time of "ruins" and now the news is good. Sometimes it takes a "ruinous season" in our own family before we can put little irritations such as mis-placed shoes in proper perspective. I almost forgot the sweetness of Aaron's baby feet and how I loved to kiss him right behind the toes.

God has gone before us through some of the difficulties of the teen years and has been our "rear guard," as Isaiah expresses it. Having those klunky tennis shoes safe at home reminds me of this. Blessed are the shoes of the feet of the messenger of good news!

God, forgive me for my impatience and for my wrong priorities that keep me from recognizing blessings until I have almost lost them. Thank you for jour-neying ahead and behind us and for being the Good News in our daily lives.

OCTOBER 8   Read 1 Corinthians 10:23-31; 11:17-29.

ON THE WAY TO GRANDMA'S HOUSE when the boys were younger, we often played a game about "what we would have for dinner." By the time the boys were teenagers, they would get it right just about every time: pork chops, corn bread—the best, with white beans and catsup on top—macaroni and cheese, and salad with French dressing. It was the delicious expectation of the familiar, and it had special meaning for us: a place of love and security, a place where you could count on things.

In his first letter to the Corinthians, Paul speaks of the meaning of what we eat and how we eat. In chapter 11, he speaks specifically about the Lord's Supper. Isn't the idea of communion that we come to the table as family?

The family table is a model of the church gathered about the communion table. Perhaps the pork chops are too greasy and the folk kneeling beside us are too worldly, but it's still a safe place where everybody is loved and the morsels are wonderfully familiar.

I hope the experiences my sons have at the Lord's Supper are as comforting to them as supper at Grandma's. I like the idea of God setting the table of mercy and love for us!

Wise and loving God, I come to your table, sometimes with great joy and sometimes with a deep shame or hurt. How grateful I am that you welcome me with the steadfast comfort of Grandma's house.

OCTOBER 9   Read Isaiah 45:2-6.

THE DAY MY OLDEST SON, HUNTER, got his driver's license and drove off by himself for the first time, I leaned against the window of the back door and claimed his baptism!

Though Isaiah doesn't speak of baptism in this passage, it is in baptism that God calls an individual "by name." It is also the event in which we celebrate that the one being baptized belongs to God.

My sons are the great gifts that God has given me, and sometimes it is tempting to believe that they are *my* sons. But I know they really are God's sons. When they were infants, I had them baptized. A servant of God put the water on their heads and, in that moment, put the "call of God," the claim of God, on each of them.

Letting them go is painful. But when I remember that they have always belonged to God and, as Isaiah says, that God is with them "from the rising of the sun" and that there is no one besides God, I can let them go in peace.

Great God, besides you there is no other. With all mothers I rejoice that our teens are claimed by you and surrounded by your presence, no matter what road they take.

OCTOBER 10   Read Luke 12:13-21.

HAVING GROWN UP IN A FAMILY of comfortable means, it has not been easy for me to learn the lesson our Lord taught about greed in the parable of the rich fool. Because I never saw our family as rich, greed didn't seem to be a feasible temptation. It wasn't until I began the struggle of letting go of my sons that I really learned about greed.

My mother tried to teach me to enjoy life at whatever age I was—rather than wish I were older. It is a lesson I was slow to learn—both as a child and later as a mother myself.

When my boys were little and were learning each new laborious lesson, such as giving up the pacifier or learning to use the toilet or tying their shoes, I found myself wishing they were beyond that already. Now that they are older, I wish I could go back and have those toddlers on my lap again!

As they became very active teenagers, I could hardly wait for them to be able to drive themselves to their many activities and events. Now that the car is so very expensive and the nights until I see it pull in the drive are so agonizingly long, I pine for the days when I was the one doing the dropping off and picking up!

Do you suppose that discontent with the child we have now is a form of greed? Are we not rich to have this child, this teen, at this moment? Do we not make a mistake similar to the rich fool in Jesus' story by thinking that somehow this child is our possession to be perfected—and only then will we be content with him or her? Jesus says that when we make this mistake, we are not "rich toward God."

How rich we are when we remember that we can only meet God in the child who "is"—not in the child who "was" or the child who is still "to be."

O God, who meets me in this present moment, teach me to see you in my teen, now. Protect me from the spiritual temptations of mothering that lure me into sad reverie or expectant fantasy, leaving me "poor" in spirit.

OCTOBER 11   Read Ezekiel 34:17-22.

MY SON AARON IS A "LEAN SHEEP"—not only because of his lanky physical appearance but also because of his character. I admit that sometimes he's too quick to get into a fight, but he's always on the side of the "weaker" ones—helping them to defend themselves against the butting horns of the "fat sheep."

When Aaron was younger, he would spot a child playing alone and join him, helping to brighten the day for that child. Later when he would go on youth retreats and a new kid would be ignored or teased by the others, Aaron would be sure to sit beside him or her and bring the kid into his group of friends.

Aaron's move to a new school in the ninth grade was an eye-opening experience for him. Unlike the harmonious inter-racial experience of his previous school, he found this school to be cancerous with racial tension. He was stunned to be ridiculed for being friendly to black students—ridiculed even by some of the black students themselves. He came home one day and announced he had a new name: "Whigger."

Aaron had encountered the fat sheep. It was a painful reality to learn that trying to befriend others whose skin was a different color than his made him unpopular. After a while, he was tempted to join in with the "fouling of the water," as Ezekiel describes. One day he admitted, "Mom, I'm starting to think like some of these racist people." It was a difficult time for him, but I'm glad to say that he didn't contribute to the muddy water. The "fat" didn't stay with him.

Our teens are surrounded by "fat sheep," and sometimes they are tempted to become "fat sheep" themselves—perhaps to be accepted, to be cool, or to be "protected." Part of our responsibility as mothers is to help keep our teens "lean"—not weak and defenseless, but strong in love and integrity. Though we can't always protect them from harm, we know that they are always in the hands of the Good Shepherd.

Lord, it hurts when my teen is rejected or ridiculed. I wish the world were not such a mean place. Please give my teen the courage always to be loving.

OCTOBER 12   Read 2 Peter 1:1-11.

THIS IS A WONDERFUL PASSAGE about "doing right." It reminds us that it is in *response* to our precious faith that we seek to "escape from the corruption that is in the world because of lust."

It has never been easy for parents to teach morality to their children, but it seems even more complicated for us today in light of the negative influences of television, movies, and other media. Some parents feel the less said about sex, the better. But this passage reminds us that goodness is supported with knowledge, which is supported with self-control, and so forth. It is difficult for our teenagers to believe that waiting to have sex until they are in the committed relationship of marriage is best; it's even more difficult for them to actually wait. If it were easy, we would not find such an involved explanation of how to live out our faith in this second letter of Peter. Even so, teaching our teens about the goodness of sex as the supreme expression of "mutual affection," which is worth waiting for, is a far stronger approach than making threats about unwanted pregnancy or disease.

Though it hasn't been easy, my seventeen-year-old son

has learned to love his girlfriend, his first real love, with mutual caring. They have experienced a lot of pain and struggle, and I have been blessed to have shared some of that with them. Yet as they continue to struggle with the gift of sexuality, they are learning a lot about faith and God and what it means to live in response to faith rather than in fear of consequences.

Living "in response" seems to lead naturally to "doing right." It's a lesson worth passing on to our teens.

God, our humanity is such a gift and such a trial. Thank you for coming in the flesh and suffering in your humanity, so that we might see how it can be done with obedience and we might believe you are merciful with us when we fail. Help us to teach our teens how to live in response to faith, and help us to be merciful when they fail.

OCTOBER 13   Read Psalm 66.

MY SEVENTEEN-YEAR-OLD PROCLAIMS that the Constitution guarantees religious freedom. He should not be made to attend church, he says—to give "glorious praise" to God. I tell him the Constitution doesn't give you rights until you're eighteen; parents give rights until then. It is a puzzling question—parentally and spiritually: Should we require church attendance, like school attendance, of a minor child?

All his life Aaron has occupied a pew in church—and sometimes he has even worshiped! I suspect that is true for a lot of adults as well. Aaron is unusually honest, and he says he loves God but hates church. I'm sure many other moms have heard a similar protest.

Glorious praise is the sacrifice God desires from us. I can require a lot of my child, but I cannot *make* him praise God—that's between him and God. What I can do is pray about it and trust God to hold him close—even when he seems so far.

Amazing God, I love to praise you, but my teen does not right now. Please hold my teen close to you until the day when holy awe works its miracle and the praise just flows.

OCTOBER 14

FOR ME, ONE OF THE SCARIEST ASPECTS of parenting two teenage sons has been handling their defiance. As a single mom, I guess I have felt especially vulnerable when one of my towering sons has declared "I WILL NOT . . . " do whatever has been demanded of him. There are only a few immediate consequences one can levy, and the stakes for rebellion mushroom each year.

Changing another person is nearly impossible—that is, unless we use the methods Jesus used with Zacchaeus. By climbing up that tree to see Jesus, Zacchaeus disclosed that he was open to influence. On a few occasions, I have found such a "crack" in the stubbornness of one of my sons. There was the time one of them asked if I'd ever had a speeding ticket. And the time the other wanted to know, "Exactly what is fornication?" And the time one returned from a short period of withdrawal to his room with a little tone of contriteness in his voice.

Unfortunately, often I leap on such openings with a lecture or too many of my own stories. Jesus simply looked kindly at Zacchaeus and affirmed him. Gosh, what a change Zacchaeus underwent!

Just imagine what we might accomplish if we tried to be a little more like Jesus.

Loving and patient God, help me pay attention to the moment of learning when my teen "climbs up in the tree to see." And when my teen is open to seeing, let me first affirm. Thank you for the love you have shown me when I wasn't too stubborn to learn!

OCTOBER 15

Read 1 Samuel 2:12-14.

ELI HAD BEEN A FAITHFUL PRIEST of God, until he had sons. When they took advantage of opportunities to take from what belonged to God, Eli couldn't bring himself to discipline them or deny them. It's a difficult choice for any parent.

Whatever their age, we are often tempted to indulge our children. Like Eli, we have to make ongoing choices. Will we give our teens an allowance or require them to earn their own spending money? Will we deny them their last years of "freedom" before they enter the rigors of adult responsibility? Will we be faithful to giving our tithe to God and therefore having less money available for the endless needs and wants of our teens?

Withholding from God what belongs to God is very much like stealing from the offerings of God's people, which is what was happening in the time of Samuel. When we fail to teach our teens the challenging lesson that self-denial is a part of earning and using money wisely, we are "cutting off their strength."

It's not an easy lesson—for them or for us.

God, you have promised to provide all that we need. Forgive our lack of trust and our inability to teach our teens the hard lessons about the limits of resources. Please teach us, so that we can teach them.

OCTOBER 16   Read Luke 8:49-56.

AARON WEARS AN APRON AND A BUTTON that advertises a big piece of pie. He's a waiter, making good tips as he stands on his feet with very little rest for eight to nine hours at a time.

One day he said he wasn't feeling well and he couldn't go to work. It was only his first week on the job. Being fairly sure that he was only feeling the aches and pains of adjusting to the physical strain, I insisted he go on to work. I later wondered if my workaholic tendencies were expecting too much of him.

Late that night my weary son returned, having stuck it out the entire shift. He reported that once he was there, he got busy and didn't feel any aches or pains the entire night. I think he was "healed" by his mother's confidence, which assured him that he would be all right.

Healing is a mysterious part of our faith. When Jairus

returned home and heard the report that his daughter was dead, the confidence he had had in Jesus when first asking for her to be healed was shaken. Then Jesus gave assurance, but "they" laughed at him for saying she was only asleep. Did Jairus laugh too? We will never know, but I do know that it was Jesus' power that made her well. And I believe that having confidence in Jesus, even when we feel like laughing cynically inside, enables us to give comfort to our children when they are ill and to allow healing to take place in our own bodies.

One thing I've learned as a mother: Fear sure doesn't do anything for healing!

Mighty God, you have made us, and in our sickness you can remake us. Grant me trust in you, that in the hours of illness neither me nor my teen will add fear to the struggle toward healing.

OCTOBER 17   Read Psalm 71:17-19; Amos 8:9-10.

BOTH OF THESE PASSAGES SUGGEST the meaning of hair on one's head as a marker of identity and relationship with God. In Psalm 71, gray hairs are a reminder of how long the journey with God has been. In the eighth chapter of Amos, a bald head is a consequence of great difficulty and mourning— almost a punishment.

Hair certainly has been a major source of "identity crisis" for my sons. During the dozen years that I have watched them proceed through adolescence, I have seen no fewer than two dozen hairstyles between them. We have been through the "tail," the frizzy look, the straight hair over the eyes, the ponytail, the shaved head, and the "cap look"— which looks more like an acorn, if you ask me. It has all been an experiment with identity.

Though it hasn't always been easy, I have never interfered with their choices of hairstyle. In my mid-forties I began to lose some of my own hair, and I experienced firsthand how very important hair is to our identity. I decided this was one fairly harmless area where I could give them some room to experiment—and another way to show them I love them for who they are, not what they look like.

Jesus chose to describe how precious and uniquely loved by God we are through the metaphor of hair: "Even the hairs of your head are all counted" (Matthew 10:30). Say no more!

Lord, forgive our impatience with our teens' strange hairstyles. Give us the wisdom to look beyond their outward appearance and see them as you see them.

OCTOBER 18   Read Colossians 3:12-17.

NEVER HAVE I MET A MOTHER of a teenager who did not pray for patience. In fact, I've never met one who claimed to *be* patient! But I think I have learned a little about patience from this great gift and challenge of motherhood.

Life is filled with waiting. We wait for grades to be announced, health reports to come back, our turn to come at the bank and the grocery store and the vehicle emissions testing site and many other places. And we wait for our half-child, half-adult teens to "get some sense." Waiting with *patience*, however, is living the faith that God's timing is best.

During pregnancy, it's easy to become impatient with the nine months, yet it is clear how very important it is to wait for the time to be right. In the same way, insisting that our teens learn behaviors and develop skills according to our timing can be as destructive as insisting that a baby be delivered prematurely.

As I have tried to teach my sons, *with patience*, how to keep their rooms straight and why it's important to do chores without reminders and to save money for important purchases, I have learned a few clues. One is to turn my attention to something else rather than become obsessed about whatever it is I wish could be done at once. Second is to review how much weight this particular issue really deserves and keep my priorities in mind. And third is to trust in God's timing by believing that God may be able to see that another learning must first take place before the particular one we desire for our teens.

It's amazing how our impatience disappears when we truly believe that God's timing is best!

My patient heavenly Parent, I like that saying, "Be patient with me; God isn't finished with me yet!" Remind me now—and often—that you are not finished with my teen either!

OCTOBER 19   Read Matthew 10:16-31.

KNOWING YOUR CHILD HAS USED illegal drugs is like knowing your child is a sheep in the midst of wolves. It is such a mixture of shock and disbelief to think that this could happen to *your* child; it is a feeling of overwhelming helplessness.

I know because I've been there. The wisdom of Al-Anon points us parents back into the arms of God, the Higher Power. It's not always easy to trust in God in such difficult times—times when our teens seem to be "rising against us"—yet we try to hold on, to endure, to trust.

When our children become adolescents, they become more and more out of our sphere of "control" and even our influence—particularly after they have the freedom that comes with a driver's license. Sometimes they stray too far and make destructive choices. In those nightmarish days and nights of helplessness, one of the faith questions that grabs a parent's gut is "Does God *really* care about this child of mine who has messed up?" In other words, "Has God turned away from this child, from whom I will never turn away?"

The answer I found is in the tenth chapter of Matthew, verse 29: "Not one of them will fall to the ground apart from your Father." Those are comforting words for every parent, whatever your worry or fear may be.

God who has never turned away from me or my child, please keep in your mighty care my sparrow who has "fallen to the ground." Help me to release my child to your care, and take away this destructive fear that has gripped my world.

OCTOBER 20   Read Proverbs 4:23-27.

I HAVE ALWAYS TRIED TO DISCIPLINE according to the seriousness of the offense, and lying has been a major infraction in our house.

When Aaron was in ninth grade, he told me he had started smoking. It was a hard truth to hear, but still it was the truth. Later when I learned that smoking pot had become part of the deal, I was again devastated by hearing the truth. Now we have come through a season of nightmares, and I think a large part of the journey toward recovery has been the practice of trying to live truthfully.

Proverbs reminds us to "put away . . . crooked speech" (4:24). It's hard to get back on a straight path if our thoughts and words are crooked. I think God was able to bring Aaron so far along the recovery journey in such a short time because Aaron was willing to be honest with himself. He was able to see, as I was, how lost in confusion and depression we both were because he had been living the illusion, the lie, that "this drug stuff makes me happy."

Often we find ourselves lying in order to avoid pain. We all do it, whether we're fifteen or forty or eighty. My own family's experience of coming to a time of "turning the foot away from evil" taught us, again, that truth-telling may be painful; but it is the way to real happiness. It is the way out of shaky, crooked living.

God, you have taught us that you are Truth and that the truth will make us free. Whenever I choose to avoid pain by speaking "crooked words," give me courage to name the truth and claim the recovery of the sure path, which is your way of freedom.

OCTOBER 21   Read Psalm 42:1-3; 126.

I CRIED ENDLESS NIGHTS OF DESPAIR after Aaron confessed to using illegal drugs and to not wanting to quit. He did not shed a tear. Then, on his own initiative, he called his grandparents to make his confession to them. When he hung up the phone, he sobbed: "I've let them down! I am such a disappointment to them!"

There are times in our lives when it is profoundly true: Our "tears have been [our] food day and night" (Psalm 42:3a). This kind of sobbing seems like an endless night. But our God is faithful, and we can claim the promise of Psalm 126: "Those who go out weeping, bearing the seed for sowing, shall come home with shouts of joy" (v. 6).

My parents were tireless in giving encouragement and love to Aaron during this terrible ordeal. They called him long distance, faithfully, to assure him of their love. Many times they did not even talk to me, which emphasized to him that *he* was their concern—this one who had disappointed them.

Today their relationship is stronger than ever. In some ways my parents have more faith in Aaron now than they did before, because he was straight with them, willing to cry the tears. Truly God has turned our tears into shouts of joy.

O God, sooner or later we all experience a time when our tears seem to be our food day and night. It is an unforgettable season in the experience of mothering. But even more amazing is the joy that you bring after the tears. When days of mourning come again, let my memory sustain my faith.

OCTOBER 22   Read Isaiah 1:2-6, 12-17.

THE FIRST PART OF THIS PASSAGE sounds so familiar: "I reared children and brought them up, but they have rebelled against me" (v. 2). I know just how the Lord feels when making this complaint. The indignity, the unfairness, the ungratefulness of children who turn against the one who has stood by them and provided for them and nursed them through their illnesses. Yeah, you tell 'em, Lord!

As I continue, reading about burnt offerings and trampling in God's courts, it occurs to me that the Lord is not speaking about my sons. *I am the rebellious one!* I am eager to make solemn vows and offer all kinds of bargains with God when my sons are in trouble. The solution to this rebellion, offered by our wise God, is doing for others.

I once read in a psychology book the theory that modern teens are deprived of the satisfaction of meaningful work. Whether or not this is true,I have found it to be true that meaningful work brings great satisfaction to my two sons.

Sometimes when I have been at odds with my sons and I have been unable to find a "connection," I have urged them to take part in some project or effort for someone else. It has always been a real changing point for them. It has reminded them of their gifts. It has given them the satisfaction of helping to bring joy to someone else. It has called them outside of self-centeredness.

It works for moms too!

Merciful God, I know that you do not seek to punish me but to love me. Forgive my stubbornness and disobedience. Remind me that my rebellion is as painful to you as my teen's rebellion is to me.

OCTOBER 23　　　　　　　Read Genesis 22:1-19.

THE FAMILIAR STORY OF ABRAHAM'S obedience to God in offering to sacrifice his son, Isaac, is profoundly meaningful to me now that Hunter, my firstborn, has left home. The day he drove off for his first year of college will forever be etched in my mind. Aaron and I stood outside the restaurant where we had had a special "last meal" together. Our "Isaac" slowly drove out of the parking lot and proceeded down the street where we had one long last look at him—and he at us. He never really came home again. He made his home in the city where he went to school. Letting him go felt like having to put a dagger in him—or in me.

I always thought that this story in Genesis was about Abraham's faith; that it was for Abraham's sake that God demanded the sacrifice of his son, for it would save Abraham from idolizing this longed-for child who had finally been born to him in his later years. But now I see that it was also for Isaac's sake.

A loving parent is tempted to let a child become "everything" in life, but no mortal can take the place of God. It *is* a great sacrifice to let a child go. In fact, it is one of the greatest gifts we can give them—and ourselves.

I have come to see that Hunter's ability to make a home for himself expresses a significant lesson that I helped teach him. How good it is to know that he can make a home in this world without needing me to make it for him. It means that I am not god for him—just as he is not god for me. I can rejoice with Abraham that my son is spared the destruction of a clinging parent.

Loving God, you seem to ask so much sometimes. You gift us with a child, let that child grow in us, and then tear the child away. I am so thankful that you have not left me to my idolatrous temptations to let this child take your place. Only you are God; my child has simply been a gift on loan from you. A good gift. Thank you.

OCTOBER 24   Read 2 Corinthians 4:7-18.

"WE HAVE THIS TREASURE IN CLAY JARS" (2 Corinthians 4:7), this treasure of life, in such fragile, wonderful bodies.

As I stood beside him in the emergency room, I watched the pain on Hunter's face from a soccer injury and heard the initial diagnosis of a split kidney. I berated myself for letting him play soccer—especially the position of goalkeeper. He was vulnerable to this kind of injury because of his fearless dives to stop the ball at the point of an opponent's striking foot.

Paul reminds us in his second letter to the Corinthians that "while we live, we are always being given up to death for Jesus' sake, so that the life of Jesus may be made visible in our mortal flesh" (4:11). In no way do I compare soccer playing to the life of Christ. But I do believe that Jesus calls us to live fully, not fearfully.

It would be easy for us to restrict our teens from activities that involve some risk, but that would be living for mom's sake—not for Jesus' sake. Little "deaths," little losses, are a regular part of life. We cannot prevent the scary moments, such as trips to the emergency room with our teens. We can only be with them when they suffer and remind them that it *is* a "momentary affliction."

I believe it is in those scary experiences that we are given eyes to see the unseen presence of the eternal in our midst.

Gracious God, for all your gifts of healing, and for your protection, I give you thanks. Through all the "little deaths," the afflictions, I am profoundly awed that you are always with us. Help me to be prepared to give others what they need when they experience the "clayness" of life—especially my teen.

OCTOBER 25   Read 1 John 4:7-21.

LOVING ONE ANOTHER IS HOW we know God. I've always said that my greatest source of God's revelation to me is through my sons, Hunter and Aaron. When each of them was born, I was overwhelmed with love—astounded at the depths of love that I felt as never before.

This letter of John, however, makes it clear that love is not just a feeling; nor is it something we have. Rather, it is a *process* that is perfected. There are some hard standards of love in this passage: having no fear (Even when our teens are working past midnight? Even when our teens enlist in the service?) and loving out of our confession of Jesus.

I think God gives us children so that we can learn how to love, and loving teenagers is the graduate level of that education! Clearly, the kind of love that involves confessing Jesus as Lord means that we love our sons and daughters the way that Jesus does.

When Hunter chose the profession of coaching soccer, I groaned. He will never have a very good salary, I thought. He will no doubt end up in a different part of the country from me, where soccer is more popular. On and on went my list of protests. But that was not showing my love for him. If coaching soccer will be fulfilling to him, I realized, then that is exactly what I must want him to do.

Letting Hunter be who God has made him to be—not made in my image of what I think he should be—comes closer to the kind of love John describes. I believe God loves me that way. And I can see God a little more clearly in this kind of loving that turns loose.

God who has given me the freedom to be me, grant me the wisdom to love my teen with that same freedom to be the individual you have created. Teach me day by day how to love. Thank you for loving me.

OCTOBER 26 — Read Psalm 63.

THIS IS ONE OF MY FAVORITE PSALMS, because it seems like troubles are always worse at night. A sick child always runs the highest fever at night. Sirens warning of a terrible wreck are more frequent after dark. A loved one who is running late only frightens us at night.

When I find myself obsessively pondering a concern about Aaron, it is usually in the dark, in the bed, when I should be sleeping. I go over and over my thoughts and fears, and I just cannot go to sleep. The trouble is that I have no other perspective, no glimpse or thought of hope, because I have become fixed on just one part of the situation.

Praying this psalm, or parts of it, has been the miraculous end to that defeating cycle for me. "When I think of you on my bed, and meditate on you in the watches of the night," writes the psalmist, ". . . I sing for joy" (v. 6, 7). We often discount some of the psalms, thinking that we have no real enemies. Yet anything or anyone that robs us of joy is an enemy. Sometimes it is even ourselves.

It is a rewarding treasure to memorize these verses, so that when we cannot find a way out of the darkness, we will have the words to get us back on track with God.

O God, you are my God, I seek you, my soul thirsts for you; my flesh faints for you, as in a dry and weary land where there is no water (Psalm 63:1).

OCTOBER 27 — Read Ezekiel 33:1-11.

MY FRIEND'S DAUGHTER—LINDY, I will call her—is nineteen. She has made some choices that have brought difficult consequences, but she's seeking help with all her energy. Now in a recovery facility where she is so very vulnerable, she is being sexually harassed. Clearly she needs to find her own way and to make some tough choices to correct the mistakes that have so muddled her life. Letting her go has, no doubt, been very hard for her mother.

But Lindy also needs help. Others in authority need to be warned of the sexual harassment she is experiencing. She needs help protesting and warning—not only on her own behalf, but also on behalf of other vulnerable young women at that place. She needs a sentinel.

Ezekiel describes the requirement God makes of all of us to be "sentinels." We mothers seem to be especially good at it. From the time our children are born, we are protecting them, watching out for them. As they grow, we learn that often obedience to God in parenting means "hands off," keep the mouth shut—particularly in the later teen years. But now and again, they still need our protection. The key is to keep watch, pay attention, so that we will know what form of obedience to God is needed.

That's what a sentinel—and a mother—is: One who keeps watch.

God, give me a watchful eye to recognize when I must not interfere and when I must speak on behalf of my vulnerable teens. As you call me to be a sentinel, give me courage and boldness.

OCTOBER 28   Read Matthew 13:24-30.

THIS WAS ONCE A VERY PUZZLING parable to me. Why would Jesus suggest letting an obvious "wrong" continue to grow? Why not "nip it in the bud," as my mother used to say? It has become clearer to me as I have struggled with how to discipline my sons. Some behaviors and decisions they have made have been very displeasing to me—such as smoking and spending a large amount of savings for an amplified base system for the car.

Even more of a struggle has been my decision to never intrude on their privacy. I have never searched their rooms or read their letters or journals or listened in on private conversations with friends. I think there are some weeds that have to be left alone, because removing them would also destroy the wheat.

I am not sure that I have always been right about my choices of discipline, but I am sure that there are many instances when we have to consider long-term consequences as more significant than short-term solutions.

Jesus was interested in the wheat, not discipline for discipline's sake, and so am I. I have always liked to think of my children "growing like wheat" instead of "growing like weeds."

God, the requirements of a disciplinarian are so very difficult. They call for so much stamina and endurance and, most of all, wisdom. Let me never destroy the person that my teen is becoming by trying to correct a behavior.

OCTOBER 29   Read Mark 6:30-32.

THE COMMANDMENT TO REMEMBER the Sabbath is a reminder of our need for times of rest. In this passage from Mark, Jesus is taking a "rest break."

Our children have done it naturally all their lives, and we have often overlooked the importance of it. When they were little, they would sometimes just sit down where they were playing and rest. Now that they are experiencing the growth spurts of adolescence, they have developed a keen desire to lie around and read or watch TV. Sometimes they are avoiding an unpleasant task. Sometimes, though, they are meeting their need for rest.

The demands of mothering sometimes speak a demonic word: Don't stop; don't rest for a moment; there is too much to do to ever be idle. Many of us feel that we must always be "accomplishing" something. Part of the Sabbath rest, however, is taking time to "just be." Our teens set a good example. I think part of the reason they spend so much time on the telephone is that they need to "just be" with friends—to rest from competing and performing and testing their skills.

We are "coming away to a deserted place" now, as we spend time in meditation and prayer. It is an important way to avoid "coming apart."

God of power and peace, be with me in silence for a while. Let me know the touch of your sweet presence, renewing me in these few moments of rest.

OCTOBER 30

Read Revelation 22:1-5;
John 7:37-39.

THESE ARE JUST TWO OF MANY passages in the Bible that use the image of the river as life-giving living water. For my family, the river is a place to ski or go fishing; it isn't essential. If we lived in the desert region of the biblical waters, however, the river would have the same critical meaning for our lives as it did for them. In our day, perhaps the image of a communication network is comparable to the river image of the Bible. Today our lives are as endangered by chaos and complexity as the ancient world was by the threat of drought.

One of the requirements I have stressed over the years has been for my sons to let me know where they are. When Aaron comes home at night from work, he wakes me up to let me know he is home—even if he is coming in very late. On a very basic level, staying in touch with our children's whereabouts is essential to our own peace of mind. On a deeper level, staying in touch with what's happening in their lives is essential to a healthy relationship with our teens. Our "communication network" with our teens is like a river in the desert. Without it, our relationship can wither up and die.

Try reading the passage from John, substituting the word *communication* for *water:* "Out of the believer's heart shall flow rivers of living *communication.*" No misunderstandings; only the thoughtful sharing of information. That I can relate to! Likewise, if in the passage from Revelation the river flowing from the throne of God is a river of information and complete comprehension, I feel much more secure. Since Jesus is the fleshly expression of God communicating with us—the "Word made flesh" (John 1:14), I don't think this too much of a stretch!

Holy God, you are pure thought-and-heart communication. If only I will listen to you, I will hear truth and perhaps learn to speak clearly. Be a spring of truth in me so that as I communicate with my teen—and with others—there will be more clarity and more life-giving sharing.

OCTOBER 31   Read Romans 8:9-11.

IN THIS PASSAGE, PAUL SPEAKS of the flesh and spirit in separate terms, and that is hard for us to live when we are attempting to put life together! But on this Eve of All Saints Day, when we are focused on remembering beloved ones who have died, it has rich meaning for us. For those of us who have lost a child or a parent or a very close friend, there is an emptiness of "the flesh" that can hardly ever be filled again. In fact, it is such a painful emptiness that it is tempting to simply refuse to think about that person.

If we remember only the "flesh" experience of the one for whom we grieve, we ourselves are living in a deadness that robs us of the life God would have us know through Jesus dwelling in us. Paul says it like this: "Life to your mortal bodies also through his Spirit that dwells in you" (v. 11). It is helpful to separate the physical from the spiritual on this All Saints' Eve in order to celebrate the gift of those who live now in eternity with God. The "body dead to sin" is not just a consequence of sinful acts, but also of dwelling in the half-truth that fleshly life is all we have.

Let us prepare for an honest celebration tomorrow of the *whole* gift of the saints in our lives: the sweet memories of their life in the flesh, now over in death, and their life in the spirit, alive again with God.

Ever living God, we cannot fully understand your resurrection plan, but you do not call us to understand; only to believe. As we recall beloved ones who are now dead, help us claim the life of spirit, which always is alive with you.

NOVEMBER

A SEASON OF THANKFULNESS

LaDonna Meinders

NOVEMBER 1   Read Psalm 8.

SEVERAL DAYS AGO, I NOTICED how drab and bare the trees in our backyard had become. With autumn in full gear, the leaves have already changed color and fallen to the ground, and the bleakness momentarily depressed me. Suddenly, one of the trees was alive with color and movement as a dozen bluebirds flitted merrily through the brown branches. Never was a Christmas tree more gaily decorated! This "miracle" spoke to me powerfully as I realized how God continually manifests himself in our lives. Out of chaos God brings order, out of despair, hope; and from seemingly dead branches, God surprises us with joy and life.

Like the bare tree, we mothers sometimes feel stripped of energy, enthusiasm, and inspiration. Sometimes we are lonely, feeling separated from our children and from friends. At times it may seem that even God has abandoned us, but we know that he never will. When we are most in need of reassurance, God surprises us with joy and hope if we will only trust him.

Dear Heavenly Father, who cares for the tiny bluebird and for me, help me see your love and goodness in the world. Help me remember, even when the day is bleak and you seem far away, that you love me and want to bless me. Thank you for the beauty all around me—beauty that sometimes hides in bare trees.

NOVEMBER 2   Read Philippians 4:8-9.

A PHRASE WE FREQUENTLY HEAR from teenagers is "get real!" Sometimes slang is more than just a "cool" way of talking. "Get real" has profound implications in our society with its superficiality and materialism.

When our children were little, they were models of simple truthfulness. Words they blurted out in front of company sometimes embarrassed us. Though they may shield vulnerable feelings in the casual wrap of indifference once they became teens, they search for truth as they determine their adult values and build relationships with others.

Today I will try to be *real* in everything I say and do. I will seek to be genuine spiritually, in my relationship to God. Then I will take care to be real with others, not speaking flippantly but with truth and meaning in what I say. Finally, I will "get real" with myself, following my best impulses as the Holy Spirit leads me.

Am I worthy to be a role model? Of course not. I don't deserve all of the blessings for which I'm thankful in this season. But, with God's help, my life and example can be positive and *real*.

Dear God, I know you are the source of all truth. Teach me and lead me, that my life will be honorable, just, and pure—an example to my children.

NOVEMBER 3   Read Ecclesiastes 3:1-11.

WHEN OUR SEVENTEEN-YEAR-OLD daughter, Lori, who was attending school in England, came home on break, we were so excited to see her. Obviously her plans centered around catching up on visiting with her father and me, right? Wrong! From the first moment at the airport until the time for her departure, her days were filled with sleeping late, appointments, and social activities. I felt hurt, even angry.

We know that we must give our children both roots and wings. Sometimes I think the roots are easier to deal with: teaching manners, helping them cope with problems, teaching them values, taking them to church—these things make us feel important and give a great deal of meaning to our lives. But the wings? This is harder. We must let go. We must trust our young to fly, giving them the space and the time to *become*. Our children still need our love, our care, our trust in them—even an occasional shoulder to lean on. But when the time comes, we must give thanks for their God-given individuality, step back, and watch them soar.

Dear Lord, I feel disappointed when I am left out of my children's lives. Give me strength and wisdom to let them grow up as you planned, and help me realize that this, too, is beautiful in its time.

NOVEMBER 4   Read Romans 5:3-5.

WHEN MY SON JOHN WAS a senior in high school, he and a friend tried out for the cheerleading team. In our town, sports was king and boys were "macho." No male had ever even thought of cheerleading there before!

John and his friend Doug practiced hard and learned some impressive acrobatic routines, so I wasn't surprised when they were named to the cheerleading team. What did surprise me, however, was the storm of protest that arose afterward. Ugly rumors spread through the school that were painful for my son and our family.

John has never been a quitter, but after his automobile tires were cut in the school parking lot, I suggested he give up cheerleading. He looked at me and said, "Mom, I can't quit. I started this, and I've got to stay with it." Although I admired his tenacity, I must admit there was a big lump in my throat! Being the object of ridicule and hate was eye-opening; John learned how it feels to be in the minority. He gained a certain comfort level just by enduring and a surprising sense of liberation.

Our teenagers feel pressure to be accepted and to be like everybody else. Breaking the mold takes courage; it can be frightening and lonely. What can we do? We can pray with our children, and offer our unconditional love. Also, we can remember that being a teenager is sometimes a very difficult experience.

Dear Lord, help our teens grow through their suffering to develop endurance, character, and hope.

NOVEMBER 5   Read Proverbs 8:10-11.

WHEN LORI WAS ABOUT THIRTEEN, she and a friend stopped after school at a classmate's house. A short time later, Lori telephoned and asked if she could spend the night. This was a school night, when overnights normally were not permitted; but Lori was a good student and I agreed to let her stay. Minutes later, she breezed in with friends to pick up her things, and I didn't see her again until after school the next day. Imagine my surprise when she told me she hadn't really wanted to stay. She fully expected that Mom would say no and she could come on home without offending her friends.

I wonder how often our teenagers come to us with requests (often of a far more serious nature) that they hope, deep down in their hearts, we will answer with a resounding "NO!" Sometimes we lose sight of our parental responsibility and slip into the all-too-easy trap of thinking our duty is just to make them happy.

Our children rely on us to provide the boundaries that help them feel secure—even though this is the last thing they appear to want!

Dear Father, I pray for wisdom and insight. Help me to know when to say yes and when to say no. In this season of Thanksgiving, I thank you for the children you have given me to nurture and love.

NOVEMBER 6   Read Luke 6:39-42.

A FEW NIGHTS AGO, JUST BEFORE falling asleep, I went through my usual prayer litany . . . naming my loved ones and asking God to bless them. Then (just so God would have all the information!) I proceeded to mention areas where I thought my husband and children needed to improve. Suddenly, a lightbulb turned on in my head and these words came to me: *Start with yourself!* Isn't it wonderful how the Holy Spirit works in the quiet little moments of our lives? All at once I realized, right then and there, that I needed to confess my own weaknesses first and seek God's guidance in overcoming them.

Part of our role as parents is to make judgments about what our children are doing. Yet, how easy it would be to overlook our own thoughts and actions, letting little habits creep in that could create a discrepancy between what we do and what we teach our children.

This month, as I thank God for all that he has given our family, I am going to be less judgmental and more careful to keep my own eyes clear of "specks" so that I can lovingly and wisely help others.

Dear Lord, the thoughts you send us are like precious gifts. Help me start with myself in becoming the person you want me to be so that I may see clearly to help my children.

NOVEMBER 7   Read Proverbs 12:18.

A FAMILY WAS ON VACATION. After weeks of planning, they were in a fishing boat on a beautiful lake where the children cast their lines and waited expectantly. A tug on the line meant great excitement as the father helped the oldest boy, almost thirteen, reel in a nice fish. Putting the slippery, flopping fish into the boy's hands, the father removed the hook. Just as he did so, the fish gave a final wriggle and slipped from the boy's hands back into the lake!

"How can you be so clumsy?" the father exclaimed angrily, and suddenly the joyous outing was not very much fun.

Our teenagers, whether boys or girls, have tender feelings they sometimes hide under a careless bravado. Egos are fragile as new identities are being formed and new challenges faced. Words flung out in a moment's anger can hurt as surely as a blow. In spite of the old saying that words can't break bones, they *can* break hearts.

In this month of thanksgiving, I will be thankful and appreciative. I will control my tongue when I am about to say something that might hurt someone so that I may build up and not tear down.

Lord, help me never to be reckless in my speech, but always slow to anger, thoughtful and wise, that my words might bring healing.

NOVEMBER 8   Read Psalm 51:6.

A *FRIEND OF MINE, WHO IS* a minister, told of having lunch with his four-year-old grandson. The conversation had gone like this:

"I love you, Keegan."

"I love you too, Grandpa, but not all the time."

"Well, I love you all the time, Keegan."

"I don't. Sometimes I love you and sometimes I don't."

This is a great example of how painfully truthful children can be! Our teenagers, when they were small, went through the same phase when they were completely transparent and open. Then the myriad influences of growing up began to make them more "sophisticated," and they lost the childlike openness that is so adorable—and sometimes so frustrating!

We want our children to be honest. But do we allow them to express thoughts without judging or condemning? And most important, *are we honest with them?*

At age four, Keegan's world is uncluttered by guile or deceit. He doesn't worry what someone might think. In the teen years, what others think becomes very important. When we encourage a truthful exchange of ideas—a two-way street—we help our children build integrity.

Dear Heavenly Father, I know that you love me all the time, even when I am unlovable or forget about loving you. Help me to be honest with my children so that they may build trust and truthfulness.

November 9   Read Colossians 3:23-24.

I GUESS WE'VE ALL BEEN THERE: when it seems we spend most of our time driving our kids from one event to another. Between school activities, piano or dance lessons, soccer practice and you-name-it, we get little done except play chauffeur for the family!

Isn't it funny how the same teenagers who have absolutely nothing to say at home can talk non-stop when their friends are around? I've learned it can be a good time to tune in and find out what's going on in their lives when several of them are crowded into the car and I'm at the wheel taking them somewhere . . . again! Just by listening, I can find out what they think is "cool," who in their group has been acting either great or stupid, and, generally, how the world looks from their vantage point.

Sometimes, being a silent chauffeur is the best way to hear what's going on with our children. Besides, aren't we thankful deep down that they have all this energy? Don't we know deep down that even this too will pass? Haven't we been told that soon these young ones will be grown and we'll look back fondly to this hectic time? In the meantime, remember: They also serve who only sit and drive!

Dear God, help me see my tasks, however humble, as a way of serving you. And please, dear Lord, be with me every time I slide behind the wheel to watch over those you have placed in my care.

November 10   Read Psalm 118:24.

THREE WORDS THAT REALLY set me off are, "Mom, I'm bored!" When we allow ourselves to be bored, we cheat ourselves out of each special, singular, non-repeatable moment. We narrow our vision, missing all the exciting and wonderful things that surround us.

We can help our teens see that boredom is a choice they make, just as they can choose not to be bored. It's like the old story about getting out of life what we put into it: people and places will be interesting if we are interested in them. If our teens understand boredom as a choice, they may decide to choose better things. Any of us can choose to be filled with the energy and excitement of life or to turn a cold shoulder to the world. The difference means focusing on something beyond ourselves.

This month is an especially good time to help our teens think of others and how they might help them, while being thankful for the blessings in their own lives. The more our family can put our emphasis on others, the less time we have for self-pity and, yes, for boredom.

Dear Lord, help me recognize every day as a gift from you—truly the day the Lord has made! Help me give my children the ability to see life as a wonderful, exciting adventure.

NOVEMBER 11   Read Psalm 119:9-11.

ONE OF THE GREAT THINGS ABOUT computers is how they help us understand the marvelous God-given human mind. When I can't remember something or can't think of a name, my faithful subconscious goes into the search mode and comes up with the name when I'm not even trying to think of it, just as the computer searches through information stored in its memory. If we put bad information or errors into our memories, we will get bad information and errors back.

We have the responsibility of teaching our teens to put "good stuff" into their minds, just as we taught them to eat their vegetables and drink their milk. Responsible parents do monitor what their kids watch on TV, and they encourage them to read and listen to things that are wholesome, not destructive. It's pretty simple: the garbage we put in is the garbage we'll get back. When we face temptation or difficult questions, we draw from what is stored in the memory-bank of our minds. Wouldn't it be great to have our computer-brain full of good reserves?

Father, sometimes it's hard to keep my thoughts and motives pure. And if I can't, how can I help my children? Help us keep your word in our hearts that we might not sin against you.

NOVEMBER 12   Read John 13:15.

ONE OF MY FAVORITE PHOTOS is a picture of my son Joe when he was about three years old. He wore his grandfathers' big shoes on his feet, his grandfather's big hat on his head, and a great big smile on his face. He was trying to be just like Granddaddy!

Even when our teenagers show disdain for our advice and we think the last thing in the world they would ever want to do is be like us, the example we set is the most powerful one they will ever experience. Consciously or unconsciously, they will often "walk in our shoes" and pattern themselves after many things they have observed in us. Of course, we parents always hope our children will learn from the good, forget the bad, and be better than we are!

Role models are tremendously important. Teenagers may try to look like favorite models or movie stars, or copy mannerisms from someone whom they consider smart or popular. The fact is, they are constantly "trying on" new identities as they develop their own character, personality, and individuality.

When I consider the many things for which I am thankful at this season, being a mother is right at the top of the list. God has entrusted us, as mothers, with a very special responsibility, and God will guide us, so that our steps will not lead our children astray.

Lord, help me pattern my life after you so that I may be a good example to my children.

NOVEMBER 13   Read 2 Timothy 4:7.

MY HUSBAND AND I USED TO OWN and manage a bowling center. One of the things I learned in my weekly bowling league was the importance of "following through" when releasing the bowling ball. We can release the ball at just the right spot on the lane, but if we do not follow through with the arm, the ball does not roll true. I don't understand this; I only know it works every time.

One of the hardest lessons in life is learning to follow through. Often, our children will start some activity—a sport, or lessons of some kind—only to tire of it and want to drop out. There is great value in learning to finish what we start, to follow through and give our best effort. Dedication will help our children when they grow up and have jobs, develop relationships, and try to live out their Christian faith.

Jesus taught the value of following through, of finishing the course and being faithful. As we pray daily for our children and give thanks for our family, God will show us ways to teach them these important truths. Sharing Scripture passages (many references are in the letters of Paul) is a great way to help them understand this.

Help me to teach my children patience and perseverance, Lord, so that they may finish the race and keep the faith, following through with their good intentions with your help.

NOVEMBER 14   Read Isaiah 40:28-31.

ARE YOU TIRED TODAY? Is this one of those days when you'd really love to crawl back into bed and pull the covers over your head, hoping no one will find you? Or maybe you'd like to sit on a sandy beach and just "count your toes" for a while.

Being a mother is not only stressful and tiring it is also constant! Maybe you get tired of always being "up" and always being the one everyone runs to with their problems. Maybe you'd like to be held and comforted yourself. Is that selfish? No, it's just normal!

Sometimes taking a few moments off and finding a quiet place (the bathroom or your bedroom or even a closet) can give you the respite you so desperately need. Get comfortable, close your eyes, breathe deeply, clear your mind, and let peace and quietness wash through your whole being. It might be helpful to remember a few Scripture verses (perhaps some you learned long ago) and to say a simple prayer. Then, just let yourself "Be" as you feel the stress flow out of your limbs and your mind. A few minutes can help you feel wonderfully renewed and ready to face the day again. It's really important to take care of yourself if you're going to take good care of your family.

Dear Lord, thank you for understanding when I feel tired and frustrated, and thank you most of all for your Spirit that renews me.

NOVEMBER 15   Read Matthew 7:24-25.

FAMILY VALUES! THIS IS A popular and widely discussed issue that we hear from all sides these days—from senators, news commentators, ministers . . . just about everybody!

So, what do we really mean by the term "family values"? We mean love, compassion, honesty, cooperation, unselfishness, and peace, among other things.

We have the opportunity to build good family values every day. In fact, we are building values constantly whether we like it or not. If we don't instill our values in our children, they will absorb them from other influences. This month is a great time to upgrade our family values as we share with one another the many things for which we are thankful. We can build family values other ways, too, such as creating time for family Bible reading and prayer and setting aside time for just being together. All that we say and do when we are together becomes part of our history as a family and defines our values. Let's make the most of this sacred responsibility to pass good values on to our children, building our house on a rock that will never be shaken.

God, as I spend time with my children today, help me to share values that will guide and strengthen them all of their lives.

NOVEMBER 16   Read Matthew 6:5-6, 9-13.

WHEN THE DISCIPLES ASKED CHRIST to teach them to pray, he gave the wonderful model we call the Lord's Prayer. Still, we often need to be taught *to pray!* Too often, we just don't do it.

Can I teach my teenager how to pray? How can I keep from feeling embarrassed or self-righteous? The answer is to use the simplicity of talking to a friend, not changing our voices to sound "churchy." Family prayers can be said in a comfortable and accepting atmosphere, so no one will ever feel self-conscious; each person should feel free to pray aloud or remain silent. Parents can take the lead by saying a brief prayer in everyday language about everyday things, asking God to help us with attitudes or problems and then thanking him in a sincere way.

When we share prayer time with our teenagers, we invariably feel closer as a family. Little disputes tend to melt away and irritations become unimportant. What is important is that when we pray with our children, we put into their hands the most important key they will ever possess: the ability to pray.

Lord, I ask you, even as your disciples did, to teach me to pray. Help me to share this wonderful experience with my family, knowing you will hear us and bless us.

NOVEMBER 17   Read Psalm 1:1-3.

ON THE FARM WHERE I LIVED as a child, we often saw large tumbleweeds which the autumn wind would send rolling across the yards and fields. Though the plant grows during the spring and summer, its root system is weak and breaks off in the fall. This is nature's way of spreading the seeds. When I watch tumbleweeds, they seem to have no weight or substance, tossing this way and that at the whim of the wind. They aren't going anywhere in particular, just aimlessly traveling to and fro.

We also had big oaks and cedars on our farm. Some of these trees had been there since my Dad was a boy. Their root systems were deep and solid; the trees were able to withstand winter blizzards and even a few Oklahoma tornados.

Our teenagers will face storms of every kind: temptations, disappointments, and difficult decisions. The only way they can weather these storms is to develop roots that will sustain them in tough times—as they practice integrity, face up to their responsibilities, deepen their spiritual lives, and learn to be considerate of others. And don't we all want more for our young people than drifting through life like tumble-weeds?

Father, I am grateful in this Thanksgiving season that you have given me my family to love and cherish. Please help them grow up like mighty oaks planted by the streams of living water, able to withstand the storms of life.

NOVEMBER 18 Read Matthew 6:19-21.

THE LITTLE BOY HAD COMPLETED his school project. As he got ready to walk to the bus, his stepfather noticed that the bulky article was hard for the boy to manage. "If you'd like, I'll give you a ride to school so you won't have to carry your project on the bus," he said.

"No, that's OK. Maybe I could ride the bus and you could bring my project to school later."

The man finally realized that the boy didn't want to be seen arriving at school in the old beat-up car his stepdad drove. So the boy struggled to carry a bulky parcel onto the bus when he could have had a ride.

When we become overly concerned with appearances, we can create heavy burdens for our families. Teenagers are keenly aware of the "status rating" of clothes, cars, and houses. One of the hardest lessons in life is giving *things* their true value. How do we react to our teen's requests for things we can't afford?

To prepare for Thanksgiving, plan some sharing time to talk about things for which each family member is thankful.

Guide the discussion to consider real and true "treasures" as opposed to material, temporary things.

Dear God, the world constantly tempts us with material things. Help me lead my family to focus on things that are real and lasting.

NOVEMBER 19 — Read Genesis 1:27.

KRISTEN ALWAYS KNEW SHE WAS ADOPTED. Her Mom and Dad told her when she was very young that she was a "chosen" child, and she was happy. Yet when she reached adulthood, she had a natural curiosity about her birth mother. I had the privilege of being with Kristen and her birth mother after they met—one as a middle-aged woman, the other a young adult. Although there had been no communication during Kristen's developmental years, it was amazing how similar the two were in many ways; even their laugh was the same. In the miraculous moment of conception, all these characteristics were indelibly established in the person whom Kristen would become.

When God made us—you, me, our children, and everybody in the whole world—he stamped each one of us with certain characteristics. Daily we have the opportunity to impress upon our teenagers that God made them and, as a delightful poster proclaims, *God doesn't make junk!* We should teach them that God loves them, that God will give wisdom for making life's choices and strength to face the trials that come their way. God does this because he made us and indelibly established his likeness upon our hearts. Isn't it great to be the imprint of God!

When I feel tired and frustrated, Lord, help me to remember that I am your child and that you always care for me. Help me to share this faith with my family.

NOVEMBER 20 — Read Genesis 31:49*b*.

A FRIEND OF MINE WAS IN the army, stationed in Korea. Although there was no particular reason for his mother to worry, she was awakened one night by a vivid dream in which her son was in danger. The dream was so real that she placed a call to her son's commanding officer to inquire about him. Surprisingly, the young man was, in fact, in the hospital and had been instructed to call his parents. We might wonder: was this sheer coincidence, or was it one of those gentle nudgings of the Holy Spirit at work? If we truly believe that God is love, can we ever limit the scope of that love?

It is comforting to know that even when our children are out of sight and beyond our influence, God watches over them and, in ways that we can't even begin to understand, binds us together in love. Can you think of some ways that God has shown special care for your family? Talk about this together—perhaps around the table or at evening devotions. The Thanksgiving season is a wonderful time to re-commit our family to God as well as thank God for his loving care.

God, your care for us is so great that it is beyond our comprehension. Thank you for watching over us! And thank you most of all for love: your love for us and our love for one another.

NOVEMBER 21   Read Jeremiah 1:4-9.

AFTER MY SON MARK COMMITTED his life to Christ, he was eager to witness to his friends. When he was a freshman, just before his fourteenth birthday, he was asked to serve as high school chaplain. Feeling that he might be too young, he prayed about it and asked the Lord to give him a sign. As he opened his Bible, the words from Jeremiah 1:4-9 fairly leapt out from the page: *"Do not say, 'I am only a boy"* . . . *Now I have put my words in your mouth.' "*

Taking the verses seriously, Mark accepted the responsibility and was able to help many other students come to know the Lord. If he had continued to feel unsure or inadequate, he would have missed a great opportunity to serve God and to develop Christian leadership skills.

Sometimes our teens are enthusiastic about new challenges before we feel they are ready. We must keep in mind that God has special things for each of us to do. For many of these tasks, the only prerequisite is our willingness to serve him.

As we continue to prepare our hearts for Thanksgiving, let us thank God for the Bible that speaks to us in powerful ways, guiding us and our families.

Dear Lord, help me to encourage my teens as they face new challenges. I know that you call all of us for different tasks and that you can use us at any age, old or young.

NOVEMBER 22   Read Luke 10:25-37.

ON APRIL 19, 1995, there was a horrible explosion in downtown Oklahoma City that devastated a federal building, killing and injuring hundreds. At my home, several miles away, the house shook and the power of the bomb could be both heard and felt. Turning on the radio to hear the news, my first reaction was one of relief that none of my loved ones were in the area of devastation. Then it hit me: all of those people whom I later saw on the television screen, streaming out of the wrecked building with blood pouring from their wounds, *were someone's loved ones—someone's neighbors.* My selfish thoughts were replaced with concern for those who were hurt, and I remembered Jesus' teaching about neighbors.

It is only too easy to close our eyes to suffering around us if it doesn't affect "us." But if we follow Christ's teachings, we must be neighbors to everyone who needs our help. So what if we've never met them? So what if they are of a different color or nationality, or even if they are not Christian?

We are thankful when our family is well and safe. But how often do we care for people beyond our familiar circle, and be neighbors as Jesus taught us? Discuss with your teenagers ways, such as helping serve Thanksgiving dinner to the needy, that you can practice Christian love.

Father, help me to be caring and compassionate to all whom you would have me call neighbor.

NOVEMBER 23   Read Proverbs 27:1.

IN THE AFTERMATH OF THE HORRIBLE bombing in Oklahoma City, during the long hours that loved ones waited for news of survivors and rescue workers searched for bodies through several floors of compressed debris, many people called the TV stations to share their feelings. In particular I remember a woman who called in to say that ever since the explosion she had just hugged her children over and over.

None of us knows when we get up in the morning what the day will bring. None of us can afford to tell a family member goodbye in the morning while holding a grudge in our hearts; we may never have an opportunity to forgive and make up. Life offers no guarantees.

All families have stressful times, times when we quarrel and say things we really don't mean. Yet, when something happens to make us recognize how fragile life is, those little disagreements seem unimportant. A great concept to share with your teenager today comes from the Latin phrase *carpe diem*, which means to make the most of the present, or "seize the day." By making the most of each day as a true gift from God, we can focus on the little things that give life its meaning and recognize every moment as the precious gift it is. From this viewpoint, every day can be truly a day of Thanksgiving!

Lord, I can't see around the corner to tomorrow; I trust that to you, knowing you will be with me. Help me to see the sacredness in today, and teach my children to do the same.

NOVEMBER 24   Read Matthew 18:21-22.

THERE IS A KOREAN CUSTOM for the New Year in which the people write all of their burdens on a kite, let it fly, then cut the string and let the wind carry it away. The symbolic "letting go" is a wonderful enactment of release. Wouldn't it be great if we could release our burdens of anger in the same way, listing the things that make us angry and then letting go of those feelings?

Teenagers are very sensitive to slights from friends, or to being excluded and made to feel like an outsider. Sometimes those they consider best friends hurt them most. Quarrels flare up between siblings or between parents and children, and getting even is much more appealing than forgiving!

It might be helpful, as a family, to write down things that have made us angry, then either literally or figuratively let the wind carry them away as we forgive one another. When we ask God to work in us, the "wind" of the Holy Spirit brings about reconciliation. And isn't this season of Thanksgiving a wonderful time to practice forgiveness?

Dear God, I know you expect me and my family to be forgiving, but it's so hard to do! Help us to let go of our burdens, and fill us with your love and peace.

NOVEMBER 25   Read Deuteronomy 30:19.

PART OF GOD'S PLAN for our teenagers is their strong desire to take charge of their own lives. Authority and control are not their favorite words! Still, we can help them see that, even though there are rules to follow and certain standards we expect them to meet, the important choices in life are theirs alone. They can choose to be happy or sullen. They can be excited about life or cynical. They can live fully or just mark off the days. Each of us chooses our attitude, and attitude makes all the difference!

We must provide our teenagers with information to help them make good choices. They face choices about organizing their time, setting limits for themselves, even making friends. When they fall in love, they face the tough choice of respecting themselves and their partner enough to wait for sex—and deferring gratification is not a natural tendency!

My children and I can choose to tune in to life, tune in to love, and tune in to our relationship with God. We can reject negative thoughts. We can choose gratitude or "gripey-tude"! Our choices will make all the difference.

Lord, you know that I sometimes make poor choices, choosing fear over faith, or discouragement over trust in you. Help me express my thanks not just in this season of Thanksgiving but always, and help me to encourage my children as they make important choices.

NOVEMBER 26   Read Proverbs 22:6.

SO YOU'RE THE MOTHER of a teenager. So things don't always go the way you'd planned. So your child has a mind of his or her own and is even rebellious! So . . . *what else is new?* Letters written in ancient times complained of the rebelliousness of teenagers. We can't blame it on TV or electronic communications! Teenagers have always bristled with independence.

It's comforting to read this passage from the book of Proverbs; it offers hopes when teenagers stray away from our teachings. As I read this verse carefully, it occurs to me how important are the words "in the way he *should go.*" It doesn't say "in the way *we think* the child should go." The most important—and sometimes most difficult—challenge for parents is to recognize the uniqueness of each child. Many lives have been ruined when parents tried to force a young person into a family business or particular profession when the young person longed to follow another dream. If we really train a child in the way *he should go,* we have God's promise that he or she will not depart from it. Thank God for that!

God, grant me wisdom in guiding my children. Help me see each child as a gift from you and encourage them to become, with your help, all that they can be.

NOVEMBER 27   Read Proverbs 17:22.

I MUST CONFESS I WAS SURPRISED, and perhaps a bit defensive, when my grown-up daughter told me she thinks our family always takes ourselves too seriously! But you know what? She is right! Oh, we have pranks and fun, but overall I don't think we give humor enough space at our house. And even the mournful writer of Ecclesiastes (in chapter 3) says there is a time to laugh! Someone has said that a day without laughter is a day lost.

When a family looks back on its history, there are big, important events everyone remembers. And then, invariably, there are the pranks and funny things that we love to recall. Humor has a way of binding us together and keeping us close. Humor can help us get over disagreements; sometimes a silly grin between husband and wife can dissolve what might have grown into a bitter argument.

When our children develop a sense of humor, they can rise above many hurts and disappointments and they will be sought after because people gravitate toward a cheerful person. Even though your family is very busy, take time to laugh together. It's the best kind of health insurance!

Another reason for Thanksgiving, Lord! Thank you for giving us the ability to smile, laugh, and play together.

NOVEMBER 28   Read 1 Corinthians 13:4-7, 13.

THREE LITTLE WORDS: I LOVE YOU. Even though these words may be spoken glibly or insincerely at times, they are still just about the most important words in the English language.

A dear friend told me that his father never once said to him the words "I love you." This man achieved great prominence and became a highly respected professional man, but he still finds it hard to understand why his father never told him he loved him. We've all heard stories about people who wish, after a loved one died, that they could have just one more chance to say "I love you."

At this Thanksgiving season, we should put love high on our list of blessings. This would be a perfect time to gather the family together, hold hands, and express our love for one another. If your family is one that doesn't do this kind of thing easily, just jump in and try it anyway! It can be so meaningful, and it can help to make it easier for your children to express love throughout their lives.

O God, forgive me when I withhold love from my family because I am angry, or busy, or just careless. Help us understand more of your love for us, so that we may truly love one another.

NOVEMBER 29 Read Acts 3:6.

MANY YOUNG PEOPLE HAVE WALKED out the door of very humble homes to go on to outstanding achievement. What contributed to their success if not the advantages of opportunity, family name, or wealth? What is there that makes some kid, whose family literally had nothing, rise to the top of his or her field? Of course, we have to recognize those things that come from within: initiative and commitment. But what went on in that little house to give that young person the will to win? If we could draw back the curtains and listen in at the kitchen table, we might have heard things like this:

"I believe in you."

"You can do it!"

"I love you."

"Go for it!"

If you can't give your teens great monetary gifts, don't despair. Give them the really important things: love, faith in God, confidence in their abilities, courage, and respect for other human beings. These are the things your teenagers need more than anything else in the world. When they pack their suitcases for the road of life, these are things that matter most of all.

Heavenly Father, help me give good and lasting gifts to my children, gifts that are eternal in value. I have a tendency at this time off year, with Thanksgiving in the air and Christmas rushing toward me, to focus on material things. Remind me to be thankful for those who have loved me and believed in me, and to give these same gifts to my children.

THANKSGIVING IS PAST. HOWEVER, there are certain "leftovers" that I want to keep this year. I want to keep giving daily thanks for small blessings. I want to keep a sense of gratitude that I can feed and clothe my family, and deep thanks for God's love and care every day. I know it will be hard to focus on these things as the Advent season rushes along, catching me with its own busy excitement.

Yes, it's time to make those Christmas lists. And, yes, I know we spoil our children with too many material things. Just stop and think a minute: How many of last year's gifts do your children still use and enjoy?

The Scripture today reminds us of the great gift we can give our children when we give them faith in the Lord. We give of ourselves by example. We give unconditional love and help them develop self-control. We can teach them that God loves and cares for them. Then, no matter what problems they may face in life, they will know where to turn and whom to trust, because they have seen us trust God. This is the greatest gift of all.

Lord, help me share the greatest gift of faith with my children. Help me be like the mothers and grandmothers of the Bible, who passed on to their children a sincere faith.

DECEMBER

MIRACLES AND MUSINGS IN THE LIFE OF A STEPMOM

M. Garlinda Burton

DECEMBER 1   **Read Habakkuk 3:17-19;**
Matthew 3:7-9.

WHEN I WAS IN MY EARLY TWENTIES I learned that I could not have children. Contrary to all the stories about lack of fulfillment and ticking biological clocks, I accepted the news with little sadness. As the oldest child of bitterly divorced parents, I've played second mom to my younger siblings since age twelve, and I have considered my years of relative freedom after the young ones grew up and became independent a blessing. Until I married at age thirty-three, I had built for myself a satisfying single life full of friends, community service, and extended family.

I also discovered that "barrenness" is a state of mind, and confidence in God's plan can fill any emptiness. I've never had a period in my life when I wasn't surrounded by the love of children. When I lived and worked in Dallas, my church unexpectedly nominated me as chairperson of children's ministries and asked me to teach first-grade Sunday school. I still hear from "my children" as they pursue successful college educations or start families of their own.

About the time I moved to Nashville, my best friend, Toni—a single mother of a nine-year-old son, Robert—was contemplating a second marriage. Partly because of my childlike spirit and partly because of his insecurity about the new man in his mom's life, Robert reached out to me. We saw movies together and talked by phone. As he grew older, I taught him to drive a stick shift, talked him through his first traumatic breakup with a girlfriend, and amazed him with my knowledge of rap music.

Then, just as Robert was heading for college and life on his own, I met the man who was to become my husband, a man with two daughters of his own and adoring nephews and nieces. Again I was thrust happily into the roles of surrogate mom and aunt.

Though Mary's cousin Elizabeth did not become pregnant until she was older—and even if God had never given her children—she was still most likely a valuable lover and partner for Zechariah, a confidante for Mary, and an inspiration to people who knew her. Instead of sighing in relief at being "validated" by biological motherhood, I imagine she laughed when she learned of her pregnancy, expressing her joy at God's "icing on the cake" of her life. Her years of being friend, sister, daughter, wife, and self had been rewarding, duty-filled, and blessed. She brought to the role of mother her rich experiences from all the relationships in which God had placed her.

When I'm at my best, I start the day by asking God who needs me as friend, sister, daughter, or surrogate mother; and I ask God to show me the way to those friends, sisters, daughters, and mothers whom I need. I've never known a time when God did not provide.

God, today I give you thanks for the people to whom I am friend, sister, daughter, and mother (name them individually). Please be present with us as we face life's challenge together.

DECEMBER 2   Read Psalm 90:14.

ON THE MORNING OF MY WEDDING, I awoke to a ringing phone. It was fifteen-year-old Heather, my soon-to-be stepdaughter. I had always been a little intimidated by her. She is stunningly beautiful and popular, like her mother, and she has her father's devastating smile. Having been born "plain" (but with a "stunning wit and intellect," my mother always adds), I grew up in awe of beautiful girls and women, afraid that they, like the rest of the world, would evaluate me based on my physical beauty and that I wouldn't quite measure up.

I was also uncertain about Heather's rather breezy displays of affection. From the moment she first met me, she had been pleasant, bestowing hugs and answering my questions in a patient, detached way. She seemed unbothered by our plan to marry, was flattered by my invitation to be a bridesmaid, and made only one comment about our future as a family: "Maybe you guys will have a baby. I'd like a brother."

Then, on the morning of my wedding the phone rang. Yes, she had had a good night; she and her grandmother had had breakfast together. Yes, her dress was ironed; yes, she liked the color—she knew purple is my favorite, so lavender silk was not entirely unexpected. She talked with ease, but I was nervous somehow. She had never called me just to talk; there was something she wanted to say, I could tell.

"I just want you to know that I'm glad you're marrying my dad. I can tell he's really happy, and I'm glad he found you," she said.

Those are still among the sweetest words I've ever heard. What a decision of purest love—to share and rejoice in her father's happiness, to love because he loves! Heather's words soothed and comforted me. I dressed and prepared myself for my wedding, reflecting on my good fortune. I was gaining a wonderful husband and two wonderful daughters.

O loving God, who bids children to come, thank you for the gift of families joined not merely by blood, but by their commitment to love, work, fight, and struggle together. Help me to remember the love that binds our family together, even when the storms of life are raging.

DECEMBER 3   Read Psalm 72.

BY THE TIME WE MARRIED, Larry's oldest daughter, Kelia, had moved away from home and, at age seventeen, had married.

Her marriage was rocky from the beginning. Now she is in a battle for custody of her three-year-old daughter, Shermana.

I don't know Kelia's ex-husband well, but I know that both of them were—and still are—too young to be married. Although I am not an advocate of divorce except as an absolute last resort, I was convinced that their marriage was "dead on arrival."

Larry and I, of course, have sided with our daughter. She wants to keep her child, and we think she is devoted to being a good mother. At the same time, we feel Shermana's father must love her too if he is willing to try for custody. And I know in my heart that it is unfair to assume that women are better parents just because of their gender. I also know that whoever is granted custody will need the help of extended family and the cooperation of the other parent in order to rear little Shermana.

At times like this, I know how the psalmist must have felt in asking prayers for the judges, kings, and other decision-makers. I don't envy the judge who will ultimately decide our daughter's case—who must explore the financial, emotional, and spiritual resources of both parents in order to place Shermana in the best environment possible. I resonate with the first line of Psalm 72: "Give the king your justice, O God."

Parents, teachers, counselors, judges, ministers—all those who have responsibility for the lives of our young people—need our prayers. Some days the obstacles and challenges seem so great that even the wisdom of Deborah or Solomon is insufficient. All we can do at those times is ask for God's wisdom, God's justice, and God's peace to come into the hearts and lives of our youth and all the people in their lives. When the storms of life are raging, sometimes you just need to grab your child's hand and pray.

God, thank you for the life of my child and every child with whom I come in contact. When adversity and conflict come into our lives, help me to remember that you have given us to one another to comfort and keep one another. Help us to remember that when everything seems to have gone wrong, you are still there with your wisdom and justice.

I WAS A BOOKISH, UNATTRACTIVE teenager, blessed with National Honor Society membership and a quick wit. Still, I was desperate to be part of the popular crowd of good-looking, never-without-a-date "party girls" in my high school.

I remember one day when my shot at popularity presented itself. This really cute, popular guy in my history class needed help with his homework. I was assigned by our teacher as Rob's study partner. He wanted better grades, and I relished spending time with one off the "in crowd"; so we studied together for several weeks, and Rob got a B on our mid-term exam.

During those weeks of studying together, Rob and I talked a lot. He got to know me and I him. He was actually kind of nice, I discovered. He liked me, too, I think, because—in a fit of gratitude or something—he asked me to our junior prom. I was thrilled and went into "prom overdrive"—buying an outfit, trying new hairdos, practicing charming chatter, even rehearsing the good-night kiss.

As it turned out, Rob and I did not go to the prom together. As I later found out, Rob was nearly laughed off the school bus when he told the girls in his crowd that he'd asked *me* to the prom. He avoided me for weeks after that, but I continued to plan, purchase, and hope.

Then one day a mutual friend relayed the message that Rob wanted to bow out gracefully. I waited, hoping that he'd have a burst of gallantry, but finally Rob cornered me in history class and said he couldn't go to the prom with me because he'd already asked another girl.

I was mortified, but I played it off very well. My mother will learn now for the first time that I went to the prom by myself. I asked a male friend to pick me up; he was in the band and had to be there. I sat alone bravely all evening, laughing and making nice conversation with a few classmates. Finally, I asked another friend who had come alone if he would drive me home. I thought it was the worst night of my life.

Now, many years later, I have the luxury of looking back at that night and smiling. Still, whenever I find myself with a group of children or youth or college students, I find myself drawn to the plump child with braces or the lanky boy with acne or the girl having a perpetual "bad hair day." And I am amazed and bewildered by the number of *adults* who will shatter a teen's fragile confidence with one mindless refrain, such as, "You're putting on a little weight, aren't you?" or "Too bad you didn't get your father's eyes."

What happened to the dazzling beauty and sacred worth that all of us have as children of God? Remember the awkwardness, the self-doubt, the longing to be loved and accepted that you may have felt as a teen. What can you do to affirm the self-worth and ease the fears and insecurities about the physical appearance of your own teen?

Dear God, each of us is fearfully and wonderfully made. Show us how to share your loving kindness in ways that help others to discover the loveliness imparted to all children of God.

DECEMBER 5   Read Proverbs 1:8-9; 2:1-5.

DO YOU KNOW THAT FUNNY FEELING you get when you hear the voice of your mother coming from your own adult mouth? My diatribes to Heather and Kelia—and to all of my other "surrogate kids"—about taking responsibility, getting good grades, and learning to be self-reliant sometimes sound so much like my mother that I have to glance in the mirror to see just who's doing the talking!

All kidding aside, I am so grateful for the lessons taught to me by my mother and father, my grandmothers, and other mentors—especially now as I seek to advise the young people in my life. Heather made better grades the second semester of her freshman year in college after we threatened to withhold funds (a tactic of my mom's that worked like a charm on *me* during my freshman year). Kelia's marriage is ending, but we're encouraging her to go back to school and offering to provide child care for Shermana—because we both had mothers who went back to school when they were in their fifties. My father encouraged me to learn a second language, which has opened many career doors for me, and I've gladly passed that wisdom along to my "adopted son" Robert.

In Proverbs we read, "Hear, my child, your father's instruction, and do not reject your mother's teaching; for they are a fair garland for your head, and pendants for your neck" (1:8-9). Although I tease my mother about her "ghost" occupying my body from time to time, I am grateful that she—and my father—shared knowledge and wisdom worth passing on to our crew. For it is through wisdom that we "understand the fear of the Lord and find the knowledge of God" (Proverbs 2:5).

One of my favorite Advent hymns, "O Come, O Come, Emmanuel," celebrates the wisdom embodied by Jesus Christ. I offer one verse as a prayer of thanksgiving for every piece of sound advice passed from parent to child.

O come, thou Wisdom from on high, and order all things far and nigh; to us the path of knowledge show and cause us in her ways to go. Rejoice! Rejoice! Emmanuel shall come to thee, O Israel.

(Stanza 2 of "O Come, O Come, Emmanuel," written by Henry Sloane Coffin, 1916.)

DECEMBER 6   Read Isaiah 11:1-10.

WHEN I WAS IN HIGH SCHOOL, "troubled teens" were the ones who drank cheap wine at parties, got into fistfights, experimented with pot in the bus parking lot, and—in pretty rare cases—ended up pregnant.

Today, in my local paper, I read an article about a twelve-year-old who shot a classmate in an argument over designer athletic shoes. A friend reports that her daughter has had two abortions. My "surrogate daughter" reveals to me that her best friend is being sexually abused by her mother's boyfriend.

These days, the parental chorus of "When I was your age . . . " often rings hollow in a world where grammar-school children smoke crack, where teen suicide is on the rise, and where too-early, unprotected sex not only puts kids at risk for pregnancy but also could mean their very lives.

Still, the Bible is fraught with stories of trials and adversities, a hint that our world has never been a simple, safe, and eternally happy place for all God's children. The prophet Isaiah lists the travails of God's people under political oppression, personal fear, and doubt. Isaiah also tells the story of a promise fulfilled, of good triumphing over evil, of a Savior who will usher in the reign of peace.

The problems our young people face are real. The perils in their schools and on the streets are real. But just as real is the assurance that these adversities are not the end of the story: A time is coming when "the wolf shall live with the lamb" (Isaiah 11:6a), and we as people of God can play a role in bringing God's realm to earth.

Sometimes I don't have an answer for Heather or Kelia. I don't know why bad things happen, why AIDS attacks young people, why violence and evil sometimes seem to win, even with all our prayers, actions, and good intentions. At those times of confusion and doubt, I simply say what I know for myself: That God has equipped us with the spiritual tools to face adversity; that God has never left me alone; that good always overcomes evil; that all we can do is live faithfully and share God's love with everyone we meet. I don't know much about many things, but, as I tell the girls, I know that God still leads and guides all those who seek God's counsel.

God, our mighty fortress, sometimes all I can do is pray for the safety and health of my children. I offer this earnest prayer: that you will, this day, keep every mother's child safe in your arms.

DECEMBER 7   Read Isaiah 2:1-5; Psalm 122.

ANDREA, SIXTEEN, CALLED IN the middle of the night. Her mother, a frequent user of illegal drugs, had physically attacked Andrea in the middle of an argument and had tried to knock the teenager's infant son from her hands.

When we arrived, Andrea stood beside two large plastic bags stuffed with clothes for herself and the baby. Both of them were crying. She didn't know where she wanted to go. With no job and no money, her options were limited. Still, she needed a couple of days to think things through. She stayed that day with us, until we could contact a friend who has her own apartment.

That day at our house, as we cooked together, watched her favorite movies, and listened to Larry's jazz albums, Andrea remarked several times how "quiet" and "peaceful" our home is. She's right. It wasn't until that Sunday afternoon with Andrea and the baby, however, that we realized what a supreme blessing it is to have a home where peace reigns. Sure, we have our battles, but the chaos of our home is usually happy or energizing: an argument over bills; Heather coming home from college unexpectedly, accompanied by three hungry, laundry-bearing girlfriends; me working on a project due at work on Monday and keeping the whole house in an uproar all weekend.

The teen years are fraught with exciting, awful, wonderful, and terrible occurrences; and peace is often elusive. Add to the normal "teen stuff" an unplanned baby with no father, chemical abuse, and poverty; and navigating through the teen years becomes even more treacherous. Peace seems a foreign concept, a pie-in-the-sky dream.

But God provides each of us the ability to locate or create a peaceful haven for ourselves. Andrea's determination led her to find a place of her own, first in a housing project, then in her own apartment. Now she is working as a hair stylist and is saving to buy her own house someday. Her home may be more chaotic than mine, with friends and customers coming in and out, but she has found the peace that comes with security—with taking the loaves and fishes God gives us and making it into a feast.

I think the best gifts we parents and mentors can give to teens are self-confidence, self-determination, and faith in a loving God. Gifts that we all need to overcome adversity. Gifts of peace.

Dear God, grant peace to those teens and their parents who are struggling today with hunger, want, anger, misunderstanding, and frustrated ambitions. Help them to find the ways of peace. And help me to know how I can help my own teens find peace and security.

DECEMBER 8   Read Isaiah 7:10-16.

"FOR . . . THE CHILD KNOWS how to refuse the evil and choose the good" (Isaiah 7:16). Isn't this every parent's fervent prayer—that we will raise our children to know right from wrong? But how do we get there from here?

Recently I spoke to a consortium of administrators and teachers of wealthy, private high schools on the issue of racial and cultural diversity. Though each person there declared her or his commitment to creating classrooms that welcome all students, they admitted being afraid to address issues of racial tensions in their schools.

One teacher complained that it does not good for him to champion a racially diverse classroom when many of his students come from homes where parents are members of racially exclusive country clubs and other exclusive social and civic groups. An administrator told me privately that she fears loss of income from wealthy "legacy" families if she "pushes the integration issue to hard."

One teacher, however, who also happened to be the mother of a teenager, declared, "If we don't have the guts to stand up to racism ourselves, we don't have the right to call ourselves educators. We can't teach what we're not willing to learn ourselves."

How true that is. In order for our children to learn right from wrong, they need to witness parents who are willing to struggle to understand and advocate what is right, and to challenge and correct what is wrong. Ask yourself, "Am I the kind of parent who only talks a good game, or am I teaching goodness and rightness by my example?"

Lord, help me to show *my teens by my own example how to refuse the evil and choose the good.*

DECEMBER 9   Read Matthew 11:2-11.

IN MATTHEW 11, JESUS HAILS John the Baptist as one predestined to "prepare the way" for the Savior. In much the same way, we mothers are, for the most part, "way makers" for our children. However, as we help to pave the way for our teens to become adults, we often make the mistake of denying or sacrificing ourselves for the sake of our sons and daughters.

I don't believe, however, that this is always what God intends for us as God's children. As the second mom for two girls, I find nothing incongruous about being both a way-maker for them and a seeker of my own fulfillment, growth, and freedom. At a mother's best, she makes a way for her children *and* sets a fine example of self-respect and self-fulfillment in the bargain. Boys who grow up in homes where women are respected are more likely to become men who respect women; girls whose mothers are loving and attentive without being overly self-sacrificing are more likely to avoid being abused and taken for granted by their husbands and children.

My own mother went back to college when I was still in high school, causing our family some financial stress and requiring my siblings and me to shoulder some household duties. Naysayers criticized her for inconveniencing her family and being a "bad" mother. But I learned to cook and clean and care for my baby sister. And my brothers learned to keep house without being dependent on a woman. (In fact, my married brother does most of the cooking at his house now.) We all learned the importance of an education, and we saw first hand what one can accomplish if one is determined to overcome obstacles. Our mother prepared a way for us by making her own way from financial dependency and lack of education to greater self-sufficiency and academic competence.

Just as John the Baptist lived the kind of life that prepared a way for Christ, so must we live our lives in ways that promise better, richer, and more fulfilled lives for our children. Yet, like John, we must be open for God to lead us down some unexpected pathways. Sometimes preparing the way for someone else means becoming better navigators in our own lives.

As you called John the Baptist to be a way maker, dear God, teach me to lead my teens down right paths, illuminating their way with the light you shine through me.

DECEMBER 10   Read Romans 1:1-12.

HEATHER'S A SOPHOMORE IN COLLEGE now, still at the age when kids run in packs. When she comes home on holiday, she brings no fewer than three other girls. While I hate the prospect of preparing meals and arranging shopping trips for four picky coeds, I love watching them interact. A typical evening finds them sprawled on the couch, both the TV and stereo blasting, with them shouting to one another over the din.

They are as natural as air in the way they braid one another's hair and swap advice on boys, grades, and how to charm money out of their parents. They haven't yet become obsessive about germs and privacy; so they drink Coke from the same bottle, share hair brushes, and try on each other's shoes.

Larry and I both know how important these moments are. Our friends from high school and college remain the most intimate, most trusted people in our lives. Rarely since college have we made ourselves that vulnerable, that open to strangers. Rarely, then, have we made the kind of lifelong friends we attained when we were still young enough to travel in packs to one another's homes, or to sleep ten to a hotel room on spring break.

Paul's letter to the Romans extols the rewards of "encouraging one another." Next time your teens and their friends are just "hanging around," talking to one another over the blast of the stereo, watch closely. A lifelong bond might be in the making.

Everlasting Friend, I celebrate the people you brought into my life at times I needed companionship. Help me to affirm, celebrate, and encourage my teens as they seek to find lifelong friends.

DECEMBER 11   Read Ecclesiastes 4:9-12.

I AM BLESSED WITH AN ABUNDANCE of friends but, as I've said, my closest and most intimate friends are those from high school and college—with only a few exceptions. With them I share a history, an evolution of life stories. I know their families; they know my siblings' full names and the intimate details of my first date.

When I got my first job after college, it was "the two Cheryls and Tammy" with whom I celebrated. The four of us were considered the posse in college. I was the first person Sheree told about her first pregnancy, and that was on the same day I called to tell her I was engaged to be married. Sally, a friend since seventh grade, was the first one to learn that my first book had been published.

Remember what it took and still takes to build those intimate friendships? Laughter, disagreements, sleep-overs, double dates, all-night study sessions, all-night crying sessions; pooling quarters to buy pizza, helping one another convert crates and planks into furniture for your first apartments. Shared joys, sorrows, triumphs, and defeats are the stuff that lifelong friendships are made of.

"Two are better than one," declares the writer of Ecclesiastes—*better* meaning stronger, better able to withstand adversity. As the lives of friends become intertwined, every member of the extended family has more shoulders to cry on, more hands to hold, more mirth to spread, and a richer family story to tell.

Who are your teen's friends? Whom does your teen imitate in dress, speech, and habits? On whom does your teen rely for comfort, affirmation, and secret-telling? Understanding your teen's friends will give you insight into her or his desires, hopes, and needs. If the friends are good and true, you may rest easier knowing that your teen's life will be strengthened through these relationships.

Ultimate and Divine Friend, thank you for the gift of human companionship in my life. My prayer this day is that my teen will find loyal, loving, positive, and Christ-like friends and that I may help my teen to become a Christ-like friend for others.

DECEMBER 12   Read Psalm 103.

AS A TEENAGER, THE CHARACTER CELIE in Alice Walker's *The Color Purple* experiences with patience and faith a harshness in life that is far beyond her years. But when she is pushed too far, she lashes out. A good friend advises her to think of the beauty of God's world—a flower, a rock, a tree—whenever she is feeling angry or discouraged. Celie, however, has hit bottom; and even God's creation fails to move her. "Every time I conjure up a rock," she says, "I throw it."

Anger is one of the emotions that comes with parenting, particularly for someone like me who was not born with patience. When Heather was still living at home, often I would ask myself, *Why can't Larry back me when I lay down the law? Why doesn't she help around the house more? Who gave her permission to use my best perfume? Why do I have to negotiate with my husband's ex-wife to plan even a simple family vacation? What possessed me to marry in the first place?*

Like Celie, I found that conjuring up rocks and flowers does little to assuage my anger. What has worked most times is time alone to reflect on the joys of marriage and family— joys that far outweigh the headaches. I loved being single, but I always wanted to find someone to share my life with. I have that with my wonderful husband. Though I never imagined myself as a mother, being a stepmother has given me not only two wonderful daughters but also two wonderful young friends. Yes, our home was often hectic; but more often than not, that chaos was more welcome than the lonely silence I experienced when there was no one I could talk with—or even argue with—at 2:00 in the morning.

Instead of conjuring up rocks and throwing them, I have found that exorcising my anger is as simple as conjuring up the gifts of love and giving thanks for them.

"Bless the Lord, O my soul, and all that is within me, bless his holy name." I give thanks, O Lord, for your many gifts of love.

DECEMBER 13   Read James 5:7-10.

I WAS NOT BORN WITH PATIENCE. That gene, I'm convinced, was omitted when God was constructing me in my mother's womb. As a child, I hated waiting for my parents after church when they wanted to visit with friends and I wanted to get home to see the afternoon monster movies on TV. I was in agony in those weeks between Thanksgiving and Christmas morning when I could finally open my presents.

I carried this impatience into my adult life. I refused to learn to sew, vowing to always have enough money to buy ready-made clothes. If a guy was shy or awkward on the first date, he never got a second chance.

My husband, Larry, is patient. Unlike me, who gulps meals down so I can get back to the book I'm reading, he prefers to linger at the table, talking about his day. I drive everywhere like I'm going to put out a fire. He makes every car trip a pleasure, singing along with his favorite music. I worry myself to distraction planning family gatherings; he "goes with the flow" and has a lot more fun.

His patience is rubbing off on me. Or maybe it is the combination of his influence and the frenetic energy of our girls that is making me slow down. For the first time in my life, I planted an herb and vegetable garden last summer—weeding, spraying, and feeding them for weeks before the seeds became food. Instead of buying new furniture, Larry encouraged me to buy some antiques and refinish them. Not computer-literate for years, I've nonetheless relearned the computer at home.

Patience, as the writer of James observed, offers the rewards of harvest, home, and a job well done. One of the serendipities of adjusting to a husband and a ready-made family has been that I've grown more patient and, I hope, closer to what God wants me to be.

O God, give me patience as I try to be the mother you would have me be.

DECEMBER 14   Read Psalm 146:5-10.

MY VARIED TASTES IN MUSIC HAVE made me a hit with Heather and Kelia, who marvel at my ability to hold an intelligent discussion of 90s-style rap and rock music, even while humming along with Rodgers and Hammerstein's *Cinderella* soundtrack. When listening to the music of my daughters' generation, I especially enjoy some of the stories told in the poetry of rap music.

A favorite of mine by the group Arrested Development is "Mr. Wendal," a story told by a young, middle-class college student who encounters a homeless man and learns that each has something to share with the other. In the song the student laments that, although many young people attend college, they often graduate "confused" about their spiritual calling and social responsibilities.

Have you ever seen kids on the street harassing a person who is homeless or begging for food? Where did they learn to devalue people who are dirty, ragged, and without a roof over their heads? How do your teens see you react to homeless people and others who are visibly poor? Do you ignore them? Do you offer them aid? Do you support organizations and agencies that offer assistance?

An exciting trend in many high schools, church youth groups, and colleges is working vacations, where students spend their spring break or part of their summer repairing the homes of the poor and elderly people, tutoring younger children, or volunteering in soup kitchens. Such programs help put a human face on words like *poverty* and *welfare recipients* and reinforce a sense of compassion and humanity in our children.

What can you do or say to help instill a sense of compassion and love for all of God's children in the hearts of your teens?

O God, you are Lord of all. Regardless of our earthly possessions, we are all your children. Help me and my children to have more compassion for those in need and to find more ways to reach out in love.

DECEMBER 15   Read Proverbs 12:25; 16:24.

WHEN I WAS IN HIGH SCHOOL, I was stunned to learn that such a beautiful girl—a friend I'd always envied—was starving herself to death.

Those of us on the outside looking in admired her athletic figure, flawless skin, and raven-dark hair; but when she looked at herself in the mirror, she saw fat cheeks and heavy thighs. At family reunions, instead of celebrating her good graces or quick wit, uncles laughed that she was getting fat; aunts warned her to watch her weight, lest she end up— gasp!—without a boyfriend. Those offhand comments, coupled with her parents' well-intentioned push for her to compete with "prettier" girls, echoed in her mind; and so she refused to eat.

At our age our biggest worries should have been homework; but every television show, magazine article, and casual glance by boys in our class seemed to increase our feelings of disgust and disapproval with our physical appearance. My beautiful friend almost died. Thank goodness a caring teacher noticed her sunken eyes and the loose sweaters worn to hide her skeleton-like frame. The teacher intervened, saving my friend's life.

Today my beautiful friend volunteers her time talking to teenage girls about self-esteem. She witnesses to God's love by explaining that we are all fearfully and wonderfully made in God's image (Psalm 139:13-14), and that we need not starve ourselves physically or emotionally to live up to some superficial notion of what makes girls—or boys—beautiful.

The psalmist often compares Israel to a vine that is tended carefully and lovingly by God. As laborers in God's vineyards, part of our task as parents is to give our children the emotional and physical nourishment they need to survive. Just as plants must be tended regularly to protect them from weeds, drought, and disease, so must we be the ones to build our children up with our words, rather than beat them down with too much criticism. And perhaps no time is more important than the critical "growing season" of the teen years.

God, the Potter who never molds junk, let my words be positive, affirming, encouraging, and loving when they are directed to my teen. Yes, I want to urge my teen toward the perfection to which you've called us, but help me learn when to stop pushing.

DECEMBER 16   Read Psalm 96.

WHEN MY MOTHER WAS A TEENAGER—and my grandmother was the age I am now—"good girls" in small-town North Carolina did *not* pierce their ears. So, when my mother got her ears pierced, my poor little grandmother had a conniption. She swore my mother would grow up to be a loose woman with no morals and would become an exotic dancer or a prostitute—all because of a couple of gold studs in her ears.

Grammy was wrong. Today my mother is heading toward retirement after forty years as a respected nurse and mother of four pretty straight-laced children (a journalist, an office manager, an engineer, and a deejay). Mom is a pillar of her church, and she can't even dance regularly—much less exotically!

Larry gripes incessantly about Heather's clothes. These days she leans toward those clunky boots and short skirts and wears her hair shorter than his. He's convinced that she's trying out for a music video, although she tells us she wants to produce TV news.

This is our kids' time to experiment with clothing and hair. This is their time to make mistakes. This is their time to sing a new song—not that we've done too badly in our day, but we haven't written or sung the last word of celebration in God's world. And after hearing our songs of life, I'm not sure God wouldn't love to hear a song with a new beat for a change!

The psalmist was probably considered pretty radical when he advocated singing a new kind of song in celebration of God's goodness. It's a little scary to consider a time when ours is not *the* theme song of life. But if you've lived to the best of your ability, it's not as hard to make room for the kids and their expressions.

Sing to the Lord a new song? Please do. And I'll be grateful for just enough energy to pat my feet.

Lord, keep me from stifling the "song" that my teens want to sing. Help me to give them the room they need to experiment with self-expression, for only then will they discover the unique persons you've created them to be.

December 17   Read Proverbs 4.

WHEN MY HUSBAND, LARRY, was growing up, he was the nightmare of every father of a teenage daughter. He was, and still is, a charmer: polite, deferential, courtly—the kind who could make you really believe that the reason your daughter was home three hours after curfew was because he had a flat tire, the kind of young man a nervous father watched like a hawk.

So it is only fitting that Larry is now the father of two attractive young women. His fair is attractively but prematurely white! When Kelia and Heather were teens, he lectured about the importance of obeying curfews, staying home to study on school nights, and delaying dating. One summer he put all of Heather's dates through a rigorous interview, concluding with the stern admonition, "I was a charming young man once. Don't make me have to deal with you!"

Though the girls have griped about their father's concern through the years, they also have found it comforting to talk with him about the pitfalls and problems of male-female relationships. It is both amusing and wonderful to watch them have serious discussions about how to set ground rules with young men, how to know if a man is sincere, and what to "watch out for." The girls expect—and receive—much more candid advice from their dad because he has had first-hand experience as a girl-chasing, parent-charming rogue. And he is able to offer more informed, practical, loving advice.

Ah, wisdom! It is what comes with experience, long life, and desiring to love, cherish, and protect the ones most precious to you. No wonder early theologians described wisdom as the intuitive, caring, loving manifestation of our God. When we celebrate Christ's coming on earth, we also celebrate Christ's personification of wise love that can inform, nurture, and protect.

"Rejoice! Rejoice! Emmanuel shall come to thee, O Israel." For your wisdom, dear God, which you offer to us and to our teens, we give you thanks.

From "O Come, O Come, Emmanuel."

DECEMBER 18   Read Proverbs 29:25.

A CHURCH IN MY CITY IS KNOWN for its inspirational billboards. One of my favorites reads, "Fear is a darkroom where *negatives* are developed."

I used to be afraid of drawing attention to myself because I wasn't perfect. As a teen, I was often dismissed—audibly by my mother's friends at church, no less—as being too fat, too brainy, too melancholy, too concerned with serious things, too odd in my choices of clothing and hairstyles. As a result, I would get butterflies in my stomach every time I walked out of the house in a new outfit or changed my hair or raised my hand to answer a question in class. I even began to resent and berate those girls who could do those things with confidence. A girl who was really pretty was a "flirt." One who was too loud and boisterous was "rude." And the girl who made valedictorian was "snotty."

I nearly let my fear of self-revelation and failure turn me into a mean-spirited, prejudiced person. Thank God that a loving mother, caring teachers, and a patient youth minister helped me overcome my fears so that I could overcome my negativity.

So much of what I see today, such as the resurgence of hate groups among our youth, reminds me of that time in my life. Behind the name-calling and the bizarre stereotypes and myths, I recognize the self-doubt, pain, and fear of failure of many young people—perhaps exacerbated by overly critical parents.

What is your teen afraid of? Could there be fear and doubt behind your teen's negative words and actions? What are you doing to help him or her overcome that fear? How can you increase your teen's feelings of security and trust?

Dear patient, loving God, help me to think before I speak. Help me to build up rather than tear down my teen with my words. Don't let me erect a darkroom of fear where my teen develops negativism. Open my eyes to the needs I can fulfill in my teen's life.

DECEMBER 19   Read Psalm 62:1-7.

ONE OF THE MOST BEAUTIFUL SERMONS on parenting I've heard was the reading of the children's book *The Runaway Bunny!* In the story, a bunny declares his independence and his intention to run away from his mother, even if he has to become another entity to elude her. The mother, however, patiently and lovingly promises that wherever her child goes, she will be there as a refuge, guide, anchor, and defender. If the bunny becomes a sailboat, she pledges to become the wind which blows him in the right direction. If he becomes a fish, she will cast about looking for him. When he threatens to become a bird, she vows to become a tree that will always be a home to him.

At our best, we parents should become like the mother rabbit: guides, defenders, shapers, refuges in the storm for our growing children. The trick is knowing when to let our children venture out, even if they fail, so that they may mature, learn, and become. We are like God's hands on earth, caring and affirming while gently nudging our children toward independence.

Even if we do our job right, we never quite let them go. Part of enabling is maintaining something of an open-door policy so that our children, like the runaway bunny, know that they can still find assurance, forgiveness, and love in our arms—no matter how old they are. It is what God offers us; we should endeavor to offer it to our children.

O God, may I be your hands on earth for my teen. Help me to provide the security and love my teen needs without stifling the growth that is part of your wonderful plan.

The Runaway Bunny by Margaret Wise Brown (New York: Harper & Row, Publishers, 1942)

DECEMBER 20   Read Romans 9:25.

MY MOTHER IS IN HER SIXTIES and I am pushing forty, but she tells everyone who will listen that I am still her baby. Sometimes this annoys me.

But whenever the political wrangling of my office becomes unbearable or housework or domestic squabbles threaten to overwhelm me, I go home to North Carolina to be with my mom. I make no apologies for being a spoiled brat pushing forty. Sometimes the only thing that will comfort me is to curl up on Mom's bed and talk over old times or confess aloud to her that I don't have it all together, even though I may want the rest of the world to think I do.

My mother makes few demands when I'm home. I can sleep all day, leave my bed unmade, let the answering machine get the phone. Even with my hair matted to my head and the remote control clenched in my fist, my mom loves me. She still kisses me good night and tucks me in. She radiates unconditional love, an unspoken but clear message that nothing on earth, nothing I can do, can change her love for me.

I can't always get home to Mom, and she won't always be there. I know that deep in my soul. So I'm learning to reach deep inside myself and find the place where God resides. The place where God says it's OK, for the moment, to be the child and not the parent. I've learned to take a day off now and then and curl up in bed with a good book, or journal about old times or problems I'm having. I'm learning to find that place where I can hear God's words of assurance and acceptance. I come back stronger after these times with God. I come back ready to tackle the office, the marriage, the kids, the responsibilities.

Where do you go to be rejuvenated?

God, even us moms need mothering. Even the caregiver sometimes needs care. Enfold us in your arms in these moments, and help us to feel your love. Renew my spirit so that I can press on in my roles as mother, worker, wife, daughter, volunteer, and friend.

DECEMBER 21   Read Psalm 148.

I RECENTLY READ ABOUT A CHURCH youth group that launched a citywide campaign to stop manufacturers from dumping industrial waste into a local river. The teens painted and posted colorful signs, produced a newsletter, sold T-shirts and buttons, held a fundraising dance, and trained a delegation to take up the issue with the city council. All this between homework, dating, and chores at home!

I find it so refreshing—our youth placing such an emphasis on environmental stewardship. When I was fifteen, I'd never heard the word *recycle;* but now it is discussed and practiced by teens around the world. As I read about that youth group, I was reminded how so much of our earth is misused by adults. Have we forgotten that we are not the rulers of the planet but are simply minding these precious resources for our children and our children's children?

"Praise the Lord from the earth. . . . Mountains and all hills . . . Wild animals and all cattle, creeping things and flying birds!" (Psalm 148:7, 9-10). There is something awesome in this psalm and in the knowledge that we, like the birds and cattle and all other creatures, are called to treat the rest of God's creation with reverence and a sense of profound responsibility. What better way to praise God than to care for—and teach our children to care for—God's earth!

Dear Creator, I join the sun and moon and stars and children in praising your name. Let me be awestruck by the majesty of your earth, as a child discovering the wonder of snowflakes and blades of grass for the first time. As you sent Christ as a shepherd to lead us, help us to take the lead in caring for your creation.

DECEMBER 22   Read Luke 2:1-14.

THESE DAYS IT'S AN ORDEAL for Larry and me to find time or energy to take a simple weekend trip, three hours one way, to visit in-laws. Not so with our daughters. I marvel at how they will pick up at a moment's notice and go.

Once, after studying every night—all night—for a week before finals, Heather decided, spur-of-the-moment, to ride eight hours to Atlanta with friends for a sorority party. She returned, exuberant and exhausted, barely in time to take her final exams. She passed them and then passed out, spending half of her spring break in bed. She still declares it was one of the best weekends she's ever had.

It is that kind of impulsiveness and exuberance that I recall when I read about the shepherds abiding in the field that Christmas night. Sleepily keeping watch, they were just waiting for something new and exciting to call them away from the mundane. But would they be ready at a moment's notice when the unexpected happened?

Then the star appeared, and the angels sang. With the impulsiveness of teenagers looking for a party, they ran to the stable. And their lives were never the same again.

Sometimes the impulsiveness of our girls is unnerving. While I'm trying to make sense of their plans, they are executing those plans or changing them midstream. But I'm learning to be a little more flexible and a little more impulsive by watching them, because they seem to have the best times in those spur-of-the-moment moments.

Dear God, I'm celebrating new life, hope, and joy! I'm celebrating young people who help me feel young again! I'm celebrating the wisdom you have given me to accompany graying hair! I'm celebrating the unexpected shine of a star, a mother's struggle, the Savior's birth, the impulsive visit of lowly shepherds. I'm celebrating life!

DECEMBER 23   Read Luke 1:47-55.

ACCORDING TO EVERYTHING I'VE READ on the subject, Mary was a teenager when she risked Joseph's lack of understanding; composed a song of praise to God that is still the most beautiful on earth; and finally, bore Jesus, the Savior of the world.

Mary's wisdom and deeds as a teenager amaze me, because the most profound thing my almost-grown stepdaughter, Heather, has done lately is to raise her college grade point average from a D-minus to a C and decide that maybe she can find a decent pair of jeans for under $100. It's hard to imagine her doing her own laundry, much less becoming a responsible adult and parent who determines God's will and follows it.

Still, I have to remember that it was years before people realized how much Mary and her child would impact the world. The innkeepers who turned her away from their doors surely did not realize that there was more to this teenager than appearances indicated. Before God spoke to him in a dream, Joseph had his doubts. And the people who crucified Mary's son obviously had no idea whom they were dealing with.

But, as Mary predicted, "generations" since have continued to bless Mary and her child. From the "low estate" of teen mother, Mary rose to the status of one of the most important women of all time.

"Everyone was young once; you'll be amazed what a difference a year can make," my mother often reminds me when I become exasperated with our girls. She's right too. Once a hunted refugee and mother of a son who was executed for treason, Mary is now called "blessed" by the Christian world. I think about that, and I look at my girls with new eyes.

Some days, God, it's hard to see responsible, mature adults in the eyes of our teens; but we trust that they're lurking there, waiting to blossom. In the meantime, help me to love them and guide them, remembering that they are blessed gifts to the world from you.

DECEMBER 24   Read Psalm 117.

IT WAS THE WORST CHRISTMAS of my life. I was nineteen, home from college and trying to maintain my famous holiday spirit in a home where my parents' turbulent twenty-two-year marriage was falling apart.

We had a beautifully decorated tree, home-baked cookies scenting the house with vanilla and sugar, and favorite holiday music playing around the clock. I had even made the most fabulous present for my parents: a beautiful wood and glass table from a design I had found in a magazine. Still, with all the trappings, my parents fought; my brothers and I moved like ghosts through our new, built-just-for-us ranch-style home; and my mother cried herself to sleep for two weeks.

I survived that awful Christmas and, praise God, have lived to celebrate many more joyous ones. But the pall of that holiday looms. Sometimes when the girls are with us now and I see them venturing into their own relationships, I find myself hoping and praying that they will never have to endure an unhappy holiday.

But I know it is not possible to spare them the occasional emotional and spiritual pain that accompanies adulthood. So my prayer for them is that they have learned enough from their father, their mother, and me to know that the living God is always there to comfort and guide them, especially in those hours of greatest pain or challenge. The psalmist reminds us that "great is his steadfast love . . . and the faithfulness of the Lord endures forever" (117:2). With that assurance, every Christmas can be blessed, even if the celebrations fall short.

Lord, you are always with us, even though the most difficult times. Remind us that even when relationships are strained, we can experience the joy of Christmas. Fill us with joy so that we may praise you with glad hearts.

DECEMBER 25   Read Luke 2:1-7; John 1:1-5.

WHAT IS IT WITH THE LETHARGIC, bored-with-everything persona that some teens adopt? Just try to get the youth group at my church to go Christmas caroling, and they roll their eyes in exasperation. The only thing they seem happy about is being out of school. Is that joy to the world, or what?

On the other hand, this middle-aged cookie baker becomes a veritable elf around Christmas time. During the Advent season, I can be found singing Christmas carols, putting together the nativity scene, wrapping presents with a giggle, hanging mistletoe, baking cookies, and decorating the house—I decorate my tree as soon after Thanksgiving as is respectable. I have loads of Christmas cheer, and I find myself having little patience with anyone who doesn't think that Christmas is the best thing ever.

Kelia and Heather, however, were more like their dad at Christmas time during their teen years. They would watch me in quiet amusement, patiently declining my invitations to build a snowman or string cranberries (I know. I know. Sometimes I sound like a Norman Rockwell painting gone mad). They would slouch in front of the television watching ball games while I hung tinsel on everything that stood still, including our dog.

But in recent years, their Christmas cheer has grown. I'd like to think that perhaps some of my enthusiasm has rubbed off on them! Last Christmas, I was surprised to see Larry's eyes shining like a child's as we exchanged gifts of love. Our ultra-cool Heather, who had accompanied her mother on a much-anticipated trip to California, called us on Christmas morning, breathless, to wish us merry Christmas and thank us for her gift. And Kelia, whose daughter, Shermana, is now three, is more enthusiastic in her Christmas celebration than I am. Once as lethargic and non-chalant about Christmas as the youth group that rebels when I suggest they sing "Away in a Manger," our girls now have reached the age when the Christmas story provides a lasting beauty in the bleak midwinter—the light shining in the darkness.

I guess that for those who are past the days of childhood, Christmas kind of grows on you as you begin to realize how much joy—true joy—is ours all because of a tiny baby born in a barn two thousand years ago. I can't wait until the kids in the youth group are old enough to become wide-eyed children again at Christmas!

God, there have been both good and bad times in my life, but every day you provide is a good gift. I'm especially grateful for Christmas and all that it means—not only to me and my family, but also to my whole earthly family. Help me to share the joy of Christmas with those who may not yet appreciate the real beauty of the season.

DECEMBER 26   Read Hebrews 2:10-18.

I HAVE A PLAQUE IN MY KITCHEN that reads "I will honor Christmas in my heart and keep it all the year." Even for someone like me, who listens to Christmas music in July, that's a tough one. It's hard to maintain my joy after the Christmas pageant and worship service are over, the presents are opened and put away, the tree is stripped of lights and chopped up for mulch, the relatives have gone home, and I'm back at work.

I wonder, too, how Mary and Joseph maintained the joy of Jesus' birth. Almost immediately their baby was marked for death by Herod, forcing them to flee as refugees to Egypt. Even after that crisis had past, they must have found it hard to sustain their joy, knowing the prophecy of Jesus' turbulent life and death. What a burden for the parents of young Jesus, knowing that there was nothing they could do, ultimately, to protect their child from the Good Friday that loomed on the horizon.

Even as we rejoice in the lives of our children, we have a sadness in knowing that we cannot protect them from every hurt. The good news is that God knows our suffering; God knows the pain that accompanies our children's lives even into their adult years, and he is always there—even when we can't be.

Knowing that God is always there for me and my children brings a smile and a sigh of relief all through the year, even when Christmas seems so far away.

God help me always to keep the joy of Christmas in my heart, trusting that you walk with me and my family through all our days.

DECEMBER 27   Read 1 John 2:9-11.

IT WAS A TYPICAL CHURCH-SPONSORED youth event. The teens spent the day painting the homes of elderly residents, teaching children to make paper chains and clay figures, and picking up the trash in a city park. By the end of the day when the food arrived, members of the group wee feeling pretty good about themselves. Pass the potato chips and the halos! We've done our good deeds for the day.

As the teens and we adult chaperones enjoyed the summer evening in the quiet park, we noticed some laughter and tittering in our ranks. Several of the youthful do-gooders were laughing nervously at two disheveled, obviously homeless men who had wandered toward our end of the park. Those who weren't laughing looked a little frightened—we'd all heard warnings about vagrants wandering the city. Even some of the adults, as they shushed the giggling kids, suggested that we take our picnic to safer ground.

But two boys in our group simply rose, grabbed a couple of extra boxed dinners—along with their own—and headed in the direction of the two homeless men. We watched them as they took a seat beside the two men, handed them the unopened boxes, and began an animated conversation. After a moment's hesitation the two men took out sandwiches and chips, and the four of them talked. Nothing heavy—sports, mostly, and a little about how church had changed since the men had been part of a youth fellowship. There were frequent bursts of laughter and even a couple of arguments about which NBA team would win the playoffs.

For all our do-gooding that day, those two boys probably did the best job of giving. Instead of seeing those men as objects of mission and charity, they saw them as brothers—down on their luck and dirty, but still brothers enough to share the universal talk about sports and growing up.

I hope I'm teaching the young people in my life that sometimes the most charitable acts happen when you're not trying to be charitable. Sometimes you do the most good when you simply treat a stranger as you would a friend. It's no big revelation, but I'm amazed how often I forget that.

God, help me and my children to see all of your children as brothers and sisters and to reach out in love.

DECEMBER 28   Read Job 12:13.

AS A KID I HAD THE DUBIOUS REPUTATION of being a "know it all." Ask me any question and I'd answer; introduce any topic and I'd expound on it; name any person in my hometown and I had the "inside story" on him or her.

As I've gotten older, I've begun to understand the saying,

"The older you get, the less you know." On the one hand, maturity has given me the confidence and willingness to forgive myself many weaknesses. On the other hand, I'm often reluctant when it comes to handing out advice and wholesale wisdom.

Part of my reticence has to do with the young people in my life. It is no longer for the entertainment of others and the joy of hearing myself talk that I engage in advice-giving and wisdom-spouting. Many times Kelia and Heather and the "surrogate children" in my life come to me with complex, important questions that require me to pray, think, and draw on experience, reason, and spiritual disciplines for a response. I have been asked for advice on everything from abortion to college majors to divorce. Quick, well-crafted answers that show off my vocabulary or my own past experiences are not what are needed. More often, mature, prayerful, loving, tough answers are what the situations warrant.

Prayers for wisdom and courage are common among those of us who parent, mentor, love, and sometimes wrangle with teens. I pray silently whenever one of them confronts me with a potentially life-altering question, and I sometimes invite the teen to join me in prayer. What do I pray for? A hymn by Harry Emerson Fosdick, "God of Grace and God of Glory," captures my fervent petition for wisdom and courage to help the youth in my life walk through the valleys with assurance, power, and faith: "Grant us wisdom, grant us courage, for the living of these days."

O God, my daily prayer is that you will give me wisdom for the living of these days.

DECEMBER 29   Read 1 Corinthians 4:10.

AH, TO BE A FOOL FOR CHRIST! I mean, if you're going to be foolish anyway—and most of us are at one time or another—why not be the class clown?

I know a high school student who is the undisputed

clown of his church school. As sure as he's named a wise man in our Christmas pageant, he shows up wearing a Mickey Mouse robe and matching towel as his costume. He makes up silly words to familiar carols and makes goofy faces at the children as they rehearse their speeches. But Derek is a favorite among the younger children. They follow him everywhere. And if he shushes them during the prayer, they stay quiet.

For the adult coordinators of the Sunday school, Derek is a refreshing disruption. Most times, it is our laughter at his cut-ups that cause an uproar. Unlike many of his compatri-ots who feel they've outgrown the Christmas and Easter productions, Derek always volunteers. If no one else will play the donkey at the manger, Derek will, braying and snorting as if his winning an Oscar depended on it.

God bless the class clowns! Often mislabeled as immature attention-seekers, they are more often the ones who love to see others smile. And in a world where sadness is too often the order of the day, sharing the gift of laughter is as much a ministry as sharing bread.

Lord of laughter, smiles, and hugs, bless all the class clowns who make your world more mirth-filled and bright. Oftentimes they are our teens. Where there are wounds that can be healed with a kind word, a funny story, or a silly face, send your fools for Christ's sake. Help me not to squelch their laughter but to encourage it.

December 30   Read Deuteronomy 6:4-9; John 13:15.

How do you talk to your teens about their faith? How do you help budding adults nurture a faith that is both practical and spiritual; a faith that will speak to them in every situa-tion, from making choices about sexual responsibility to how to treat one another? How can you help them find the balance between the knowledge of eternal life and learning to create a meaningful life here and now?

Parents of teens know that it does precious little good to "preach" to them about anything. Adolescence is a time of exploration, self-expression, and self-discovery; and although what parents say is important, our kids are stubbornly trying to find their own way through life. How, then, can we help them find their own way to a life-sustaining faith in God?

We parents must remember that our own expression of faith is critical to helping our children develop their faith. What can we do? Consider these ideas.

Practice your faith—don't preach. I have a friend who, for years, dropped her children off at church on Sunday then went home to sleep until the service was over. She was a hard-working mom and, no doubt, needed some rest. However, her example said to her kids that church is "kid's stuff," and they stopped going as soon as they were old enough to make their own decision—even though she nagged them about the importance of going to church.

Tell your own faith stories over dinner or during quality family times. (If you also have younger children, tell your own faith stories in place off reading bedtime stories.) Talk about how the love of Christ helps you make decisions, overcome adversities, and cope with real-life situations. Personal witness is still the most potent evangelism tool. Your children will remember your stories long after they have families of their own.

Set aside time for family devotion and prayer. Even with our busy schedules, we parents should model a healthy prayer life. It may be prayers before meals, offering thanks and celebration. It may be prayers before bedtime. It might even be a comforting word of devotion said first thing in the morning, just before the mad dash for the bathroom and breakfast. Family prayer and devotion do not have to be time-intensive to have a lasting impact on your children's faith.

Find a faith community that places an emphasis on its youth. If you want your teens to nurture their faith, you can help them by joining a church where youth are visible, active, and involved. If their peers are active in church, they are more likely to see church and the life of faith as relevant to their lives.

Now spend a few moments in prayer, allowing God to reveal other ways you can help your teens nurture their faith. And trust that God will provide whatever you require to make it happen.

God, I want my teens to have a strong faith, but sometimes I don't do my part to help make that happen. Help me to be a better example in their lives, and show me the specific ways that I can nurture their faith in you. (Wait in silence, listening for God's response.)

DECEMBER 31   Read Psalm 111.

I GREW UP BELIEVING THE SUPERSTITION that whomever I was with on New Year's Eve would be with me throughout the year. It was a belief shared by my mother and grandmothers. So, when I was growing up, I spent at least part of almost every New Year's Eve at church. The women in my family believed in starting the year right.

Watch night service, a tradition in many southern and black churches, still holds a kind of holy mystery for me. It is the time when you cleave to God, give thanks for the bounty of the past year, and ponder "how I got over," as the spiritual says.

In my mother-in-law's small, rural town last year, watch night service was especially poignant. Teenage girls came dressed for parties, with sequins and lavish hair styles. One man had liquor on his breath, and he sat respectfully at the back door of the sanctuary. Others came straight from work, still wearing mechanic, waitress, and hospital orderly uniforms—most of them lacking the luxury of taking vacation during the holidays. Farm laborers tucked their dirty shoes underneath the rough pews and bowed in earnest prayer.

But they all came, like my mother and grandmothers and our family had come in my childhood, to give witness to God's goodness in the last year, to pray for God's mercy in the coming year, and to ask God's forgiveness for always.

Tears of joy for the blessings; tears of sorrow for those who didn't live to see another year; tears of anguish for lost jobs, ailing parents, wayward children all flowed together at watch night. Even the small children rose to give thanks for "Mamma takin' care of me" and "Granddaddy's new plow."

As we sang the gospel hymn "Hold to God's Unchanging Hand" and I remembered the old superstition about spending the year with whomever I shared December 31, I realized how smart my grandmothers, mother, and mother-in-law really were. I love the parties and the celebrations of the holidays, but I hope I will always take a moment to give thanks on the last day of every year I'm allotted. If God's grace abides all year, surely I can corral our family to church on that one special night to give thanks for a year's worth of blessings.

Have a blessed new year!

Today "I will give thanks to the Lord with my whole heart, in the company of the upright, in the congregation." I praise you, Lord, for your bountiful blessings and mercy. May your peace go with me and my family during the coming year.